HEALTH CARE IN THE EUROPEAN COMMUNITY

Health Care in the European Community

ALAN MAYNARD

UNIVERSITY OF PITTSBURGH PRESS

First published in Great Britain 1975
by Croom Helm Ltd Publishers

Published 1975 in the U.S.A.
by the University of Pittsburgh Press
© 1975 Alan Maynard

Library of Congress Catalog Card Number 74—17701
ISBN: 0—8229—1119—1

Printed in Great Britain

CONTENTS

To Liz, Justin and John

PREFACE

The aim of this book is to analyse the finance and provision of health care in the nine member states of the European Economic Community. There may be argument about the meaning of the term 'health care'; this book is primarily concerned with the finance and provision of medical care — what are usually known as 'benefits in kind'. Short-term sickness benefits have also been discussed because in some countries their finance and provision is integrated with the provision of medical care.

Why are the health care systems of other countries of interest? Firstly because of knowledge for its own sake. It is good to know how other societies allocate scarce resources in the pursuit of 'good health'. This quest produces many insights into how societies react to similar problems of choice. The second reason is utilitarian. By studying how other countries allocate their health care resources, solutions may be suggested to common problems. Where countries use different policy instruments to pursue solutions to these common problems a comparative analysis of their success can be interesting and useful if prosecuted with caution.

For the administrator, the doctor, the politician and the social scientist interested in health care, this book offers a glimpse of how other people in different countries react to similar problems. Hopefully it will precipitate a desire in the reader to further his knowledge.

University of York
September, 1974

ACKNOWLEDGEMENTS

The author would like to thank everyone who has helped him during the preparation of this book. The book is derived from a report prepared by the author for a consortium of five bodies: the International Federation of Voluntary Health Service Funds, the British United Provident Association (BUPA), the Office of Health Economics (OHE), the Blue Cross Association and the National Association of Blue Shield Plans. These five organisations funded a research grant to the author which enabled him to acquire the basic data from which this book is derived.

At the individual level the list of those people who have been helpful to the author is long. Perhaps the greatest debts are owed to John R. U. Green (formerly of BUPA), Walter McNerney (President of the Blue Cross Association, USA), George Teeling-Smith (Director of OHE, London), Robert van den Heuvel, Marc Smout, An van Overschelde (all three of whom work for the Christian Mutualities Federation in Belgium), Elizabeth Liefman-Kiel (University of Saarlandes, West Germany), Derek J. Morris (Department of Health and Social Security, United Kingdom), Miles C. Hardie (Director of the Kings Fund Health Centre, London), W.A.J. Farndale (Polytechnic of the South Bank, London), Brian R. Bricknell (BUPA), Franco Illuminati (Director of the National Sickness Insurance Institute, Italy – INAM), Gilberto Muraro (University of Padova, Italy), Shaun Trant and Paul Turpin (Department of Health, Dublin), G.W. de Wit (Nationale Nederlanden, the Netherlands), F. Schrijver (Nederlandse Vereninging Van Ongevallen En Ziekverzekaraars), L. Andriessen (Nederlandse Unie van Ziekfondsen), Jean Hasse (Social Affairs, European Economic Commission, Brussels), M. Mode (L'Inspecteur-General Chargé de la Direction Régional de la Sécurité Sociale de la Région Parisienne, France), M. de Mourgues (Caisse Nationale D'Assurance Maladie at Maternité des Travailleurs non Salaires des Professions non Agricoles) and John J. Carroll (Assistant Commissioner US Department of Health, Education and Welfare). These patient and helpful people, together with numerous civil servants in the health ministries of Western Europe, have given me data, pertinent comments on previous drafts, and encouragement to continue with my endeavours.

Finally I would like to acknowledge the help of my colleagues at the University of York, England – in particular Alan Peacock, Jack

Wiseman, Douglas Dosser, Alan Williams, Leslie Godfrey and Tony Culyer who, knowingly and unknowingly, helped me to complete my work. Many thanks also to H.C. Wright for his help.

The property rights in any omissions or errors of interpretation that remain in this book are vested in the author, and are in no way the responsibility of the named and unnamed assistants mentioned in the preceding paragraphs.

1 INTRODUCTION

The objective of this book is to provide a systematic analysis of the finance and provision of health care in the European Economic Community. Although the subject of the book is health care (i.e. benefits in kind or medical care, and cash benefits or sickness insurance) the principal component of the study is medical care. Short-term cash sickness benefits have been included throughout because in some countries their finance and provision are fully integrated with the finance and delivery of medical care and consequently their exclusion would have created ambiguities.

In order to facilitate the analysis of health care in the European Community there is a common structure to Chapters 2 to 10 of this book. The purpose of this brief introduction is to acquaint the reader with this structure and to indicate the nature of the final two chapters which, to some extent, summarise the book.

Each chapter begins with a brief introduction outlining the evolution of the health care system in the country with which the Chapter is concerned. The intention of this is to describe the significant changes of the last century or so. This is followed by the first substantive part of the Chapter which is concerned with the administrative structure of the system. Here an attempt is made to discuss central and local government activity, the activity of autonomous institutions such as the sickness funds and the relationships which exist between these bodies. In most cases the structure is summarised in terms of a simple diagram. For some Chapters (e.g. Italy and the United Kingdom) two structures are described. This procedure is necessary because reform is taking place in these countries at present and the discussion is facilitated by knowledge of reform and the structures prior to and after this reform.

The second Section of each Chapter is concerned with the coverage of the health care system under consideration. The coverage of the compulsory social insurance system is discussed and, where necessary, the coverage of each component part of this system is described. The residue of the population not covered by compulsory insurance are covered by private insurance or public assistance/social aid. In some cases this residue is large (e.g. the Netherlands) but in most cases the coverage of the system is almost complete. However as is noted in the text, coverage can mean different things in different countries. Thus in Belgium the self-employed are covered for heavy risks only and in

Ireland all those citizens in the less eligible group have to pay out of their own pockets for the medical care provided by general practitioners. Consequently some caution must be exercised in interpreting the statistics.

The qualifying conditions which have to met by contributors prior to their being registered as members is the concern of the third Section. In some cases these conditions are nominal (e.g. Denmark) whilst in others (e.g. France) they are substantial. Qualifying conditions are described separately for medical care and cash sickness benefits where they differ.

The finance of health care is discussed in the fourth Section of each Chapter. The prime concern of this Section is the source of finance. The contribution regulations are analysed. This entails detailed discussion for countries such as the Netherlands where there are dynamic earnings ceilings and two types of contribution: one for general care, and one for heavy risks. In other countries, for instance Denmark, the discussion is brief as individual contributions are non-existent and the system is financed out of central and local government taxation.

The financial picture is completed in Section five where the income and expenditure characteristics of each system are analysed in some detail. The principal objectives of this system are to move towards some estimate of the total expenditure of the medical care system and to discuss the size of the component parts of this expenditure. The estimation of total expenditure is rather like an enterprise in detection. Whilst it is relatively easy to acquire statistics relating to the expenditure of the compulsory social insurance system, it is more difficult to get data about expenditures financed out of private insurance and the income and wealth of the consumer. Thus in the case of the Netherlands there is data for expenditure of the heavy risks' insurance system which covers everybody, and there is data for general scheme expenditure which covers seventy five per cent of the population. To get a complete expenditure figure an estimate has to be made of the private outlays of those people not covered by the general scheme. Similar estimates have to be made for other countries where the consumer participates in the cost of the care he receives. These estimates are fraught with difficulties and these difficulties together with problems of definition make the expenditure estimates highly tentative in some cases.

The next Section, the sixth, discusses the provision of benefits in cash and in kind. Medical care (benefits in kind) are the principal consideration of this discussion. General medical care, hospitalisation, dental care and pharmaceutical benefits are discussed in some detail. Where fee scales exist they are discussed and the participation of

2

the consumer in the costs of care is examined in detail.

The discussion of fees is complemented in the first part of the seventh Section which is concerned with the provision of medical personnel, The remuneration and the number of different types of personnel are discussed and particular attention is paid to the physician. The discussion is followed by an examination of the hospital system. This is concerned with numbers, the types of ownership and the geographical distribution of hospital facilities. The regulation by the State of medical personnel and the hospital system is analysed particularly where efforts have been made to 'plan' hospital provision.

The Chapter for each country is rounded off by a conclusion which summarises and discusses the content of the previous sections. This is followed by a bibliography.

This framework is applied to the health care systems of the nine member countries of the European Economic Community. The final two Chapters are concerned with more general issues. Chapter 11 contains a comparative analysis of the medical care systems of the Nine. Its structure is identical to that of the individual country Chapters: viz: administration, coverage, qualifying conditions, finance, income and expenditure, benefits, provision and conclusions. Tables of comparative data are provided for coverage, contributions, expenditure in absolute terms and some tentative estimates of expenditure as a percentage of Gross National Product, benefits (hospital care, general practitioner care and prescribed pharmaceutical products) and the costs of each which are borne by the patient, and provision indicators for medical personnel and hospitals.

The final Chapter is an overview in which some issues raised in the previous pages are discussed at greater length. The criterion for the selection of issues in this Chapter reflect the biases of the author. They represent what he believes to be issues of importance, for all the medical care systems. The first such issue is the insurance myth in which it is pointed out that the contributions are ear-marked taxes and the extent of reliance on such finances varies enormously within the Nine. This will create an obvious problem if financial harmonisation is attempted as prescribed under the Treaty of Rome. The other part of this myth is the sickness funds whose existence can be justified only if they represent a least cost method of meeting the objectives of society. One problem which the funds may fail to counter is the monopoly power of some suppliers of medical care. This is the second issue discussed in the final Chapter where it is emphasised that the countering of this power by State monopsonies (i.e. sole buyers) can lead to problems of a different nature but equally intractable. The final specific item in this Chapter is a discussion of the restrictive practices of professions. All three areas need more rigorous examination than has been possible in the present study, which is to be viewed as the key to the Pandora's box from which they arise. For such examination to be prosecuted efficiently the theories available to explain the behaviour of the State and other non-profit making bodies need to be more fully developed and then rigorously tested with the available data.

The analysis in each of the Chapters can be supplemented by using the data in the appendices. The first Appendix gives the rate of exchange bases to the financial data reported in the test. It is to be emphasised that all such data in the text is approximate because of the fluctuations in the rates of exchange between different currencies. The second Appendix gives a series of 'social indicators' for the Nine. These indicators range from population data, to infant mortality data and income tax data. Such indicators may be useful to the reader wishing to augment his knowledge of the countries with which this book is concerned.

The provision of health care in the Nine and the rest of Western Europe is changing rapidly. The health care structure of all countries is groaning beneath the combined pressures of inflation and escalating consumer demand. Indeed at the present rates of growth the health care systems of some countries (e.g. Denmark) will require a hundred per cent of the national Gross National Product by the end of this century. Such requirements cannot be met. However if the European Economic Community as a group, and individual countries separately, are to make choices which facilitate an efficient allocation of resources, more rigorous and clearly thought out policies will have to be devised and implemented by all concerned.

4

2 WEST GERMANY

The Evolution of Health Care in West Germany

Although social health insurance in Germany existed before the creation of the German State — Prussian legislation (in 1854 and 1876) regulated the operation of the sickness funds — its magnitude was greatly increased by the reforms of Bismarck's administration. The principles enunciated in 1883 — compulsory insurance, free services and sick benefits — are those which govern the present system of West German Social Health Insurance. At first the legislation applied to manual industrial workers only but during the succeeding twenty years it was extended to include transport and office workers. By 1903 ten million people were insured and the scheme was financed by contributions paid by employees (two thirds) and employers (one third). The scheme, then as now, was administered by autonomous bodies which, though responsible for provision of services, seldom got further than the financing of provision by independent contractors (physicians, hospitals, etc.). Further legislation in 1911 extended the scheme to cover agricultural and forestry workers, and reformed the organisation of the funds so that 8,500 disappeared. During the period 1911 to early in the 1930s the scope of insurance was extended and more sections of the community were brought into the scheme (seamen 1927). The early 1930s saw large cuts made in expenditure and this was followed by a period of Consolidating Legislation (1934-9) which dealt with organisation and finance primarily. It was not until the latter half of the Second World War that benefits were increased significantly (1941-3) and since then most medical care benefits have been available without a time limit. During the first decade of the Federal Republic, social health insurance was affected by various pieces of legislation, e.g. in 1961 sickness insurance waiting days were abolished. However all this legislation was *ad hoc* — adding to and subtracting from the Bismarck creation. No fundamental reforms of health care have taken place in West Germany since 1883 although attempts have been made (1958-62). The role of the State in the finance of health care is relatively small, but. like so many other countries, West Germany is facing escalating provision costs and a demand for greater redistribution of resources by subsidising health care. These demands, plus other factors such as harmonisation, may lead to an increase in the role of the Government in the finance and provision of health care in West Germany.

5

Throughout this chapter benefits in kind will be referred to as medical care, benefits in cash as sickness benefits and the two types of benefit together as health care.

1 Administration

(a) The Public Sector

Diagram 1 *The Administration and Financial Organisation of Health Care in West Germany*

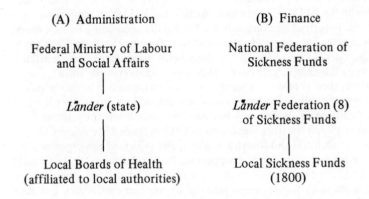

(A) Administration	(B) Finance
Federal Ministry of Labour and Social Affairs	National Federation of Sickness Funds
Länder (state)	Länder Federation (8) of Sickness Funds
Local Boards of Health (affiliated to local authorities)	Local Sickness Funds (1800)

The social insurance of health care in West Germany is administered by a dual tripartite structure (see diagram 1). At the apex of the administrative pyramid the Federal Ministry of Labour and Social Affiars (*Der Bundesminister für Arbeit und Sozialordnung*) concerns itself with 'general supervision'. The next tier is the *Land* (or State) Ministry of Work and Social Welfare which is responsible for the enforcement of the law and regulation of the *Land*. It is the *Land* which has responsibility for administering the health services. The health departments of the *Länder* are supervised by chief medical officers who are responsible to the *Land* Minister. The lowest administrative authorities are the local boards of health which are affiliated to the local authorities. These boards are in charge of caring for specific groups (e.g. the handicapped, the chronic sick, addicts, etc.), provide specific services (school health, public health, sanitary inspection) and supervise all hospitals. The financial base of the structure consists of the sickness funds. There are over 1,800 sickness funds arranged in a variety of ways: local, occupational, establishment, agricultural and miners funds exist.

Table 1 *Sickness Funds*

Type of Fund	Number	Membership Total	Average size of funds (in thousands)	Percentage of all members in
1. Local Sickness Funds *(Ortskrankenkassen)*	401	15,715,000	39.18	52.6
2. Rural sickness funds (agricultural) *(Landeskrankenkassen)*	102	438,000	4.29	1.4
3. Guild sickness funds *(Innungskrankenkassen)*	179	1,385,000	7.73	4.6
4. Company sickness funds *(Betreibskrankenkassen)*	1147	3,995,000	3.48	13.3
5. Seamen's sickness fund *(Seekrankenkasse)*	1	76,000	76.00	0.2
6. Miner's sickness funds *(Knappeschaft Uche Krankenkassen)*	6	1,126,000	187.66	3.7
7. Substitute sickness funds* *(Ersatzkrankenkassen)*				
(a) for blue collar workers	8	328,000	41.00	1.0
(b) for white collar workers	7	6,783,000	969.00	22.7
TOTAL	1,851	29,845,000	16.12	22.7

Source: *Bundesminister fur Arbeit und Sozialardnung.*
*   These are mutual insurance associations registered before 1st April 1909 and officially authorised as sickness funds

Table 1 shows the general characteristics of the funds. There are seven basic types of fund of which the Local Sickness Funds (OKK) are the most important with 52.6 per cent of total membership and an average fund size of over 39,000. If OKK membership is added to the membership of the Company Sickness Funds (BKK) with 13.3 per cent of members, and the White Collar Workers Substitute Funds (Ek. An) with 22.7 per cent of members it can be seen that the aggregate membership of all the other funds is only 11.4 per cent of total membership. The biggest funds are in the Ek. An. employers' substitute fund type and overall the average fund size is very small: just over 16,000.

Table 2 *Membership of Types of Fund**

Year	OKK	LKK	BKK	IKK	KnK	SKK	Ek Ar	Ek An	Total
1938	13,524	1,817	4,097	676	762	59		2,287	23,222
1950	13,838	670	2,300	398	1,128	21	81	1,764	20,200
1955	16,143	540	2,960	660	1,335	46	145	3,071	24,900
1960	15,433	469	3,600	936	1,402	70	231	4,919	27,060
1965	15,441	418	3,874	1,244	1,318	71	290	6,082	28,740
1966	15,272	420	3,869	1,294	1,286	72	302	6,307	28,924
1967	15,115	426	3,766	1,329	1,226	74	399	6,452	28,698
1968	15,332	434	3,832	1,367	1,253	75	319	6,615	29,123
1969†	15,715	438	3,995	1,385	1,126	76	328	6,783	29,845

Source: *Op. cit.* (1970, 1971).

* Yearly average in thousands.
† Latest available data.

OKK	Local Sickness Funds	SKK	Seamens' Sickness Fund
LKK	Agricultural Funds	Ek Ar	Manual Workers' Com-
BKK	Company Sickness Funds		pensation Fund
IKK	Guild Sickness Funds	Ek An	White Collar Workers'
KnK	Mineworkers Sickness Funds		Compensation Fund

Table 2 shows the evolution of the membership of each type of fund over the period 1938-69. The funds with the most rapid growth have been the substitute funds. During the period 1950 to 1969 the Manual Workers' Fund (Ek. Ar) grew from 81,000 members to 328,000 i.e. by 304 per cent. The White Collar Workers funds grew from 1,764,000 members to 6,783,000 members, i.e. by 284 per cent. The Mineworkers' Funds and the Company Funds experienced a slight decline in membership if terminal year membership data is compared with 1938 data. All the funds are self-governing corporations managed by elected representatives of the insured persons and the employees.[1] They are grouped into eight *Länder* and one National Federation. All these funds administer the same health insurance scheme (based on the 1883 Social Insurance Act) and provide roughly the same range of health care benefits. The separate insurance institutions of the *Länder (Länderversicjerungstantalten)* are responsible for the finance of services for which the *Land* is responsible i.e. care of psychiatric and tuberculosis patients.

8

(b) The Private Sector

In many European countries the private sector seems to be in the process of contracting due to the expansion of social health insurance. Germany is no exception. It would seem that the private sector will be increasingly involved in supplementing the public cover. As we will note below, recent changes have, in some ways, increased the *per capita* flow of resources to the private funds but even so their role is small in comparison to social insurance.

In 1969 there were fifty-eight companies providing sickness insurance. Eight of these companies were joint stock companies and the remainder were mutual societies. The premium income of these companies totalled £618m. in 1969[2]. In addition there are several hundred small insurance associations. These generally operate on a local basis and according to the International Labour Office their revenue is less than one per cent of the total revenue of private insurance.

2 Coverage

In March 1970 the public insurance scheme covered approximately 17.8 million employees (see Table 3). In addition to this 7.9 million pensioners were insured on a compulsory basis and about 4.6 million persons were insured on a voluntary basis. These 30.3 million people[3] plus nearly twenty-four million members of their families made up about eighty-eight per cent of the total population. Thus out of every hundred insured persons, fifty-nine were compulsory members, twenty-six were old age pensioners who were compulsorily insured and fifteen were voluntary members.

Table 3 *Membership by Groups of Insured Persons**

Year	Total	Compulsory Members Excluding OAPs	OAPs on Compulsory Insurance	Voluntary Members
1938	23,222	19,769	-	3,453
1950	20,200	13,235	4,734	2,464
1955	24,900	16,292	6,663	2,982
1960	27,060	17,655	5,504	3,901
1965	28,740	17,201	5,885	5,654
1966	28,924	17,791	6,023	5,110
1967	28,698	17,019	6,241	5,439
1968	29,123	16,697	7,384	5,042
1969‡	29,766	16,501	7,767	5,497
1970†	30,287	17,769	7,913	4,604

Source: *Op. cit.* (1970,1971).
* Yearly average in thousands.
‡ Figures for 1st July 1969.
† Figures for 1st March 1970.

9

Table 3 shows the development of the three main categories of members. These figures show marked peaking in certain categories. The total number of compulsory and voluntarily insured persons (excluding OAPs) fell back to the 1960 level in 1969 (21.7m and 21.6m). A peak was reached in 1966 (22.9m). This peaking seems directly attributable to the increase in the earnings ceiling (see Table 5), the effects of which appear to peter out slowly until the small 1969 increase was enacted.

This coverage has been further extended. The implementation on January 1st 1971 of the dynamic earnings ceiling resulted in another one million white collar workers becoming subject to compulsory sickness insurance. These new members, plus their dependents, further increased coverage of social insurance at the expense, in most cases, of private insurance. Furthermore all white collar workers who from the beginning of their careers earn in excess of the ceiling can opt to join the social insurance scheme and, by so doing, gain access to all its benefits. This right of entry was offered in 1971 to all those white collar workers who were in employment and not in the scheme because their earnings were in excess of the ceiling. Many opted in.

Various other sections of the population could claim medical treatment through sickness insurance by virtue of their being in receipt of other welfare benefits.

Namely:

1. Disabled war veterans, members of severely disabled war veterans' families, survivors of persons killed in the war.
2. Recipients of welfare under local agreements.
3. Accident victims and sufferers from occupational diseases.
4. Invalids at home.
5. Those receiving compensation benefits.
6. e.g. skilled workers, clerks, seamen, and apprentices (even if they are in receipt of no wage).
7. e.g. office staff, clerical workers, actors and musicians and administrative staff (*Angestellte*) in the educational, health and welfare professions.
8. Officers and men of inland shipping are subject to the rules cited above i.e. those who are not classed as blue collar workers and are in receipt of earnings in excess of DM 22,500.

10

Table 4 *Resident Population by Type of Cover*

A Sickness Insurance Fund (or other type of insurance)
B Total
C Compulsory Insurance
D Voluntary Insurance
E Insured persons
F Insurance Cover
G Health services for the Police and members of the Armed Forces
H Insured dependents
K Without cover

A	B	C	D	E	F	G	H	K
General local Sickness Funds, district, guild, and agricultural Sickness Funds	30,238	10,391	1,823	5,249	-	-	12,775	-
Company Sickness Funds including those of the Post Office and Railways and Operations & Administration Sickness Fund of the Federal Ministry of Transport	8,526	2,625	1,008	791	-	-	4,102	-
Mineworkers' Sickness Fund	2,109	381	27	614	-	-	997	-
Compensation Funds	10,956	3,282	2,550	581	-	-	4,543	-
Private Sickness Insurance	5,945	-	3,312	-	-	-	2,633	-
Students' Sickness Fund	211	-	200	-	-	-	1	-
Other Insurance† Cover	844	25	10	-	729	60	19	-
Not insured against sickness	842	-	-	-	-	-	-	8
TOTALS	59,580	16,703	8,928	7,238	729	60	25,080	8

Source: *Op. cit.* (1970, 1971).

* Covered as recipients of welfare, war disablement pensioners, etc.
† Including foreign sickness funds.

All data as at April 1968.

According to the mini-census of 1968 (see Table 4), 98.6 per cent of the total population (i.e. about 59.6 million people) were insured against sickness and of these eighty-one per cent were in receipt of public cover. of the total population twenty-eight per cent (16.7 million) were compulsorily insured under the legal sickness insurance scheme, 12.1 per cent (7.3 million) were compulsorily insured as old age pensioners and 9.2 per cent (5.6 million) were insured on a voluntary basis and 37.6 per cent of the population (25.1 million) were covered as associate members. Other legal arrangements provided cover for a further 1.3 per cent (0.8 million) of the population. Private sickness insurance schemes insured 5.9 million people against sickness. Of these about 1.1 million were civil servants (excluding relatives) — it is to be noted that this section of the labour force can recoup part of the costs of treatment by way of assistance from their employer, i.e. from public funds. Approximately 1.4 per cent (0.8 million) of the population were not insured against sickness.

An analysis of each type of insurance is set out in more detail below:

A.   *Compulsory Insurance*

By law five categories of people are compulsorily insured.
(a)   employees (eighteen million)
(b)   old age pensioners (eight million)
(c)   the unemployed (a fluctuating total)
(d)   apprentices and specified female trainees
(e)   the self-employed.

(a)   Employees: The first group of employees includes all ordinary or blue collar workers (*Arbeiter*) regardless of the amount of their annual earnings, and those white collar workers (*Angestellte*) with regular earnings of up to DM 22,500 (£3,762) per year (about ninety per cent of white collar workers in 1974). The officers and men of sea-going vessels are insured compulsorily regardless of the amount of their annual earnings. The miners' fund require that all their blue and white collar workers are compulsorily insured against sickness.

Before the end of the 1970s the relatively fixed compulsory insurance limit (see Table 5 in Section 4) for white collar workers repeatedly led to their 'growing out' of compulsory insurance as earings' levels proved more dynamic than the compulsory insurance limits. Many such workers maintained their public cover entering the voluntary insured category despite its costliness in some cases (see Section (B) (c) below). At present the ceiling is tied to the corresponding ceiling of the old age and disability pension scheme at seventy-five per cent of that ceiling. Thus each year the ceiling will be changed in accordance with a formula that takes into account movements in national wage levels.

12

(b)   Old Age Pensioners: Sickness insurance for old age pensioners
was introduced in 1941 and revised in 1956 and 1967. In 1967 a
contribution by pensioners towards their sickness insurance was re-
introduced but this was set aside as from 1st January 1970. Basically
pensioners in the ordinary workers' old age pension scheme and the
white collar workers' old age pension scheme are covered against
sickness. The cover under the public scheme begins from the date of
the submission of a claim for the old age pension (formal membership).
Until the pension is authorised the pensioner must continue to meet
contributions himself, but these are repaid from the beginning of the
pension. Special regulations affect the benefits of the widow or an
orphan of the insured person who had been drawing pension. If the
widow applies for a widow's pension, or if the orphan applies for an
orphan's pension before the age of eighteen and if such pensions are
not taken up, formal membership of the sickness insurance scheme
ends. Old age pensioners in the mineworkers' old age pension insurance
scheme are given sickness insurance cover without any further
formalities. If old age pensioners continue to work after the retirement
age and if they are obliged to insure, then their sickness insurance is
continued.

(c)   The Unemployed: The unemployed are insured against sickness
if they draw an unemployment allowance or unemployment benefit.
Participants in occupational further education or retraining schemes
who are drawing maintenance allowances are also covered for sickness.
Membership of the public scheme for employees who are compulsorily
insured remains intact as long as they are entitled to a short contract
work allowance or a foul weather allowance (building trade).

(d)   Apprentices and Specified Female Trainees: Special regulations
insure female trainees in education, infant and child care, midwifery
and home help.

(e)   The Self-Employed: Various categories of the self-employed are
compulsorily insured provided their regular income is less than the
earnings ceiling of white collar workers (DM 22,500), e.g. those in
domestic industries, artists, midwives, independent teachers, tutors,
musicians and self-employed persons in the health professions, home
help, infant and child care, who employ no staffs in their business. The
latter categories include nurses, physiotherapists and masseurs provided
they work alone. If they work in groups they are generally insured on
a compulsory basis as employees.
    Until recently, self-employed farmers were outside compulsory
social health insurance.

B   Non-Compulsory Insurance

(a)   Exempt Professions: There are several categories of workers who
are exceptions to the rule of compulsory sickness insurance; civil servants, other employees of public bodies and the clergy of religious
bodies recognised as public law corporations are not compelled to
insure provided they are members of other schemes which guarantee
retirement and widow's benefits. Other exceptions include members
of religious societies, Sisters of Charity, and Sisters of the German Red
Cross provided they 'devote themselves to the care of the sick or to
activities in the common good out of predominantly religious and
moral motives'. Trainee executives, medical aides, students and
Referendare[4] do not have to insure during 'scientific training for
their future profession'.

(b)   Contracting Out: For white collar workers, tutors, musicians,
artists, midwives, persons incidentally active in the health professions,
home helps and infant and child care workers, there exist opportunities
to contract out of the compulsory sickness insurance scheme provided
they have private insurance which assures them, and their relatives of
benefits which are at least equal to those of the compulsory scheme.
After the raising of the earnings ceiling in 1970 only one per cent of
the 1.025 million people affected chose to contract out — i.e. ninety-
nine per cent joined compulsory sickness funds.
   The other cause of contracting out is where earnings rise faster
than the earnings ceiling. The member can remain in the State scheme
but until recently if he did so he could cease to benefit from the
employers' contribution (some employers continued to contribute) and
became liable for the whole contribution. However, since 1971 the
employer has had to contribute fifty per cent of the workers' contribution up to a maximum of half the contribution of a worker at the
ceiling. This provides a further inducement for workers 'overtaken' by
the ceiling to remain in the State schemes.

(c)   Contracting In: The right to contract into the compulsory sickness insurance scheme exists for all white and blue collar workers whose
income is above or below the earnings ceiling. These categories cover
such groups as: new entrants to the labour force (school leavers),
members of the family of an employer who work for him without pay,
the self-employed in skilled trades, company directors, those who
complete their service in the armed forces and the border police and
those who are State financed to undertake education and training for
their subsequent careers. It is to be noted that in these cases the funds
cannot impose age or health qualifications on the entrants.

14

C   *Private Insurance*

We have seen that the public scheme has increased in coverage of late. It would seem that a likely estimate of those with private insurance cover at the end of 1971 was ten million. This is an approximate figure because some people have more than one policy – in 1969 there were 18.97 million insurances, of which about six million were comprehensive. The 1969 income from the premiums of sickness insurance was about DM 3,700 million (£618 million) of which eighty per cent was returned to the insured population by way of benefit funds. During the last few years the number of comprehensive private insurances has declined due to the expansion of social insurance. Many of these policies have been replaced by partial insurances to ensure the individual a more comprehensive range of benefits that social insurance per se affords.

The net effect on private insurance of the recent legislation is difficult to assess. On the one hand the insured and their dependents may have been gathered up into the State scheme by its expansion or may have opted into the scheme during its 'open period' in 1971. This will have reduced both the membership and the resources of the private sector. However, another facet of the new regulations has expanded the employers' obligation to pay fifty per cent of their employees' contributions to health insurance schemes. Now the employers have to contribute fifty per cent of the workers' contribution up to the maximum of half the contribution of a worker at the ceiling. If workers are not in the State scheme they can use such contributions to pay for private insurance cover.

This 'boost' to private insurance is supplemented by circumstances. similar to those in the United Kingdom. The characteristics of the benefits (see Section 6 below) is such that individuals have been buying private insurance cover to supplement their public cover. Thus rather than go into a 'third-class' hospital bed the individual can purchase superior accommodation and pay for it with public benefits supplemented by private benefits.

D   *Social Aid*

Those people who are compulsorily insured (eighty-eight per cent of the population) and privately insured (ten per cent of the population) can with the remaining two per cent of the population benefit from the Social Aid programme. Social Aid sets out to meet the full cost, without limitation, of whatever measures may be appropriate and its administration is carried out by *Länder* officials. The benefits are means-tested and the criteria vary from one part of West Germany to another. Those whose benefits expire or who have no benefits on which to rely can go to their local *Land* office.

E   Summary

(a)   The public compulsory sickness insurance scheme covers all manual or blue collar workers and those white collar workers earning less than the earnings' ceiling (DM 22,500 at 1st January 1974). Pensioners, the unemployed and the self-employed are covered. All those covered are required to become members of one of the appropriate sickness funds (1800). Contracting in and out of the scheme is possible for certain categories of workers in certain circumstances.

(b)   The private sickness insurance cover can be purchased by those not in the public scheme and by those who are in the public scheme and wish to supplement their cover.

3   Qualifying Conditions

The sickness insurance funds provide medical care on the following conditions:

(a)   Members: The only condition necessary for a person to acquire a benefit is that they should be a member of the fund.

(b)   Dependents: are entitled to benefits if the person on whose insurance the claim is made is a member of the fund, if the dependent is entitled to benefits under the rules and if the patient has no legal claim to such benefits from another source.

4   Finance

In theory all German social insurance benefits are financed by contributions from employers and employees, and, as we shall see in this section and that which follows it, reality bears a close resemblance to this theory. All contributions are income related but they are not assessed on full but on insurable earnings limited by the ceiling which which reference was made above. On 1st January 1974 the ceiling was raised to DM 22,500 i.e. DM 1,875 (£313) per month. The evolution of the earnings ceiling over the period 1904 to 1974 is shown in Table 5. Since 1970 the earnings ceiling has been dynamic in that it is automatically adjusted to a level of seventy-five per cent of the ceiling of the old age and disability pension scheme. The latter is adjusted *via* an agreed formula for changes in wages and prices.

16

Table 5 *Compulsory Insurance Limit for White Collar Workers in the Sickness Insurance Scheme*

From	DM per year
1.1.1904	2,000
1.1.1914	2,500
12.1.1925	2,700
1.10.1927	3,600
1.6.1949	4,500
1.9.1952	6,000
1.10.1957	7,920
1.9.1965	10,800
1.8.1969	11,880
1.1.1970	14,400
1.1.1971	17,100
1.1.1972	18,600
1.1.1973	20,700
1.1.1974	22,500

Source: *Op. cit.* (1970, 1971) p.125 and *European Economic Community Commission* (1973), p.152.

Within the various earnings ceilings the total insurance deduction from employee and employer represents about twenty-seven per cent of insurable earnings. Health insurance deductions are eight per cent of insurable earnings according to most published sources.

However this figure is misleading. Each sickness fund annually fixes its contribution rates for the various categories of insured persons, taking into account the risks and the anticipated inflation in expenditure. Employers and employees pay an equal part of the contributions, except in the case of the employee who is either doing a year's voluntary social service or earns less than DM 65 per month (DM 15 per week). In the latter cases the employer pays all the contribution.

Tables 6 and 7 refer to the 1960s, i.e. the period before the guaranteed wage. The latter's creation has led to the reduction of contribution rates which is reflected in the first line of Table 7. Obviously the contribution rates of those workers not covered by the guaranteed wage is higher than the contributions of those so protected.

Table 6 *Movements in the Average Contribution Rate**

Date of Application	Sickness Insurance as a whole	OKK	BKK	LKK	IKK	SKK	KnV	Ek Ar	Ek An
1.4.1960	8.4	8.6	8.2	6.9	7.8	5.8	8.2	8.8	7.9
1.4.1961	8.6	8.7	8.3	7.2	7.9	5.8	8.2	8.9	8.5
1.4.1962	9.6	9.8	9.4	7.9	8.7	6.2	9.7	9.7	9.9
1.4.1963	9.7	9.8	9.5	8.1	8.8	6.2	9.6	9.8	11.0
1.4.1964	9.7	9.8	9.5	8.3	8.8	6.6	10.0	9.9	11.0
1.4.1965	9.8	9.9	9.7	8.7	8.8	6.6	10.7	9.9	11.5
1.4.1966	9.9	10.0	9.6	9.2	9.0	6.6	10.0	10.0	12.0
1.4.1967	10.1	10.2	9.9	9.7	9.2	6.6	11.0	10.3	13.1
1.4.1968	10.2	10.3	9.8	9.8	9.3	6.6	10.9	10.6	12.8
1.4.1969	10.4	10.5	10.0	10.0	9.8	7.8	12.0	10.8	14.1
1960 – 69									
Increase (as %)	23.8	22.1	22.0	44.8	25.6	34.5	46.3	22.7	78.5

Source: Spitaels *et al* (1971) p.555.

* in per cent
OKK Regional   KnV Miners
BKK Company   Ek Ar Manual Workers Compensation
LKK Agriculture   Ek An Staff workers Compensation
SKK Seamen

Table 6 shows the evolution of the manual workers' contribution rate up to 1969, and prior to the guaranteed wage. As can be seen from this Table the overall mean contribution rate increased by over twenty-three per cent in the period 1st April 1960 to 1st April 1969 and the average rate at the latter date was 10.4 per cent. The skew of the funds rates around this mean is small because the Regional Sickness Fund (OKK) had over sixty-seven per cent of the total number of insured persons in its ranks in 1969. The average contribution rate of the OKK was 10.5 per cent.

Table 7 *White Collar Workers – Average Contribution Rates**

Schemes	Rates %	Share of total Nos. of Insured Persons
Overall	8.5	
OKK	7.8	27.2%
BKK	7.3	10.3%
LKK	8.6	
IKK	7.4	
SKK	6.6	

18

Table 7 *(Cont)*

KnV	10.0	
Ek Ar	7.9	
Ek An	9.1	54.9%

Source: Spitaels *et al* (1971) and *Bundesminister für Arbeit und Sozialordnung*
(1970, 1971).

* As at 1st April 1969, i.e. prior to the guaranteed wage (see text).

Table 7 shows the average contribution rates of white collar workers
(as at 1st April 1969). Most of these workers (54.09 per cent) belonged
to the relevant substitute fund (Ek An). Of the rest 27.2 per cent
belonged to local funds (OKK) and 10.3 per cent belonged to comapny
funds (BKK).

With the fund's discretion to vary the contribution rates within
limits it is impossible to talk of a contribution rate. There are contribution rates and they average (early 1974) about 9.5 per cent to ten
per cent of insurable earnings (Eichhorn [1974] page 16).

The pensioners' contribution towards the cost of sickness insurance
is paid by the relevant pension insurance organisation and it is
equivalent to two thirds of the contribution of the corresponding
group of insured person. Because pensions are related to lifetime
earnings, the individual contributions vary greatly.[5] During the first
six years of the 1960s the average contribution rose slowly from DM
18.4 per month to DM 31.6 per month. During the period 1967-70
pensioners were made to contribute directly towards their sickness
insurance and the rate rose to DM 38.6 in 1967 and DM 39.6 in 1968.
The net effect was that between 1960 and 1968 the average total
contribution rose by 109.8 per cent (Spitaels *et al* [1971]). Since
1970 pensioners have made no direct contribution.

Similarly the unemployed person is compelled to pay two thirds
of the contribution of a corresponding active person and this contribution is paid on his behalf, this time by the Federal Labour Office.
The latter also reimburses the sickness funds for their payment of
sickness allowance and household allowance during the unemployed
person's period of illness.

By and large the direct contributions of the Government[6] are
minimal. The State can channel resources to health funds in four ways:
maternity insurance (for every payment of maternity allowance the
State pays DM 400 to the fund), the supplementary contribution made
by the Federal Treasury towards the mineworkers' scheme (an additional payment of one per cent of the workers earnings assessable for

insurance is made by the State), indirectly in compulsory insurance of pensioners (the pension insurance scheme is partially financed by the Federal Funds); and, since 1970, a lump sum subsidy (about DM 175 per year for the period 1970-72) is paid to the joint liability compensation funds of small companies (less than twenty employees) so that the effects of the guaranteed wage legislation are alleviated. Additionally the State (and the *Länder*) can channel resources to the providers of health care. As is noted below (see Section 5) this method is being used to improve the quality and quantity of hospital beds available.

5 Revenue and Expenditure

The financial impact of the contribution arrangements reviewed in the previous section is outlined in Table 8. This table shows the development of revenue for sickness, maternity and death insurance during the period 1960 to 1968. As can be seen total contributions increased by over 167 per cent during these nine years. Contribution income amounted to 95.2 per cent of total revenue in 1960 and 92.4 per cent of total income in 1968. Overall contribution revenue was growing at nearly ten per cent per annum. Contribution revenue for the various categories grew at varying rates: that of voluntary members grew at only 6.7 per cent per annum. This difference is due to members changing category (from compulsory to voluntary) due to the relative stability of the earnings ceiling in the period under consideration.

Table 8   *Movements in Sickness, Maternity and Death Social Insurance Revenue 1960-68*   Contributions (in millions of DM)

Year	Compulsorily insured	Voluntarily insured	Sub-total	Compulsorily insured Pensioners	Total Contributions	Contribution by the State**	Various	Total
1960			8,840	1,341	10,181	105	406	10,692
1961	7,584	1,402	8,986	1,551	10,537	117	415	11,069
1962			10,184	1,849	12,033	129	551	12,713
1963	8,819	1,801	10,620	1,984	12,604	135	648	13,387
1964	9,379	1,915	11,294	2,156	13,450	141	1,006	14,597
1965	10,641	2,103	12,744	2,355	15,099	142	975	16,215
1966			15,000	2,704	17,704	197	970	18,871
1967	12,340	2,956	15,296	3,340	18,636	222	1,224	20,082
1968*	12,716	3,524	16,240	3,583	19,823	265†	1,373	21,461
1960-1968 increase (as %)			83.7	167.2	94.7	152.4		100.7

Source: Spitaels *et al* (1971) p.558.

** In connection with benefits provided by the sickness funds in application of paras 11 and 13 of the Protection for Maternity Act, and reimbursed by

Table 8 *(cont)*

the State. Since 1968, they have, for the most part, become regular benefits of sickness insurance; the State reimburses expenditure on maternity allowances.
* Provisional figures.
† Total subsidy 260 million DM + allocation of 5 million DM to cover earlier liabilities.

During the same period the annual average growth in expenditure was 10.6 per cent, the lowest rate of increase in the European Community.[7] Table 9 shows the changes that took place in health service expenditure in the period 1960-68. As can be seen expenditure increased in all categories. The relative importance of pharmaceutical services and hospital services is obvious from this table. The former consumed fifteen per cent of total health care expenditure and twenty-one per cent of medical care expenditure. Hospitalisation (accommodation costs) consumed twenty per cent of total expenditure and 28.2 per cent of medical care expenditure. Not only were their total shares larger, their annual rates of growth (14.6 per cent and 13.6 per cent) are substantial also.

The Federal Ministry expected the share of hospitalisation to increase and the deficits, already apparent in 1968, to worsen. Their figures are reproduced in Table 10. The most significant change in this table is the fall in the share of total expenditure of cash sickness benefits. This is a result of the implementation of the guaranteed wage which shifted the burden, on paper at least, to the employers. The share of hospitalisation in total expenditure in the period 1960-73 increased by nearly one hundred per cent. The share of appliances, dentures and medicines increased by over sixty per cent. This increase was possible partly because of the reduction in the cost of the cash sickness benefits paid out by social insurance. Despite the leeway offered by the reduction of sickness benefits it can be seen from the table that social sickness insurance was in deficit for each year in the period 1968-73. However the magnitude of this deficit in relation to the total budget is small.

If columns 5, 6 and 7 are added together it can be seen that the 1973 Federal Ministry expenditure estimate for medical care was DM 24,826 million (£4,151m). Of this large budget medical and dental care consumed 32.6 per cent of the total; medicines, dentures and appliances 33.3 per cent and hospital treatment 34.3 per cent.

It can be seen that the figures in Table 10 are based on an arbitrary definition of health services, e.g. they exclude private expenditures. However, the problem, as with all semantic arguments, is to decide the 'correct' definition of health services. An alternative definition of health care and an alternative set of expenditure estimates is given by

Table 9 *Social Health Insurance Expenditure 1960-68 (in DM thousand million)*

	1960	1961	1962	1963	1964	1965	1966	1967	1968*	Increase as %	Average Annual growth rate (%)
(a) benefits in kind											
including:											
medical services	5,767	6,455	7,281	8,041	8,995	10,425	12,509	13,745	15,363	166.4	13.1
dental treatment	1,874	2,083	2,268	2,426	2,748	3,195	3,797	4,036	4,378	133.6	11.2
pharmaceutical services	468	518	658	716	783	953	1,313	1,364	1,446	209.0	15.1
dental appliances & false teeth	1,093	1,241	1,390	1,555	1,726	2,021	2,437	2,757	3,255	197.8	14.6
false teeth	269	281	311	345	341	401	503	568	619	130.1	11.0
hospital service	1,568	1,777	2,036	2,295	2,572	2,947	3,397	3,851	4,336	176.5	13.6
(b) cash benefits											
including:											
cash benefits	3,128	3,526	3,902	4,002	3,959	4,366	4,773	4,329	4,888	56.3	5.7
sickness allowance	2,572	2,915	3,221	3,281	3,166	3,501	3,791	3,301	-		3.6
TOTAL	794	891	979	1,066	1,126	1,248	1,397	1,506	1,371	72.7	7.1
including death		165	171	217	229	257	311	341	383		12.7
maternity		456	501	564	624	679	794	850	988		11.7
Administrative costs	515	581	619	696	734	815	899	956	1,025	99.0	9.0
OVERALL TOTAL	9,680	10,872	12,162	13,109	14,080	16,039	18,679	19,580	21,622	123.2	10.6

Source: Spitaels *et al* (1971) p.560.

* Provisional Figures.

Table 10 *Social Insurance Income and Expenditure 1938-73 (Selected years)*

Year	Income	Expenditure	Deficit/ Surplus	Types of Expenditure Medical & Dental	Medicines Appliances	DM million Hospital Treatment	(% of total expenditure)* Cash Sickness benefits
(1)	(2)	(3)	(4)	(5)	(6)	(7)	(8)
1938	1,803	1,787	16	526 (29)	205 (11)	205 (11)	397 (22)
1950	2,422	2,278	144	568 (24)	438 (19)	438 (19)	469 (20)
1955	4,617	4,627	-10	1,276 (17)	826 (17)	709 (15)	938 (20)
1960	9,524	9,513	11	2,342 (24)	1,568 (16)	1,362 (14)	2,572 (27)
1965	15,961	15,785	176	4,148 (26)	2,947 (18)	2,422 (15)	3,501 (22)
1966	18,554	18,362	192	5,109 (27)	2,940 (16)	3,397 (18)	3,791 (20)
1967	19,738	19,236	502	5,400 (28)	3,325 (17)	3,851 (20)	3,301 (17)
1968	21,195	21,513	-318	5,844 (27)	4,390 (20)	4,384 (20)	3,967 (18)
1969	23,315	23,734	-419	6,284 (26)	4,989 (21)	5,042 (21)	4,186 (17)
1970	24,120	25,583	-1,463	6,598 (25)	5,660 (22)	5,748 (22)	1,580 (5)
1971	25,863	26,322	-459	7,074 (26)	6,422 (24)	6,553 (24)	1,607 (6)
1972	28,404	28,695	-291	7,526 (26)	7,288 (25)	7,470 (26)	1,687 (5)
1973	31,245	31,550	-305	8,038 (25)	8,277 (26)	8,516 (27)	1,771 (5)
	(£5,224)	(£5,275)	(£51)	(£1,344)	(£1,383)	(£1,424)	(£296)

Source: *Bundesminister* (1971) p 142

* The expenditures do not add up to the years totals (or 100%) because only the most important categories are listed. Exemptions include cash maternity and death benefits, administrative costs.

Table 11 *The Cost of Health 1968*

	Total	State	Other Social Insurance	Legislative health Insurance	Private health Insurance	Employer	Private Households (employees)	Organisations without earning capacity
A Preventative Medicine	4.5	1.1	1.8	1.3	-	0.2	0.1	-
1 Duty of the Public Health Service	0.9	0.9	-	-	-	-	-	-
2 Public Health Welfare	0.5	0.2	-	0.3	-	-	-	-
3 Prevention of Unemployment	2.0	-	1.7	-	-	0.2	0.1	-
4 Maternity Care	1.0	-	-	1.0	-	-	-	-
5 Accident Prevention	0.1	-	0.1	-	-	-	-	-
B Treatment	25.8	4.0	0.5	14.5	(2.0)	-	4.9	1.9
1 Doctors & Dentists	9.0	0.1	0.2	6.4	(0.9)	-	2.3	-
2 Hospitals	10.6	3.5	0.2	4.3	(0.6)	-	0.7	1.9
3 Medicines	6.2	0.4	0.1	3.8	(0.5)	-	1.9	-
C Consequence of illness	15.7	1.4	7.2	4.0	0.1	3.0	-	-
1 Sick Pay, sick benefit	9.1	1.4	0.6	4.0	0.1	3.0	-	-
2 Pension for early invalidity	6.6	-	6.6	-	-	-	-	-
D Training & Research	2.5	2.2	-	-	-	-	0.2	0.1
1 Training of specialists	2.2	2.0	-	-	-	-	-	-
2 Training of all other medical staff	0.2	0.1	-	-	-	-	-	-
3 Research Institutes	0.1	0.1	-	-	-	-	-	0.1
TOTAL	48.5	8.7	9.5	19.8	0.1 (2.0)	3.2	5.2	2.0

Source: K. Szemeitat (1970) p 676 Table 1 (corrected for arithmetic errors).
The figures in brackets: refund to private patients. Beside the amount shown in the Table the author also proposes the addition of lost production due to illness estimated at DM 20 Mrd. All data is in thousand millions, e.g. 48.5 = 48,500,000,000.

Szemaitat.[8] He expands the definition of health to include preventative medicine, invalidity payments, training and research and private expenditure. Also he attempts to provide estimates of the costs of various units.

As a result (Table 10) the official Government figure for social sickness insurance is augmented and escalates from DM 21,195 million (£3,544m) to DM 48,500 million (£8,110.36m): an increase of 128 per cent. This difference between the social insurance expenditure (which is often the basis of international comparison) and Szemeitat's estimate of the cost of 'good health' highlights some of the inherent difficulties which exist for those interested in carrying out exercises which compare expenditure between countries. The identification of the 'correct' figure depends on the readers' interpretation of the word 'health'.

It is apparent that the figures for expenditure and revenue for the social insurance system are not an adequate means of determining total health care figures in West Germany and the tendency of some writers to use this figure in international comparison must be avoided. The conclusions to be derived from the official statistics are important nevertheless. The primary method of funding is the contributions of the employee and the employer. Although the contribution rates in many cases fell in the early 1970s the 'dynamisation' of the earnings ceiling means that absolute contributions of some workers is higher now than it was in the late 1960s. Even though it may increase in the late 1970s out of necessity, the role of the government as a financer is, as yet, quite small. The expenditure trends are rising and in some component parts of the health budget, rising rapidly. The Federal Government's Social Budget shows a projected expenditure growth similar to that of the other sections of the social budget (e.g. pensions). This is despite the 1970 reforms which made the employers liable for the payment of the first six weeks of sickness pay (the guaranteed wage). The DM 3,000 million (£836m) expenditure cut which resulted from these reforms has been compensated by cost expansion of medical care benefits. The provision of medical care is labour intensive and wage inflation plus the demand for better standards of care is increasing the costs of care in West Germany, as in other countries.

6 Benefits

Social health insurance in West Germany provides medical care benefits and cash benefits as a result of the membership of a fund and the payment of one contribution. Each type of benefit will be dealt with separately. Medical care is considered in Part (a) and cash sickness benefits are the subject of Part (b).

(a) Medical Care

Attempts by the sickness funds to set up their own health centres run by doctors paid by lump sum methods precipitated such medical opposition that the funds' activities in this are now regulated by law. Apart from these health centres the funds have no medical infra-structure as they own few hospitals and employ few doctors. Thus the funds' major role is that of financier. The provision of health care facilities rests in the hands of the doctors and the owners of the hospitals.

In principle a person is entitled to benefits only if he acquires a medical certificate (Krankenschei) valid for the current quarter before he consults a doctor. If such certificates are unused they can be surrendered for a cash refund of DM 10 per quarter up to a limit of DM 30 per annum. This arrangement is likely to be terminated as it has had little impact in curtailing consumption (see *Bundesartze-kammer* [1972] 'Tatigkeitsbericht' 1971-2). Usually the funds have required employers to issue these certificates to employed workers and, of late, they have begun to issue books of certificates to insured workers. These certificates are used as evidence of membership and for billing for the medical services provided. Each certificate is sent by the doctor to his association of registered doctors. The association pays him according to rates agreed with the sickness funds. Usually the physician is paid a fixed sum per item of service. If the individual maintains his membership of the fund he is entitled to benefits for an unlimited duration in all cases except that of hospitalisation where a limit of seventy-eight weeks over three years for the same illness is in operation.

If the individual gives up his membership of the fund during treatment, benefits can be obtained for up to a maximum of a further twenty-six weeks. (For dependents this period is thirteen weeks, with the possibility of an expension up to a maximum of twenty-six weeks and the exclusion of an older children, according to the fund's rules).

The benefits derived from membership include medical and dental consultations, home visits, laboratory analyses, special services and surgical operations. Most of these benefits are provided free of charge if they are administered by sickness fund doctors (*Kassenartze*) who are members of an association of registered doctors. Unregistered doctors can act in an emergency. The patient has free choice of general practitioner, specialist, dentist and optician, to the extent that he can change at the end of each quarter; changes within the quarter are only permitted by the fund if the patient can provide a satisfactory rationale of his desire to change or he obtains a transfer note (*Uberweisungsaschein*) issued by the practitioner who is being consulted at the time.

Pharmaceutical products when prescribed by a registered doctor, are obtained on payment of a fixed sum. The insured family and his dependents pay twenty per cent of the cost of the drugs up to a maximum of DM 2.50 per prescription.[9] For pensioners, the chronic sick (as per legal list) and those insured persons who have been unfit for work over six weeks, there is no charge.

In the case of lapsed membership the general rule continues to apply to the insured member for the maximum period of twenty-six weeks referred to above. However his adult dependents may have to contribute thirty to fifty per cent of the cost of the drugs depending on the fund's rule. As in the UK some attempt is made to constrain doctors from prescribing expensive drugs. A Federal Committee (*Bundesausschuss für Artze und Krankenkassen*) urges doctors not to exceed an average prescription rate which is calculated as a guide line. This average is applied to all prescriptions of a particular doctor and if the norm is exceeded the doctor must show justification to his association of registered doctors who supervise the operation of the scheme.

The sickness fund is required to provide hospital care when the patient requires treatment which his family cannot provide by reason of the nature of the services required in infectious cases and where the patients condition requires constant care. The hospital is paid a fixed amount per day. The patient is usually provided with Third Class Ward admission and is entitled to treatment for up to a maximum of seventy-eight weeks in any three year period for one disease. For more than one disease the entitlement exists separately. The amount paid varies according to the type of hospital and different *Landes* have differing categories of hospital — the number of categories varies between six and twenty. The fixed sum so paid does not take account of all the costs of care. Depreciation on buildings and equipment, loan interest, and the building up of reserves are all ignored. Such liabilities were met by the owners, the Land, the local authorities and religious or other bodies. Recently legislation has been introduced to provide state finance for hospital treatment *via* direct subsidies or non-returnable payments to meet the cost of debt finance (see below).

Hospitalisation and the medical care of the doctors is supplemented by other types of care. The funds can attempt to take the initiative in providing home treatment when they regard hospitalisation as unnecessary. However in practice this is apparently rare because of the lack of auxiliary medical staff.[10] In addition to such care the Health Insurance funds pay for the regular examination of infants to detect physical and mental abnormalities up to the age of four years. Also women over thirty and men over forty-five are entitled to a free annual cancer check. A peculiarity of the German system is the discretionary provision of *Kuren* or cures. This is the treatment at spas and in convalescent homes. There are two hundred spas in West Germany providing either mineral or mud baths. Also there are several hundred approved convalescent homes.

Dental treatment and medical appliances are covered by a variety of regulations. Dental treatment is dichtomised into two types of benefit: standard and supplementary. The former benefit covers preventative treatment, extractions and fillings. Here the funds cover one hundred per cent of the cost of treatment. Supplementary benefits – e.g. false teeth and crowning – can also be fully covered by fund benefits in some cases. In each case in this category cover depends on the regulations of the particular fund. Usually the fund meets about one third of the cost and may pay a further one third on behalf of the Pension Fund. Treatment can be given only by registered dentists and a special insurance certificate has to be presented by the insured person prior to treatment. The dentist is usually paid on a piece-rate basis.

Spectacles are covered by the same regulations as for pharmaceutical products, i.e. twenty per cent of the cost up to DM 2.50 except for the exempted categories noted above. Artificial limbs and hearing aids are financed in accordance with the funds regulations. Once again a cash grant may cover the entire cost of approved purchases. The patient submits the prescription to the fund and the services are treated by the funds in two cost categories. The cost dividing line varies from fund to fund and was between DM 80 and DM 100 in 1969. Services in the lower price range are free of charge. Services in the upper range require patient contribution but the fund's guaranteed minimum contribution is equal to the maximum price in the lower price range. By and large fund contributions rates vary from thirty to forty per cent. So if the fund's regulations fix an upper limit to the lower range at DM 100 and the contribution rate at 33.3 per cent the fund will pay following sums in the three cases below:

1) An appliance costing DM 98 – all.
2) An appliance costing DM 130 – DM 100 (£16).

28

3) An appliance costing DM 450 — DM 150 (£25).

This in case 3 above the individual could be faced with a bill for DM 300 (£51). However it is apparently general for a further third of the cost to be paid for by the fund and debited to pension insurance if the patient is elderly.

(b)   Cash Sickness Benefits

(i)   Outside the insurance scheme: As from the 1st January 1970 all workers received a guaranteed wage [11] for the first six weeks of sickness. The worker would not qualify for the guaranteed wage if he is sick twice in one year and the successive bouts of illness are not separated by an internal of six months.

(ii)   Inside the insurance scheme:

(a)   Sickness allowance and household allowance: A medical certificate has to be sent to the employer by the worker within three calendar days from the date shown on the certificate. The doctor should inform the relevant sickness fund immediately, certifying the nature of the illness and estimated duration. In dubious cases the fund can refer the member to the confidential medical service for verification.

During the first six weeks of illness all workers receive full wages from their employers (the guaranteed wage). The insured worker can, after this period, qualify for one of two benefits. The sickness allowance *(Krankengeld)* is compensation for loss of earnings paid due to a physical incapacity which does not necessitate admittance to a hospital. If hospital care is necessary the household allowance *(Hausgeld)* is paid in lieu of the sickness allowance to contribute to fixed household expenses. [12] These benefits amount to seventy-five per cent of previous 'regular' earnings [13] plus family suuplementation. The duration of these benefits is normally not more than eighteen months during any period of three years for the same illness. When sickness benefits are exhausted the worker is entitled to a disablement or retirement pension or Social Aid.

(b)   Maternity: A confinement allowance is paid to contribute to expenditure other than treatment expenses *(Wochenhilfe)*. A maternity allowance *(Mutterschaftsgeld)* is paid to all those women who are directly or indirectly insured (dependents). The allowance is assessed on a lump sum basis or on the basis of earnings in the case of women directly insured.

(c)   Death: The death grant *(Sterbegeld)* is paid to meet funeral expenses. Smaller grants are paid for all those dependents living under the insured's roof.

As can be seen from the above description of the benefits provided by social health insurance in West Germany, the cover is comprehensive and the degree of financial contribution from the patient is small. It is argued by some that the level of remuneration of physicians is 'excessive' because this profession gets the first, very effective, bite at the budget cherry. There does seem to be evidence of under-finance of hospitals, the critics would say as a result of the physicians' monopolistic power, and as can be seen in the next section (Section 7) this is leading to an increase in State involvement in the provision of health care.

7 Provision

This section is concerned with the detailed arrangements surrounding the delivery of various types of medical care in West Germany and with statistical indicators of various types of input provision.

(a)   Medical Personnel

Since 1970 the aspiring physician has had to undergo a course of training lasting six years (five years study). This regulation was retroactive and led to a substantial increase in the output of new physicians in the late 1960s and early 1970s, e.g. in 1969 4,923 new licences were granted (seventy-eight per cent more than in 1966). There are twenty university hospitals with about 40,000 beds and after six years training in one of these institutions a physician can undertake a further four to six years training to qualify as a recognised specialist in one of twenty-five specialisms.

The relationship between the funds and the medical profession has been quite heated at times during the recent past. There have been threats of strikes and boycotts, the rise of protective medical organisations, press campaigns and much political lobbying. The funds have a legal obligation to provide medical care and their attempts to meet this have run into the familiar problem of the physicians' attempting to maintain their 'independence'.

All physicians and dentists must join a *Land* association. These associations have the power to admit, tax, supervise, discipline, fine and expel members. The associations guarantee the standards of the medical services their members provide and enter into collective agreements with the sickness funds. The sickness funds pay the association a lump sum and this money is distributed to the doctors by the association on one of four bases:
1) According to the number of assured and the average annual number of visits — the proportional system or lump sum system
2) According to a contract for each instance of illness
3) According to a contract for each medical act

4) According to a mixed system.

The most common methods are payment by service and a proportional payment. The former method remits to the doctor a sum of money for each medical act. The proportional payment is paid by the funds to the doctors' *Land* association on a *per capita* basis or on an average number of services basis. The associations then redistribute the funds to doctors on a fees for services basis. The sums are fixed in the sickness fund medical association agreement and normally run for one year. The basis of recent rate fixing has been along the lines of that concluded at a national level in 1965 by the Federal Association of Registered Doctors (FARD) and the Federal Association of Regional Funds (FARF − OKK). This agreement − which has been followed by funds other than OKK [14] − has led to the fixing of coefficients to be applied to inflate the 1965 Federal Index. Where the two parties fail to reach an agreement on the rates the Federal Arbitration Committee will step in and their decision is binding on both parties. Many doctors are still partly paid by a lump or proportional system (especially those working in partnership with LKK, BKK and IKK). However the substitute funds (EKN) almost entirely pay in relation to the service rendered. The average medical fees in 1970 were as follows:

(a) Consultation with G.P.   DM 3.60 (£0.6)
(b) G.P. visit to patient's home   DM 10.80 (£1.8)
(c) First consultation with specialist with
     examination   DM 11.60 (£1.9)

Table 12 *Doctors, Medical Assistants and Dentists 1969*

Year	Total	Population per Doctor	Medical Assistants	Dentists* Total	Pop. per Dentist
1938**	49,732	1,379	-	35,565	1,928
1952†	68,135	735	-	27,979	1,822
1960	79,350	703	3,328	32,509	1,716
1965	85,801	691	6,613	31,660	1,873
1966	86,700	690	7,893	31,599	1,892
1967	88,599	677	8,841	31,148	1,925
1968	90,882	665	9,643	31,227	1,936
1969	93,934	651	9,476	31,220	1,960
1970	99,654	612	6,322	31,175	1,956

Source: *Wirtschaft und Statistik* (1970) Table 1.

* Until 1966 includes dental technicians.
** German Reich.
† Without Saarland.

It was estimated by survey in 1967 that the average physician was paid DM 80,000 (£13,400). However because of the skew of the distribution the central value (or modular, i.e. fifty per cent earned more, and fifty per cent earned less than this figure) of the distribution was DM 109,000 (£18,230). These figures are gross incomes and the modular net proceeds of the practice for a married physician with two children was estimated to be DM 44,460 (£7,435).

Most physicians are affiliated to the sickness funds. It was estimated that at the end of 1969 there were 94,000 doctors in West Germany (see Tables 12 and 13): 50,379 physicians were in independent practice, most of these physicians (as can be seen from Table 14) were without access to a hospital; 9,785 physicians were engaged in research and administration; 33,770 were attached to hospitals. Registered doctors accounted for approximately ninety-nine per cent of those doctors in independent practice. Some five hundred physicians, mostly specialists, appear to be unregistered and in full time private practice.

Table 13 *Affiliation of Physicians 1970 (1969) and Dentists (1969)*

Category	Active Physicians			Dentists
	Total	General Practitioners*	Specialists	Total
A in independent practice				
(a) without access to hospitals	43,876	26,814	17,062	(28,346)
(b) with access to hospitals	6,855 (6,993)	1,177 (1,259)	5,678 (5,734)	(107) (107)
(c) Assistants	(418)	351	67	(1,429)
B Full time in hospitals	38,655 (33,770)	22,938 (18,917)	15,717 (14,853)	(636)
C Public Employment	99,654 (93,934)	57,921 (53,358)	41,733 (40,576)	(31,220)

Source: *Wirtschaft und Statistik* Table 2 and Eichhorn (1973) p.85.
* Including bacteriologists, pathologists, etc.

Table 13 shows that 56.8 per cent (53,358) of West German physicians are general practitioners and 43.2 per cent (40,576) were specialists. Members of the latter group work both inside and outside the hospital and Table 14 gives an indication of their specialisms. This shows that the largest single category was internal medicine and that most of these specialists were in the community rather than working full time in hospital.

Table 14 *Specialist Physicians by Specialism 1969*

Specialisms	TOTAL Absolute	Percentage	NUMBER WHO WERE Female (%)	Independent practice (%)	Full time in hospital (%)
Surgery	5,169	12.7	4.4	30.8	63.6
Internal Medicine	10,715	26.4	13.8	53.1	36.0
Lung diseases	1,707	4.2	17.0	37.5	36.3
Obstetrics	4,231	10.4	15.4	62.7	35.4
Paediatrics	3,336	8.2	38.0	62.9	27.2
Ear, nose & throat	2,469	6.1	6.4	83.6	14.5
Opthalmic	2,417	6.0	20.3	86.9	12.2
Dermatology & VD	1,756	4.3	18.3	79.8	13.2
Nervous diseases	2,885	7.1	20.8	39.0	50.6
Neurology	108	0.3	6.5	7.4	88.9
Radiotherapy	1,716	4.2	7.2	52.2	40.9
Orthopaedics	1,626	4.0	6.9	72.8	20.3
Urology	851	2.1	0.7	62.6	35.7
Dental	438	1.1	13.7	71.2	26.5
Anaesthesia	730	1.8	34.7	7.1	90.8
Laboratory diagnosis	422	1.0	13.5	45.5	29.9
TOTAL	40,576	100.0	15.9	55.6	36.6

Source: *Wirtschaft und Statistik* (1970) p.3.

The community physician — whether registered or unregistered — usually works on an individual basis. Group practices are, as yet, rare — only thirty group practices were reported to be functioning in the whole of West Germany in 1970. [15] Many doctors appear to carry out their own laboratory analyses rather than delegate such functions to specialist bodies. This practice is, in part, a function of a system of payment which is related to items of service. To delegate or divide labour under such a regime is to reduce one's own income if doctors are underemployed.

Another significant difference in the German system health compared compared with the USA or the UK is the relative lack of outpatients hospital facilities. With a few exceptions, hospitals are not licensed as institutions to treat outpatients. Semi-hospitalised care exists only for psychiatric patients.

The payment of hospital doctors depends on the type of hospital in which they work. Those who work in publicly owned hospitals are divided into three classes (chief hospital doctors [*chefartze*] , head physicians and assistant physicians) and paid a salary by the hospital board. Usually chief hospital doctors are allowed to conduct private practice and are paid directly for such services. Many hospitals are too small to provide full time employment and in these cases the physician practices outside the hospital and agrees with the hospital board to use a specified number of hospital beds. In these cases the physician is paid directly by the patient or the sickness fund.

Those physicians working in private charitable hospitals (mostly religious) are paid a salary and, in some cases, they are able to earn private fees. Usually the doctors are 'freelance' with extra-hospital practices because the size of the hospital units does not warrant full time employment of specialists. In private profit-making hospitals there is a sharper distinction between the *chefartze* (the chief hospital doctor) and his juniors. The latter are usually paid salaries whereas the chefartze is paid fees directly by the patient or the sickness fund. Often the chefartze is the owner, or part-owner, of the private profit-making hospital.

The basic fees paid to hospital doctors are governed by the fee scales agreed between the doctors' organisation and the fund. The actual fees charged can be up to six times the basic fee and are inflated by special circumstances, e.g. the difficulty of the case, time taken, the financial circumstances of the patient, etc. The actual fees can exceed the amount of the basic fee only if the patient agrees. The more affluent patients tend to have treatment in better class (i.e. 1st and 2nd Class, rather than the basic 3rd Class). Physicians' fees depend on the class of treatment chosen by the patient. However a new law (1972) has tended to blur the distinction between the classes of treatment. Single-bedded, twin-bedded and rooms with several beds are to be grouped together. Separate payments make it possible to obtain access to single or twin-bedded rooms but this does no entitle the patient to receive private treatment nor to choose a particular physician and pay him privately. Such choices can be made by the patient but he may find himself sharing a twin-bedded room with a person whose treatment is wholly financed by social insurance and who has merely paid an additional fee to be more secluded. Better class accommodation will be concomitant with private treatment only if this is specified in the head doctors' contracts concluded before 1st July 1972.

Remuneration and other factors have led to a distribution of physicians which is very uneven. This lack of uniformity has several dimensions. Firstly, as regards to where they work. In the period 1960-70 there was an increase of 31,000 in the number of physicians and medical assistants in West Germany. Most of these doctors (21,238 or sixty-eight per cent) have gone into hospital work and this flow represents an increase in the hospital doctor staff of ninety-one per cent in the decade. The second characteristic of inequality has been the relative stability in the number of general practitioners and the large increase

Table 15   *Regional Distribution of Physicians* 1970*

Region	Absolute Number	Number per 100,000 population
Schleswig Holstein	4,565	1,795
Hamburg	5,005	2,808
Bremen	1,514	2,048
Lower Saxony	11,094	1,544
Westphalia	12,015	1,709
Nordrhein	17,277	
Hessen	10,696	1,948
Rheinland-Pfaiz	5,936	1,613
Baden-Wurttemburg	16,726	1,847
Bavaria	20,039	1,874
Saarland	2,036	1,814
TOTAL	106,905	1,799
West Berlin	6,552	3,143

Source: Wolff (1970).

* Includes those who are actively practising medicine and those who are not. Thus the figures differ from Table 14 which is for active physicians only.

(thirty per cent) in the number of specialist physicians in the period 1960-70. The relative stability of the general practitioner stock is combined with the third inequality measure: that of dispersion. Table 15 shows that the West German ratio of physician to 100,000 patients was 1,799 in 1970. Apart from West Berlin, which is a special case and has a doctor/100,000 population ratio of 3,143, the distribution ranges from a high of 2,808 in Hambgurg (fifty-six per cent above the average) to a low of 1,544 in Lower Saxony (fourteen per cent below the average). The stocks below the average in quantity and magnitude of 'deficiency' are not as substantial as in some other West European countries. However it is necessary to emphasise that these statistics are highly aggregated and within the *Länder* there are large variations. In particular there is evidence of 'under-doctoring' in rural areas. These problems are familiar to any policy maker or analyst of this area of social policy. The Germans are making efforts to change the geographical distribution e.g. by increasing payments and guaranteeing a minimum income to those in rural areas. Perhaps the most surprising aspect of the distribution of physicians is the increase in their numbers in the hospitals in the period 1960-70. This has improved the doctor/bed ratio significantly but contributes substantially to the increase in the cost of the hospital service which, by its very nature, is labour intensive. To allow sixty-eight per cent of newly qualified physicians to enter a hospital service with no outpatients facilities (see below) is not necessarily very efficient.

The relationship between funds and dentists is similar to that between funds and doctors. Only dentists registered with the funds are permitted to provide treatment. Most are in independent practice (Table 14). Treatment is carried out after the presentation of special medical certificates. Payment is usually by individual services performed – i.e. fee per item of service (or piece rates).

Table 16   *The Dental Service*

Year	Nos. of registered dentists	Annual expenditure per member	Annual expenditure on false teeth per member
1960	32,509	DM 20.24	DM 10.40
1968	31,227	DM 61.74	DM 20.35

Source: *Bundesminister für Arbeit und Socialordnung* (1970, 1971) p. 131.

Figures per member relate to members with their dependents, but excluding services to pensioners and their dependents.

Tables 12 and 16 show that the number of dentists declined in the 1960s. This trend is exaggerated because prior to 1966 the data included dental technicians. Some fifteen per cent of dentists were female.

There were 104,134 trained nurses at the end of 1969 (Table 17). Also there were 14,479 male nurses, half of whom worked in mental hospitals, 15,880 children's nurses, 16,975 male medical orderlies and 36,503 unregistered nursing assistants, i.e. 187,971 in total. In 1970 there were 199,457 trained nurses of various types and 52,047 trainees. The magnitude of this annual increase (11,486 or 6.1. per cent) is not unusual. During the 1960s the number of nurses increased 57,600, i.e. thirty-one per cent.

36

Table 17 *Other Medical Professions 1969*

Year	Pharmacists in Pharmacies		Nurses				Social Workers*	
	Total	Female %	Male Nurses	Nurses	Childrens Nurses	Mid-wives	Total	Female %
1938**	11,819	-		132,288	10,633	24,377	-	-
1952†	11,414	-	7,737	92,499	9,024	11,740	7,705	96.7
1960	15,776	38.4	10,835	94,352	11,921	9,442	7,653	91.4
1965	17,725	43.7	12,532	97,527	13,282	8,230	8,894	89.6
1966	18,268	44.8	13,219	99,609	13,708	7,498	8,398	90.3
1967	18,794	45.9	13,411	101,088	14,213	7,746	8,293	90.2
1968	19,669	46.7	13,945	102,422	15,204	7,481	8,255	88.9
1969	20,151	47.6	14,497	104,134	15,880	7,182	8,276	87.5

Source: *Op. cit.* Table 7.

* Welfare office, health visitors, etc. employed in public health or working for health office.
** German Reich.
† Without Saarland.

At the end of 1969 there were 10,954 public pharmacies (one for every 5,587 people) and 20,151 pharmacists. Most pharmacies appear to be quite small (on average 1.79 pharmacists per pharmacy) and nearly half their personnel is female. This latter fact may contribute to a situation where the total number of pharmacists in West Germany is, unlike many other European countries, increasing.

(b)   Hospitals

Table 18 *The German Hospital System (Social Health Insurance Fund Fund Cases Only)*

Year	Hospital cases in	Days spent in hospital	Length of Stay	Cost of In-patient treatment (DM m)	Cost per day DM
1950	2,929	68,261	23.3	438	6.50
1955	3,555	81,833	23.0	777	9.50
1960	4,093	90,991	22.2	1,568	17.20
1965	4,445	101,324	22.8	2,947	29.10
1966	4,587	103,605	22.6	3,397	32.80
1967	4,751	106,607	22.4	3,851	36.10
1968	5,012	110,815	22.1	4,384	39.10

Source: *Op. cit.* p.133.

The hospital system seems to be in some financial trouble. In part this is due to the fact that the sickness funds refuse to contribute towards the capital costs of hospital provision. Table 18 gives some details about the characteristics of the German hospital system. The main points to note are the average length of stay in hospital (for acute beds only the average length of stay in 1969 was 18.6 days), and the inflation of costs in the 1960s. The average occupancy rate is quite high 88.9 per cent (Eichhorn [1973] p. 85).

Table 19   *Hospital: Ownership and Capacity 1960 and 1969*

Type of Hospital	Number of Hospitals	Number of Hospital Beds	Average Number of Beds per Hospital
Public			
1960	1,385	326,413	235.7
1969	1,345	370,541	275.5
Private Charitable			
1960	1,307	215,120	164.6
1966	1,281	248,779	194.2
Private Profit-making			
1960	912	41,980	46.0
1969	975	58,375	59.9
Acute only			
1960	2,656	406,022	152.9
1969	2,462	454,055	184.4
Total			
1960	3,604	583,513	161.9
1969	9,601	677,695	188.2

Source: *Bundesminister für Jegend, Familie und Gesundheit* (1971)

Data as at 31st December.

The ownership of the hospitals is one of three types: public, private, non-profit making or voluntary and private profit-making. Table 19 shows the number of hospitals and beds in each type of ownership in 1960 and 1969. Despite the fact that only thirty-seven per cent of hospitals are publicly owned (almost entirely by the *Länder*) over fifty-four per cent of the 1969 bed stock was in such hospitals. On average public hospitals are larger than their private counterparts. Some writers (Eichhorn [1973] p. 84) have argued that the optimal hospital size is 450-500 beds (which is small by UK Ministry standards). This estimate implies an optimal hospital stock of 1,450 units, i.e. 2,000 less than at the beginning of 1970. The final two rows of Table 19 show the acute hospital and bed stock position in 1960 and 1969. It can be seen from this data that although the number of acute hospitals fell the acute bed stock rose by nearly 48,000 to 453,055, and the average unit size increased to over 184 beds. The difference between the total and the acute bed stock is made up of special hospitals. Of this portion of the bed stock (thirty-three per cent in all), 117,235 were for the treatment of patients with mental disorders, 56,004 were convalescent hospital beds (often old sanatoria) and 33,628 beds were for the treatment of patients with TB.

The number of beds per thousand population is quite high by European standards. In 1969 (EEC 1973) there were 11.03 beds per thousand population of which 7.42 were in general and specialised establishments, 0.48 were for TB patients, 1.90 were for psychiatric patients and 1.23 were for the chronically ill, the aged, rehabilitation, convalescents, etc. The first sub-category of provision (7.42) was the highest in the old EEC in the late 1960s. As we mentioned above social insurance benefits, by and large, entitle the patient to basic (third class) hospital accommodation in the hospital of his choice — provided the hospital has an agreement with the insured's fund. In the 1960s the criteria by which the charges for third class accommodation were fixed were decided by each hospital, subject to Federal and *Länder* regulations (1954 legislation). This regulation was rather uncertain and arbitrary, and contributed to the financial problems of the hospitals in that it usually resulted in fees which met only part of the costs. The resultant deficits were met by *Länder* subsidies until more formal intervention was introduced since the Federal Law of 1971 (*Altenstetter* [1973] p. 47) the daily hospital service charges for third class in all areas are to be set uniformly by order of the Federal Ministry upon approval by *Länder* Governments. Additional purchasing power (either cash or private insurance) is required by the patient who requires better accommodation, e.g. single or double rooms rooms. However the various categories of room size differ with regard to aspects other than the number of beds per unit. There are differences in comfort between the groups (e.g. quality of furnishings, private bath, balcony, visiting hours and food) and also the higher classes may have the right to be treated by a senior hospital doctor. Whereas the distinctions between the types of care was sharp in the 1960s, it has been blurred by recent Federal Legislation (1972). Additional payments give the patient access to single or twin-bedded rooms but now it does not always carry with it the concomitant right to private medical care. As was noted above in the discussion of the remuneration of hospital physicians, such concomitance depends on the physician's contract with the hospital. Consequently the patient is freer to purchase more seclusion without obligation to private treatment. These types of care give rise to differing daily charges.

However despite the complexities of the system of payment the hospital system is running a substantial financial deficit. The deficit of communal, public and private hospitals in 1966 was DM 843 million. This figure was arrived at after operational subsidies of DM 650 million and subsidies and loans for investment of DM 554 million. Both sums were paid by combinations of *Lander* and local authorities. Thus in reality the deficit could be regarded as DM 2,047m in 1966. These are not isolated statistics: Table 20 shows substantial deficits (i.e. post *Land* and local authority subsidies) for various years between 1957 and 1970. However, by and large, these deficits are met quite easily by local authority grants and voluntary contributions (e.g. voluntary church taxes are paid by a high proportion of the population).

Table 20 *Hospital Deficits in Germany*

Year	Deficit (DM Million)
1957	280
1962	470
1964	785
1966	843
1970	900 (£150m)

Source: British United Provident Association Research Department.

Recent projections[16] for hospital bed requirements provides the data for Table 21 and highlights the financial problems which the hospitals face. Not only are the hospitals in a financial deficit they also face the 'need' to produce and implement very costly investment programmes.

Table 21 *Hospital Investment Projections 1969-74*

Year	Requirement	Bed Cost per DM	Total Investment Cost (DM m)
1969	21,272	80,000	1,702
1970	21,418	86,400	1,802
1971	21,564	92,800	2,003
1972	21,710	100,310	2,178
1973	21,856	108,335	2,268
1974	22,002	117,000	2,574

Source: H. Muller (1970).

This problem prompted the Federal government to promote a bill in 1971. The legislation provides for public subsidisation (one third by Federal sources, two-thirds by *Land* and local government sources) of hospital investment programmes and represents a significant increase in the involvement of the public authorities in the provision of health care in the FDR. In 1972 (the first full year of the law's operation) the total investment requirement of these hospitals qualifying for assistance was approximately DM 2,000 million (£334m). Of this DM 636 million was provided by the Federal Government. DM 1,070 million by the *Länder* and DM 400 by the *Gemainder* (districts) (*Bundesminister Gesundbeitsbericht* [1971] p. 324). It means that the State via the *Lander*, with Federal Government approval, may finance out of taxation fifteen per cent (investment and maintenance costs) of hospital care. The remaining eighty-five per cent (running costs) will be covered by health insurance and the funds are obliged to pay the hospital fees sufficient to meet these running costs in full. These subsidies are accompanied by exact accounting procedures which are to be used by all hospitals.

In addition to the financial control the State has also taken power to affect the regional location of hospitals. As in Britain, France and most other European countries the distribution of hospital beds in West Germany is very unequal. Now the plans of individual hospitals will have to fit into a regional hospital plan which has been supplied to each *Land* by the Federal Government. This plan gives a general indication of the 'necessary' number of hospital beds and their ditribution. The Federal Government is to vet each proposal and ensure that it complies with the plan and without its approval the individual hospital will not have access to *Land* funds to cover investments and maintenance costs. This policy instrument and the objectives to which it is directed are comparable with French and British instruments and objectives. Its major defect seems to be that the expansion of outpatients facilities continues to be ignored. This means that hospital facilities may not be as intensively used as they are in health systems where equipment such as X-ray facilities, electro-cardiograph machines, etc. are used to diagnose and treat both in-patients and outpatients. Also it means that physicians outside the hospital acquire equipment which duplicates neighbouring hospital facilities, and, once again, is not used intensively, or patients are 'needlessly' hospitalised so that they can gain access to hospital facilities. This 'gap' between the community physician and the hospital could be eradicated and costs of treatment reduced if habits of mind could be changed by financial incentives or coercion.

8 Conclusion

Germany, like so many countries, is suffering from a severe economic problem with regard to its health services. The demands of medical technology, rising aspirations, and inflation are throwing the opportunity costs of the health programme into high relief. The system is being reformed piecemeal and many observers believe that they can see a monolithic social insurance system around the corner. Whether these observers are accurate in their predictions is difficult to say. A vast matrix of variables affects the scene and the probable expansion paths of these variables is difficult to discern.

Whether such a development would be more efficient is difficult to say. If the observers believe that public finance and public provision will replace the present system then we can only note by way of 'evidence' that we have no evidence about the relative efficiencies of public and private involvement in any particular environment. Be this as it may, agnosticism has not prevented the Federal Government from legislating to influence the supply and demand of health care.

Attempts have been made to circumscribe demand in three ways. Firstly attempts have been made to restrict the rate of expansion of pharmaceutical expenditure (rising at fifteen per cent pa in the 1960s). However the DM 2.50 limit on the prescription charge is relatively low in relation to German incomes. It has led to a reduction in the number of prescriptions but to an increase in their average costs (*Bundesartze-kammer* [1972]). The medical profession and the pharmacists (for administrative cost reasons) are against this method of attempting to constrain the expansion of demand. The trade unions are opposed to the raising of this limit as they favour a universal approach (i.e. equal treatment of unequals) rather than a selective approach. This attitude seems to cover all attempts to increase the revenue of the funds by manipulating the price mechanism. The second method used to influence demand is negative pricing or refunds for non-use of the health care system. Unused medical certificates can lead to quarterly refunds of DM 10 up to a maximum of DM 30 per annum. Again this does not appear to be a very significant incentive for prople to avoid using the system and it is likely to be abolished due to its alleged lack of efficiency and its high administrative cost. The third major way in which demand for benefits has been cut has been achieved by altering sickness benefit regulations. The guaranteed wage, introduced in 1970, has shifted the cost of the first six weeks of income main-tenance for the sick from the funds to the employer. As has been noted this had the effect of decreasing contributions rates in 1970 but expenditure has continued to increase, financed by greater absolute contributions made possible by the dynamic earnings ceiling.

Federal and local public action has also affected supply. Regulations cover the rate fixing activities of the funds and the professions. Arbi-tration machinery is provided to resolve deadlocks. Committees attempt to influence prescribing activities by doctors. In addition to these legal constraints the state has become further embroiled in financing the system. Maternity subsidies, miner's subsidies, small firm subsidies and, more recently, hospital investment subsidies are increasing the role of the various levels of government in the finance of the scheme. The 'dynamisation' of the earnings ceiling and other reserve measures are increasing the revenue of the funds and enabling them to improve supply in both quality and quantity.

Despite these substantial changes some aspects of the system of sickness insurance in West Germany are of doubtful efficiency in relation to a least cost provision objective. There is a great diversity of funds and a degree of variation in the benefits given. Such variations will, no doubt, remain unless some form of financial equalisation between the funds takes place. As in all such circumstances financial equalisation will lead to a reduction in fund autonomy and this will be rejected by many. The trade-off appears quite stark: autonomy and inequality or equality and interdependence. If equalisation is undertaken autonomy will be reduced and perhaps Federal involvement in the funds' day to day affairs will increase (depending on the nature of the equalisation). Many people see this as a road to socialisation: as is usual in any country some welcome and some reject this road. Another bone of contention is the limitation of hospitalisation benefits to seventy-eight weeks in any period of three years for any one disease. After this period the chronic sick have to recourse to public assistance. This problem is emotive but concerns relatively few people.

The major problem is, as in all countries one which is economic in nature. What to expand, how to expand it, how much to expand it, and to whom should the benefits of expansion go? These four questions are the ones which every society has to answer and the acquisition of solutions is difficult and costly.

NOTES

1. In practice the representatives are nominated by the trade unions and the employers' associations.
2. This insurance provided cash benefits and benefits in kind.
3. Of these 30.3 million insured persons 17.7 were men and 12.6 were women.
4. *Referendare* are young lawyers attending the Courts and qualifying for the post of an 'Assessor'.
5. The contributions made on behalf of the old age pensioner and the unemployed will vary because it is two thirds of a varying benefit. Benefits vary as both the pension and the unemployment benefit are related to previous earnings levels.
6. Throughout this chapter the term Government is synonymous with the Federal (or Central) Government, and the *Länder* with the local (or State) governments.
7. Spitaels *et al* (1971). Vol. III, p. 559.

8. K. Szemeitat (1970).
9. Originally the prescription charge was fixed sum of DM 0.50 (1961-7) and DM 1.00 (1968-9).
10. Indeed we may note that the German system of health care is notable for its apparent dependence on hospital care and the, as yet, relative absence of any drive towards cheaper and perhaps more effective community care as in the UK.
11. For the purposes of the guaranteed wage the German courts have decided that regular overtime which has been worked for three months prior to incapacity for work must be reckoned in with maintained wage payments. This was decided by the Hamburg Labour Tribunal in the case of a crane driver who put in an average of fifty-five hours a week.
12. Hausgeld varies according to the composition of the household. Where there are no dependents it is twenty-five per cent of the sickness allowance. One dependent gives rise to benefits of two thirds of the allowance with an additional ten per cent for every additional person, subject to the limit that it cannot exceed the sickness allowance.
13. Regular earnings are the gross wage prior to incapacity. The maximum of the regular earnings adopted in the calculation of benefits is equal to the usual ceiling (DM 22,500 pa). The amount of benefit paid is this earnings related up to the ceiling plus family supplements (four per cent of regular earnings to the ceiling for the first dependent person plus three per cent for each additional dependent) up to a maximum of seventy-five per cent of regular earnings. A further rule stipulates that the sickness allowance cannot exceed net pay (a similar rule to the UK's 'wage stop').
14. EKN – the substitute funds – pursue a 'prestige policy' and fix rates five to ten per cent higher than those paid by other funds.
15. See 'Bundes arbeitsblatt' No 9, September 1970 (*Der Bundesminister für Arbeit und Sozialordnung*) and 'Gesunfheitswesen' Wirtschaft und Statistik Heft 11 1970 S 546 f.f.
16. H. Muller (1970).

References

Altenstetter, C. (1973) 'Planning Facilities in the United States and West Germany' *Millbank Memorial Fund Papers.*
Brakel, J. (1970). 'Das sozialbudget unter besonderer Beruchsich – tigung der Sozialversicherung' *Bundesarbeitsblatt,* September.
Bundesartzekammer (1972) 'Tatigkeitsbericht'.
Bundesverband Der Ortskrankenkassen (1971) 'Statistik der Ortskrankenkassen in der Bundes republick Deutschland 1970' Bonn – Bad Godesberg.
Der Bundesminsiter fur Arbeit und Sozialordnung (Federal Minister of Labour and Social Affairs [1970, 1971]), *Ubersicht uber die Soziale Sicherung,* Bonn.
Der Bundesminister fur Jugend, Familie, und Gesundheit (1971) *Gesundheit bericht,* Bonn.
Douglas-Wilson, I. and McLachlan, G. (1973) *Health Service Prospects.*
The Lancet and the Nuffield Provincial Hospitals Trust especially Chapter 4 'German Federal Republic' by S. Eichhorn (1973).
Eichhorn, S. (1974) *The German Health Service.* Paper presented to a seminar

References *(Cont)*

at the Kings Fund Centre, London. January.

European Economic Community Commission (1973) *Report on the Development of the Social Situation in the Community in 1972* Luxembourg and Brussels.

Kastner, F. *Monograph on the Organisation of Medical Care within the Framework of the Social Security,* Federal Republic of Germany, International Labour Office, Geneva.

Kastner, F. (1968) *Monograph on the Organisation of Medical Care within the Framework of the Social Security,* Federal Republic of Germany, International Labour Office, Geneva.

Muller, H. (1970) 'Der Zukenfrige Bedarf an Krankenhaus betten und seine Kosten', *Das Krankenhause,* October.

Spitaels *et al* (1970) 'Le Salaires indirect et la couverture des besoins sociaux', Vol III of *Le Comparison Internationale* (Allemagne, France, Italy et Pays-Bas). Editions de l'Institut de Sociologie Universite Libre de Bruxelles.

Szemeitat, K. (1970) 'Was Kostet die Gesundheit', *Das offenliche Oesundheitswen* Stuttgart.

US Department of Health, Education and Welfare (1966) *Old Age and Sickness insurance in West Germany in 1965,* Social Security Adminstration, Office of Research and Statistics, Research Report No 13, Washington.

US Department of Health, Education and Welfare (1971), *Social Security Bulletin,* June.

Wirtschaft und Statistik (1970) 'Gesundheitswesen'.

Wolff, G. (1970) 'Arztestatistik im Zehn-Jahre-Vergleich', *Deutsches Arzteblatt,* December.

3 THE NETHERLANDS

The Evolution of Health Care in the Netherlands

The development of health care in the Netherlands has resulted in a
system where both the supply of medical care and health insurance are
of a private nature. The insurers, the providers of care and the patients
are free to bargain within constraints which are defined by the law.
Like so many other countries in Western Europe, health care for the
Dutch population (13.3m) is financed by sickness funds, many of which
were founded in the nineteenth century. The interaction between the
desire of the funds to aid those with low incomes and the increasingly
egalitarian philosophy of government led to an expansion of state
regulations. The first law affecting health care (cash benefits only) in
the Netherlands was passed in 1913. By the outbreak of the Second
World War legislation had been prepared to regulate, and make
compulsory, medical care insurance. This legislation was implemented
by decree in 1941 and established an environment similar to that
existing today.

Health care (medical care and cash benefits) in the Netherlands is
regulated by four pieces of legislation. The Sickness Funds Insurance
Act 1964 (ZFW) replaced the 1941 decree powers and provides health
care in kind (hereafter called medical care) in the short term for the
seventy per cent of the population who are compulsorily insured. The
thirty per cent who are unaffected by this legislation — largely the
more affluent — are usually insured with private insurers or the public
funds. The organisation of this type of insurance is very diverse although the private insurers are attempting to achieve greater uniformity
in finance and benefits. This has been supplemented by the General
Special Sickness Expenses Act 1967 (AWBZ) which covers all the
population and provides insurance cover for serious long term illnesses.
Income maintenance benefits (hereafter called cash benefits) are
regulated by the Sickness Act 1913 (ZW) which provides short-term
benefits, and the Incapacity Insurance Act 1966 (WAO) which regulates long-term benefits. Private insurance cover provides part of the
finance to purchase private medical care and cash benefits for thirty
per cent of the population. These arrangements are described at the end
of the relevant sections of Section 6 (benefits) and the overall impression of private coverage is that adequate detail in description and
statistical detail are noticeable by their absence.

1. Administration

(a) Medical Care

Compulsory medical care insurance is governed by two pieces of legislation. The first of these, the 1964 Sickness Funds Insurance Act (*Ziekfondswet* – ZFW) provides medical care (with some time limits for hospital care) for those wage earners whose earnings are less than a certain ceiling. The administration of this care in the Netherlands is decentralised and in the hands of sickness funds. Those sickness funds whose activity extends to one or more localities are supervised by the Sickness Funds Council (*Ziekfondsraad*). This body is made up of thirty-five members appointed as follows:-

(a)   Seven by the Minister of Social Affairs and Public Health;
(b)   seven by the sickness fund insurance organisations;
(c)   seven by organisations of persons and institutions capable of

Diagram 1 *The organisation of Compulsory Medical Care in the Netherlands*

Ministry of Social Affairs and Public Health
(General supervision)
|
National Sickness Funds Council
(*Ziekenfondsvaad*)
|
National Federation of —— Joint Association of
(4) Sickness Funds   Sickness Funds (1)
|
Sickness Funds (92)

providing various types of medical benefits;

(d)   seven by the central employers' organisations;

(e)   seven by the central employees' organisations;

The Council administers the General Fund (*Algemene Kas*) into which compulsory sickness funds' insurance contributions are paid, and shares out the fund amongst the various sickness funds. Also it administers the Fund for Elderly Persons' Insurance (*Bejaardenverzckering*) into which State contributions and Fund contributions are paid. Other functions of the Council include advice and consultation with the Minister on all matters pertaining to sickness fund insurance either at its own initiative or when asked to do so.

At the regional level the general sickness funds carry out various types of activity. They provide compulsory insurance cover which entitles the insured person to benefits in kind during periods of sickness, pregnancy and maternity. They provide voluntary insurance cover for people aged under and over sixty-five years. Finally they provide complementary insurance which supplements benefits except for hospital benefits which are covered after the 350th day by AMBZ.

Each fund is governed by a Board of Directors which, subject to the approval of the Sickness Fund Council, determines the nature of the fund. There are four groups of general sickness insurance funds. The controlled sickness funds are governed by Boards of Directors, the majority of whose members are elected by the fund's members from amongst their own ranks. Doctors, dentists and chemists are represented on the Board in a few cases but are always in the minority. The second group of funds is comprised of those funds controlled by its members and by the medical professions. In many cases these funds were founded by doctors and chemists. At present their Boards are equally divided with half the members coming from the ranks of the insured and half from the professions. Company sickness funds are set up by firms or groups of firms for their own personnel. They are controlled by Board members elected by employers and employees. The fourth group of funds has been set up as public service corporations and are controlled by full time officials who are not elected by fund members or the professions.

At present there are ninety-one sickness funds and these are federated into four national organisations:

i)   The Federation of Sickness Funds controlled by representatives of insured members and of the Medical Professions (*Federatire van door Verzekerden on Medewerkers beheerde Ziekenfondsen*). The members of this federation cover about 46.7 per cent of the insured population.

ii)   The Netherlands Union of Sickness Funds was formed in 1971 and was the result of the amalgamation of three other groups. They were:-

(a)   The Central Association (*Centrale Bond van Onderling beheerde Ziekfondsen*) which originated from the Red Fund of the Socialists Union. This Association is no longer closely associated with the Union and is controlled solely by its insured members.

(b)   The Association of Roman Catholic Sickness Funds of the Netherlands (*Bond van R.K. Ziekfondsen in Nederland*).[1]

(c)   The Association of Company Sickness Funds (*Overlag van Ondernemings – Ziekfondsen*) a grouping of twelve sickness funds. The total coverage of this group is about 35.1 per cent of the insured population.

iii)   The Organisation of General Sickness Funds of the Netherlands (*Organisatie van Algemene Ziekfondsen in Nederlands*) covers eleven per cent of insured persons.

iv)   The Independent Sickness Funds Foundation (*Stichting atonome Ziekenfondsen*) covers 8.1. per cent of the insured population.

These organisations join together (e.g. to negotiate doctor's fee) in the Joint Association of Sickness Fund Organisations (*Gemeenschappelijk Overleg van Ziekenfondsorganisaties – GOZ*).

So far we have been solely concerned with the administration of the 1964 Act (*Ziekenfondswet – ZFW*) which is concerned with compulsory and voluntary medical care insurance and the medical care protection of the elderly. The General Special Sickness Expense Act (*Algemene Wet Bijzondere Ziektckosten – AWBZ*) came into force in 1968 and is a scheme of national insurance which covers the whole population against the risks of particularly expensive medical treatments associated with long-term illness (more than fifty-two weeks), and serious mental and physical handicaps. The scheme is administered by the sickness funds, by private insurers and by the public law bodies entrusted with the health care protection of civil servants. All three sets of bodies are supervised by the Sickness Funds Council.

An independent Prevention Fund (*Preventie fonds*) has the responsibility of sharing out amongst the various preventative medicine institutions the proceeds of sums paid to it each year by the bodies administering the two Acts referred to above. In 1965[2] one third of this outlay (six million florins – £918,836) went to the Institute of Preventative Medicine, twenty per cent to the mentally handicapped and ten per cent to the Cross Associations.

The latter are another legacy of the past. Originally these were created to provide domiciliary nursing services. Nowadays their role is the provision of nursing services (health visiting and home visits)[3] and the organisation of preventative health care. The latter function is

49

largely to do with propaganda and information provision. There are three large National Cross Associations – the Green (non-sectarian; 1.5 million members), the White-Yellow (Catholic; 0.780 million members) and the Orange-Green (Protestant; 0.300 million members). Altogether the Associations have a membership of three million families (1971), i.e. two thirds of the population. Their activities are financed by membership contributions (capitation fees) and substantial central government subsidies.

(c) Cash Benefits

Cash benefits are regulated by two Acts. The Sickness Act 1913 (*Ziektewet*), modified in 1967, insures all wage earners against the effects of short-term incapacity to work (less than fifty-two weeks) caused by illness, accident, maternity or physical or mental handicap. The insurance is administered by twenty-six occupational associations[4] established by employer or employee organisations acting alone or in cooperation. Such administrative bodies have to be approved by the Ministry and are supervised by the Social Insurance Council (*Sociale Verzekeringsraad*).

Longer-term illness is covered by the Incapacity Insurance Act 1966 (*Wet up Arbeidsongeschiktheidswerzekering* – WAO) which protects the insured from the financial effects of industrial accidents as well as the effects of longer-term (over fifty-two weeks) illnesses. The insurance is administered by twenty-six occupational associations which collect contributions, fix the daily earnings on which the allowances are based, and pay out the allowances. Once again the associations are supervised by the Social Insurance Council.[5] The Joint Medical Service (*Gemeenschappelik Medische Dienst* – GMD), made up of representatives of both sides of industry, assesses the degree of incapacity of potential benefit recipients, supervises their rehabilitation where possible and monitors their progress.

2. Coverage

(a) Medical Care

The Sickness Funds Insurance Act covers three categories: the compulsorily insured, the elderly and the voluntarily insured. The compulsorily insured usually excludes those workers earning more than 20,900 florins (£3,200.61 – 1st January 1971).[6] It provides insurance cover for wage earners in the private sector, invalids, sportsmen, unemployed persons in receipt of benefits under the Unemployment Insurance Act (*Wet Werkloosheidsvoorziening*) and the State Code for Unemployed Workers (*Rijksgroepsregeling Werkloze Werknemers*).

certain sections of the armed forces and widows and orphans receiving benefits from the General Widow's and Orphan's Act (*Algemene Weduwen en Wezenwet*). The dependents of the insured person are also insured, e.g. the wife, children under sixteen, children under twenty-seven who are disabled or continuing their education and who are largely maintained by the insured person, parents, parents-in-law and grandparents of the insured who live in his house. All these people (about fifty-one per cent of the population – see Table 1) receive the same benefits in kind as the insured person providing the combined income of the married couple is less than 23,265 florins (£3562.78).

Table 1 *The Sickness Funds: Compulsory Membership 1960-72*

Year	Workers	Family Members	Pensioners and their family members	Total	Total Compulsory Membership as percentage of Total Population
1960	2,554,971	3,073,382	103,797	5,732,150	49.6
1961	2,637,870	3,120,091	106,732	5,854,693	50.0
1962	2,689,936	3,105,403	112,417	5,907,756	49.7
1963	2,799,587	3,207,753	160,586	6,167,926	51.2
1964	2,859,960	3,226,449	198,699	6,285,108	51.5
1965	2,863,099	1,172,879	236,288	6,272,266	50.7
1966	2,900,922	3,205,306	268,804	6,375,032	51.2
1967	2,909,006	3,228,623	302,751	6,440,380	50.8
1968	2,964,000	3,240,000	334,000	6,538,448	51.1
1969	2,994,000	3,202,000	368,000	6,564,343	50.7
1970	3,069,000	3,238,000	419,000	6,725,692	51.3
1971	3,125,000	3,303,000	458,000	6,885,646	51.9
1972	3,099,000	3,264,000	497,000	6,860,000	51.3

Source: The yearly report of the *Ziekenfondsraad* (Sickness Funds Council), *Centraal Bureau voor de Statistiek* (Central Bureau of Statistics) and *Statistisch Zakboek* (Statistical Yearbook).

All the elderly, those over sixty-five years of age, whose annual family income does not exceed 13,407 florins (£2,053.13) can register with a sickness fund as elderly insured members (*Bejaardenverzekerde* – about seven per cent of the population). The members of their families are also insured free of charge subject to some qualifying conditions.

Finally the Act can cover persons who opt for voluntary membership (about twelve per cent of the population) because they are not permitted to register as compulsory or elderly members. Once again the family's income must not exceed 20,900 florins (£3,200.61). Many persons who can opt into membership do so.

As a result of the Act the sickness funds provide medical care insurance for about seventy per cent of the population. The largest groups excluded from membership are managerial and technical staffs whose incomes exceed the ceiling and who insure themselves privately either with the funds or commercial insurance companies. Tables 1 and 2 give more details of membership in the period 1960 to 1972. Table 1 shows that the proportion of the population compulsorily insured during the period has been quite stable. This stability remains when we examine Table 2 which looks at the movements in membership of all types of beneficiaries. Table 1 shows a 19.6 per cent absolute increase in compulsory memberships whilst Table 2 shows a 12.7 per cent increase in all types of membership. The latter is smaller because of the decline in voluntary membership which has resulted from the high individual cost of such insurance.

Table 2 *The Sickness Funds: All Types of Membership 1960-72*

Year	Compulsory Insurance	Insurance for the Elderly	Voluntary Insurance	Total	Total Membership as a % of Total Population
1960	5,732,150	667,091	1,815,381	8,214,622	71.1
1961	5,864,693	669,489	1,806,100	8,340,282	71.2
1962	5,907,756	670,527	1,802,739	8,381,022	70.5
1963	6,167,926	680,257	1,819,253	8,667,436	72.0
1964	6,285,108	688,000	1,809,306	8,782,414	71.9
1965	6,272,266	681,165	1,778,195	8,731,626	70.5
1966	6,375,032	692,916	1,730,013	8,797,261	70.6
1967	6,440,380	714,386	1,709,337	8,864,103	70.0
1968	6,538,448	729,175	1,693,110	8,960,733	70.0
1969	6,654,343	745,815	1,641,741	8,951,899	69.1
1970	6,725,692	858,021	1,512,337	9,096,050	69.3
1971	6,885,646	896,962	1,482,896	9,265,054	69.8
1972					

Source: The yearly report of the *Ziekenfondsraad* (Sickness Funds Council), *Centraal Bureau voor de Statistiek* (Central Bureau of Statistics) and *Statistisch Zakboek* (Statistical Yearbook).

The General Special Sickness Expenses Act (AWBZ) provides insurance cover for anyone residing in the Netherlands, regardless of age and nationality.

(b)   Cash Benefits
The coverage of the legislation providing for short-term benefits in cash (The Sickness Act) applies to all persons who are parties to a contract of employment of a private nature. The legislation covers trainees, unemployed persons receiving benefits under the Unemployment Act, persons working in their own homes, professional musicians, artists and sportsmen. The insured is eligible for benefits under this legislation if he continues to be in employment after the age of sixty-five. Long-term incapacity benefits (The Incapacity Insurance Act – WAO) are paid to all wage earners in the private sector until they reach the age of sixty-five and become eligible for an old age pension.

3 Qualifying Conditions

(a)   Medical Care
The only condition which has to be satisfied for a person to qualify for short-term and long-term health benefits in kind is that the insured person should be registered with a sickness fund.

(b)   Cash Benefits
Short-term cash benefits are paid if the person is incapable of carrying out a normal day's work (specific invalidity). The doctor is the sole arbiter of incapacity. The allowance is paid for fifty-two weeks, after which the insured is automatically transferred from sickness insurance (ZW) to incapacity insurance (WAO). Generally the person has to be insured at the beginning of the period of his incapacity to work and the degree of incapacity must be at least fifteen per cent. Incapacity Insurance (WAO) unlike sickness insurance (ZW) is concerned with general incapacity, i.e. inability to do work of any kind.

4 Finance

(a)   Medical Care
The rates of contribution are adjusted annually in an effort to equate the income and expenditure of the scheme. Contributions under the Sickness Funds Insurance Act depend on the category of membership. In 1973, compulsory insurance was financed by a contribution of 8.9 per cent of daily earnings up to a ceiling of sixty-eight florins (£10.41)

53

per day (17,680 florins per year is £2,707.50). Normally half this contribution is paid by the employer and the rest by the employee. However, the employer does have the option of paying a higher proportion or all the contribution if he wishes. The contribution of voluntary members varies from region to region. The contribution is fixed by the sickness funds subject to the approval of the Sickness Fund Council.[7] In 1973 it ranged from forty-eight to eighty-five florins (£7.35 − £13.01) per month payable by every insured person over the age of sixteen years. This means that in the case of married couples each partner has to pay this contribution separately. Students and invalids pay a reduced voluntary membership contribution which was at the rate of 43.05 florins (£6.59) per month in 1972.

The insurance of the elderly is available for all those who are aged sixty-five and whose income is less than 13,407 florins (£2,053.13) per year. The contribution rate depends on income and in 1973 was:-

6.30 florins (£0.96) per week (27.40 florins [£4.19] per month) for those with incomes up to 8,682 florins (£1,329.55) per year.

12.60 florins (£1.92) per week (54.75 florins [£8.38] per month) for those with incomes from 8,682 to 9,692 florins (£1,329.55 − £1,484.22) per year.

15.75 florins (£2.41) per week (68.45 florins [£10.48] per month) for those with incomes from 9,692 to 11,550 florins (£1,484.22 − £1,768.75) per year.

22.05 florins (£3.37) per week (95.80 florins [£14.67] per month) for those with incomes from 11,550 to 13,407 florins (£1,768.75 − £2,053.13) per year.

Single persons contribute 15.75 florins (£2.41) per week (68.45 florins [£10.78] per month).

These contributions give family coverage, i.e. the insured, his wife, any children under sixteen years, etc. As we show below, the contribution revenue of the elderly covers only about forty per cent of the total expenditure. Of the rest thirty per cent is met by central government and thirty per cent from the contributions of the compulsorily insured.

State intervention to in kind health insurance under the Sickness Funds Insurance Act is limited to an annual grant to aid the insurance of the elderly and voluntarily insured.

The State grant to the insurance of the elderly is related to the number of people in the lower and upper contribution rate categories. One and a half times the contributions of the lower group plus half the contributions paid by the upper group is paid to the sickness funds (in 1972 the sum was 280.7 million florins [£42m]). This State grant is supplemented by a transfer out of the compulsorily insured's scheme of a sum equal to that paid by the State. The State aid to voluntary insurance is decided each year. In 1972 the sum paid over was 22.5 million florins (£3.5m).

The activities of the sickness funds which are covered by the General Special Sickness Expenses Act (AWBZ) are subsidised. In 1972 the subsidy, linked to movements in the basic wage index, was 583 million florins (£89m). The other source of finance for the AWBZ scheme is contributions. In 1973 contributions were 2.6 per cent of earnings up to a ceiling of 24,300 florins (£3,721.28). These contributions are paid wholly by the employer at present. However, new regulations, when legislated, will compel persons aged more than eighteen years to pay a monthly contribution. This contribution will finance insurance for hospitalisation in a recognised institution for a period in excess of six months.

(b)   Cash Benefits

Short-term cash benefits (the Sickness Act) are financed by contributions which vary from one industrial or trade group to another. The 1973 average was an employer contribution of 6.2 per cent and an employee contribution of one per cent of earnings, up to a maximum of 32,500 florins (£4,977) per year. The finance of the Incapacity Act is covered by contributions which are the same for all groups of workers. The employer paid 5.28 per cent and the employee 2.55 per cent of earnings up to a maximum of 32,500 florins (£4,977) per year in 1972.

5   Income and Expenditure

(a)   Medical Care

Table 3 shows benefit expenditure under the two Acts affecting medical care during the period 1960-72.

The changes in medical care expenditure in the period 1960-72 were large, both in absolute and percentage terms. Sickness Fund Insurance expenditure rose from 634 million florins (£97m) to 4,321 million florins (£661m) an absolute increase of 581 per cent. During the first five years of its life AWBZ expenditure rose from 581 (£88m) to 1,193 (£305m) million florins: an absolute increase of 105 per cent.

Table 4 shows a time series of the composition of the income of each of the three types of compulsory medical care insurance under the sickness Funds Insurance Act (ZFW). The overall total of each of the columns in Table 4 is greater than the expenditure statistics given in Table 3 for two reasons: in some years income was greater than expenditure (see Table 5 below); and the income figures given include the contribution of people entitled to benefits under the Incapacity Insurance Act.

Table 3 *Medical Care Expenditure 1960-72**

Year	Sickness Funds Insurance Act (ZFW) Total Expenditure	Annual Average percentage increase	General Special Sickness Expenses Act (AWBZ) Total Expenditure	Annual Average percentage increase
1960	634 (97.09)	-		
1961	694	9.5		
1962	782	12.7		
1963	914	16.9		
1964	1,123	22.9		
1965	1,293	15.1		
1966	1,552	20.0		
1967	1,864	20.1		
1968	2,154	15.6	581† (£88.97)	-
1969	2,485	15.4	864	48.7
1970	2,939	18.3	1,067	25.8
1971	3,556	21.0	1,159	34.2
1972	4,321 (£661.71)	21.5	1,993 (£305.20)	36.6

Source: Central Bureau of Statistics – Social Insurance, Pension
Insurance, Life Insurance.

* This expenditure is for compulsory medical care insurance only.
† AWBZ was legislated in 1967.
All data is in millions of florins (£ million).

Table 4 shows the magnitude of State financial involvement in the
ZFW operation of the sickness funds. There is no State grant to the
compulsorily insured. The elderly's insurance income was made up in
1972 (1960) of a State grant which was 34.1 per cent (35.6 per
cent) of total income. The voluntarily insured received a State grant
equal in 1972 (1960) to 3.2 per cent (3.1 per cent) of total income.
The annual average rate of increase in the total involvement of the
State was 63.9 per cent in the elderly's insurance scheme and 33.3 per
cent in the voluntary scheme. These rates of increase are very similar

Table 4 *Income by Types 1960-72 in millions of florins (£m)*

	1960	1961	1962	1963	1964	1965	1966	1967	1968	1969	1970	1971	1972	Average annual percentage increase
(1) Compulsory Insurance														
Employers Contributions	238.1	268.2	286.4	304.1	394.4	453.1	545.9	677.6	803.8	905.8	1016.2	1207.0	1380.0	40.0
Households Contributions	250.4	280.8	294.7	324.1	422.8	491.2	599.5	754.5	898.0	1034.4	1174.9	1405.7	1674.8	47.4
Mutual Payments*	2.7	2.1	3.5	7.1	4.4	5.2	8.0	18.6	10.6	10.4	13.6	15.0	26.2	72.5
Interest	1.2	1.7	2.6	2.5	1.9	1.9	2.9	3.6	8.7	16.4	24.0	26.1	18.0	116.7
Total	492.4	552.8	587.2	637.8	823.5	951.4	1156.3	1454.1	1721.1	1967.0	2228.7	2653.8	3099.0	44.1
	(£75)												(£474)	
(2) Insurance for the elderly														
Household contribution	28.2	30.1	31.5	39.5	49.4	71.9	84.1	108.2	133.2	141.2	216.5	254.1	309.7	83.2
State Grant	32.4	35.6	37.0	46.2	57.8	66.4	76.3	95.1	112.1	118.1	187.1	236.2	280.7	63.9
Mutual Payments*	30.0	33.9	40.6	46.9	58.5	64.3	78.6	92.9	106.7	124.3	132.3	174.0	232.5	56.3
Total	90.6	99.6	109.1	132.6	165.7	202.6	239.0	296.2	352.0	383.6	535.9	664.3	822.9	67.4
	(£13)												(£126)	
(3) Voluntary Insurance														
Household Contributions	139.1	150.2	161.4	179.6	221.3	257.2	302.8	357.6	416.7	477.5	465.8	548.1	669.2	31.8
State grant	4.5	4.7	4.7	6.1	7.6	7.2	6.9	7.4	8.1	8.8	10.0	19.9	22.5	33.3
Total	143.6	154.9	166.1	185.7	228.9	264.4	309.7	365.0	424.8	486.3	475.8	568.0	691.7	31.5
Overall Total	726.6	807.3	862.4	956.1	1218.1	1418.4	1705.0	2115.5	2497.9	2836.9	3240.4	3886.1	4613.6	44.6
	(£111)												(£706)	

Source: Central Bureau of Statistics *op. cit.*

* Mutual payments are contributions paid by the working force who are compulsorily insured and which are transferred to finance the insurance of the elderly.

Table 5 *Sickness Insurance Fund Act (ZFW): Income and Expenditure 1960-72 in millions of florins (£m)*

Income	1960	1961	1962	1963	1964	1965	1966	1967	1968	1969	1970	1971	1972
Contributions	655.8	729.3	774.0	847.3		1273.4	1532.3	1897.9	2251.7	2558.9	2873.4	3414.9	4033.7
State grant	36.9	40.3	41.7	52.3	65.4	73.6	83.2	102.5	120.2	126.9	197.1	256.1	303.2
Mutual Payments	32.7	36.0	44.1	54.0	62.9	69.5	86.6	111.5	117.3	134.7	145.9	189.0	258.7
Interest	1.2	1.7	2.6	1.9	1.9	2.9	3.6	8.7	16.4	24.0	26.1	26.1	18.0
Total	726.6 (£111)	807.3	862.4	956.1	1218.1	1418.4	1705.0	2115.5	2497.9	2836.9	3240.4	3886.1	4613.6 (£706)

Expenditure	1960	1961	1962	1963	1964	1965	1966	1967	1968	1969	1970	1971	1972
Benefits	634.3	693.9	781.9	914.6	1123.5	1292.1	1551.7	1863.2	2153.4	2484.5	2938.6	3555.9	4321.0
Mutual Payments	30.0	33.9	40.6	46.9	58.5	64.3	78.6	92.9	106.7	124.3	132.3	174.0	232.5
Admin. charges	40.3	42.0	46.7	53.2	62.9	72.5	83.0	90.0	98.2	112.2	128.2	147.0	163.5
Balance	22.0	37.5	6.8	58.6	26.8	10.5	8.3	69.4	139.6	116.9	41.3	9.2	103.4
Total	726.6	807.3	862.4	956.1	1218.1	1418.4	1705.0	2115.0	2497.9	2836.9	3240.4	3886.1	4613.6

Source: Central Bureau of Statistics *op. cit.*

to the overall absolute income increase in each category and indicate a
static degree of involvement by the State over the period 1960-72.

Table 6 *General Special Sickness Expenses Act (AWBZ): Income and Expenditure 1968-72 in millions of florins (£m)*

Income	1968	1969	1970	1971	1972
Contributions	177.7	476.4	659.8	977.8	1370.8
Mutual Payments	5.3	15.7	23.4	34.6	54.2
State Grant	450.6	476.6	476.5	509.0	583.3
Interest	0.1	0.2	5.2	6.0	2.5
Total	588.7	968.9	1164.9	1527.4	2010.8
	(£90)				(£307)
Expenditure					
Benefits	581.2	864.1	1087.3	1458.7	2006.8
Admin. charges	5.7	15.6	23.1	28.1	33.0
Balance	1.8	89.2	54.5	40.6	29.0
Total	588.7	968.9	1164.9	1527.4	2010.8

Source: Central Bureau of Statistics *op. cit.*

The overall income and expenditure patterns of the two schemes (ZFW
and AWBZ) is shown in Tables 5 and 6. From Table 5 it can be seen
that ZFW was in deficit in six years in the period 1960-72. The deficit
was particularly acute in 1972 (103.4 million florins [£15m]).

Table 6 shows that the State's role in the finance of AWBZ was
quite significant. In 1972 the State contributed 583.3 million florins
(£89m) or about twenty-nine per cent of the total. This is lower than
earlier years, e.g. 1968 the State financed sixty-nine per cent of AWBZ
activity.

If the income of both schemes is aggregated we can see that the
overall significance of the State in the direct finance of medical care in
the Netherlands is quite small. In 1972 the total income of AWBZ and
ZFW was 6,624.4 million florins (£1,014m). The State gave grants
totalling 886.50 million florins (£135m), i.e. about thirteen per cent of
the total.

Table 7 shows the size of different types of expenditure under ZFW
(all types) during the period 1960-71. A familiar pattern can be seen.
The costs of drugs, physicians' services and hospitalisation are large
and increasing very rapidly. In 1971 medicine and dressings represented eighteen per cent of total expenditure (£88m). The payment of
physicians (practitioners' attendance and specialists' treatment) was
over twenty-eight per cent of total expenditure (£140m). Hospitalisation accounted for a further fifty per cent of expenditure (£247m).
Thus these three items (£477m) took over ninety-six per cent of total

Table 7 *Expenditure by Category (ZFW only) 1960-71 in millions of florins*

	1960	1961	1962	1963	1964	1965	1966	1967	1968	1969	1970	1971	Average annual percentage increase
Practitioner's attendance	89.9	101.1	109.8	121.8	138.7	151.0	171.4	213.9	247.7	239.6	332.2	383.2	29.6
Medicine and dressings	96.8	109.6	123.2	148.4	177.8	108.9	246.8	284.9	334.9	391.7	471.3	580.0	45.3
Specialist's treatment	107.1	116.9	131.2	152.4	176.0	198.5	232.4	267.1	319.7	361.7	434.8	536.5	36.4
Dental treatment	43.9	48.4	51.0	57.2	69.4	77.7	91.9	103.4	117.2	130.4	149.1	177.6	27.7
Obstetrical treatment	7.5	8.7	9.9	10.9	12.7	14.0	15.2	17.5	20.3	24.9	27.3	29.6	26.7
Hospitalisation	226.6	244.5	283.2	341.2	449.7	535.7	653.6	814.4	951.2	1109.9	1317.2	1617.2	55.8
External therapy	10.8	12.0	13.9	17.0	22.0	25.4	30.6	36.6	44.3	56.2	67.9	85.7	63.1
Prothetic appliances	10.8	11.4	12.3	14.5	16.4	17.7	22.0	23.8	26.0	29.0	33.1	37.3	22.2
Ambulance service	7.9	9.0	10.0	12.4	15.2	18.2	22.4	26.2	32.5	39.0	46.8	58.6	57.7
Nu rsing in nursing homes	-	1.2	7.4	5.9	8.8	14.7	15.9	19.3	6.1	-	-	1.1	-
Sanitorium treatment	15.7	13.5	12.9	13.4	13.3	12.0	12.2	12.8	12.0	12.0	10.8	10.3	3.2
Maternity Care	9.2	9.6	9.5	9.9	10.0	9.8	28.9	33.9	36.1	41.8	45.6	52.2	42.1
Retraining expenses benefits	6.7	7.0	0.6	7.4	6.9	7.0	6.8	6.4	0.5	0.2	0.2	0.3	8.7
Collecting, administration and supervision expenditure	40.2	41.9	46.6	53.2	62.9	72.5	82.4	89.4	97.7	111.6	127.6	145.6	23.8
Special expenses	0.8	1.1	0.8	2.0	3.6	3.7	3.6	4.7	7.3	6.3	8.3	9.4	92.0
Overall Total	674.5	736.5	823.0	968.4	1154.4	1367.6	1636.8	1955.1	2254.3	2603.6	3072.2	3202.2	34.1

Source: Health Insurance Fund Council;
Central Bureau of Statistics — Statistical Yearbook of the Netherlands.

Table 8 *Sickness Act Income 1960-72 in millions of florins*

	1960	1961	1962	1963	1964	1965	1966	1967	1968	1969	1970	1971	1972	Average annual percentage increase
Employers' contributions	268.0	312.5	326.6	384.2	502.3	610.9	893.1	1122.5	1325.3	1533.8	1907.5	2320.0	2513.7	96.8
Households' contributions	132.6	149.3	156.4	173.9	220.5	229.2	227.9	280.9	322.0	367.7	422.6	475.0	520.0	24.3
Mutual Payments	7.5	5.9	8.0	12.4	8.8	11.4	18.0	17.9	25.6	28.1	39.6	45.8	61.3	59.8
Interest	5.0	5.2	6.5	5.3	5.8	5.1	7.4	17.6	27.5	34.5	35.6	48.0	50.0	75.0
Total	413.1 (£63)	472.9	497.5	575.6	737.4	856.6	1106.4	1438.9	1700.4	1963.3	2405.3	2885.8	3145.0 (£481)	55.1

Source: The Central Bureau of Statistics *op. cit.*

Table 9 *Sickness Act Expenditure 1960-72 in millions of florins (£m)*

	1960	1961	1962	1963	1964	1965	1966	1967	1968	1969	1970	1971	1972	Average annual percentage increase
Benefits	366.9	389.2	448.2	530.4	651.3	788.5	901.7	1075.9	1490.6	1826.5	2127.0	2430.0	2855.0	56.5
Mutual Payments	1.7	1.7	1.8	9.0	11.6	10.8	13.7	15.9	28.5	42.2	50.3	63.5	80.0	383.8
Administration charges	44.1	48.8	55.2	82.6	75.2	86.9	98.5	104.3	115.6	136.1	154.4	176.0	204.0	30.2
Balance	0.4	33.2	-7.7	-26.2	-0.7	-29.6	92.5	242.8	65.7	-41.5	73.6	217.3	6.0	116.7
Total	413.1	472.9	497.5	575.8	737.4	856.6	1106.4	1438.9	1700.4	1963.3	2405.3	2888.8	3145.0	55.1

Source: Central Bureau of Statistics – Social Insurance, pension insurance, life insurance.

ZFW expenditure (£490m). The equivalent statistic for 1960 was seventy-seven per cent, with medicaments and dressings taking 14.3 per cent (£14m), physicians' services 29.2 per cent (£30m) and hospitalisation 35.5 per cent (£34m).
The overall annual average rate of increase in expenditure during the period 1960-71 was 34.1 per cent (Table 7). This increase in expenditure was in part due to the inflation on the costs of medical care. An EEC report (EEC 1973 (a) page 2) shows that the Netherlands medical care cost index was 100 in 1960 and 298 in 1968. For hospitalisation alone the index rose from 100 to 378 over the same period. The movement of prices of medical care services has been higher than the movement of prices generally in the economy.

(b)   Cash benefits
Tables 8 and 9 show the income and expenditure details of the short term cash benefits scheme (Sickness Act). The income data shows that the employers paid a larger share in both absolute and relative terms at the end of the period than did the employees. The income from employers increased annually on average by nearly seventy per cent.
   Benefit expenditure increased by an annual average percentage of over fifty-six per cent. Overall the scheme was able to finance transfers to other schemes and remain solvent except during the period 1962-5 and in 1969.

Table 10   *Incapacity Act (WAO) Income 1967-72 in millions of florins (£m)*

	1967	1968	1969	1970	1971	1972	Average annual % increase
Employers' contributions	438.3	966.8	1224.1	1437.7	1679.2	1828.2	21.7
Households' contributions	99.7	221.3	399.0	495.7	622.0	655.6	45.8
State capital transfer	3.0	-	1.1	-	-	0.3	19.0
Mutual Payments	4.0	10.9	11.4	15.6	17.9	28.6	51.5
Interest	10.0	21.0	22.2	20.0	20.0	-	20.0
Total	555.0 (84.9)	1220.0	1657.8	1969.0	2339.1	2512.7 (384.7)	25.3

Source: Central Bureau of Statistics *op. cit.*

Table 11 *Incapacity Act (WAO) Expenditure 1967-72*
in millions of florins (£m)

	1967	1968	1969	1970	1971	1972	Average annual % increase
Benefits	407.0	1108.5	1399.0	1676.1	2200.4	2830.3	49.5
Out of work pay	3.9	13.7	14.9	14.1	12.9	10.5	6.9
Compensation*	100.6	13.2	20.7	10.1	10.0	8.0	-19.2
Mutual Payments	36.0	60.0	60.0	60.0	88.8	0.6	-19.8
Administration charges	33.3	53.3	64.1	74.9	83.3	103.7	11.1
Balance	-25.8	-28.7	99.1	133.8	-56.3	-440.4	150.7
Total	555.0	1220.0	1657.8	1969.0	2339.1	2512.7	25.3

Source: Central Bureau of Statistics – Social Insurance, Pension
Insurance, Life Insurance.
* Surrender of accident benefits.

The propensity to increase the relative contribution to the employers
cannot be seen from the income and expenditure details of the Incapacity Act shown in Tables 10 and 11 (the data is for the years
1967-72 – as the Act did not come into force until July 1967).[8]
The contribution of employers fell from 78.9 per cent to 72.7 per
cent of total income. The average annual increase in contribution funds
from the employees was greater for the employees (nearly forty-six
per cent) than for the employers (nearly twenty-two per cent).[9]

The foregoing describes the income and expenditure detail of the
four schemes. It is to be remembered that thirty per cent of the
population is outside the scope of the Sickness Funds Insurance Act:
here medical care is financed by private insurance (estimated premium
income: 1,200 million florins [£183m]) and out of savings (no estimate
of the magnitude of this is available). Cash benefits are purchased
privately, but once again, we have been unable to acquire a recent
estimate of their magnitude. In conclusion it is possible to say that
expenditure on medical care (ZFW, AWBZ and private insurance
excluding private consumption out of saving) was approximately
7514 million florins (£1150m) in 1972.

6 Benefits

(a) Medical Care

The Sickness Funds Act (ZFK) gives the right of short-term medical, pharmaceutical, dental, hospital and other types of care to the insured person and his dependents. Every insured person is required to register with a physician approved by the Fund to which he belongs. Most general practitioners work alone as group practice is unusual. The choice of doctor by the insured is free provided the physician is attached to the Fund, has a list of less than 3,000 patients and practices in the insured's locality. In 1966 the average list size was 2,856, of whom 1,999 were insured with a sickness fund.[10] The services of the physician are provided free of charge and the Fund usually reimburses the doctor directly. Any physician can apply to be attached to the Funds in his locality. The attachment is by contract of a standard form established by the Funds and the doctors' professional organisations. The contract sets out the obligations of each of the parties and includes provisions regarding the level and method of payment and fees. The fees are fixed by negotiations between the doctors and the Joint Association of Sickness Fund Organisations (GOZ).[11] Most fees are paid on a *per capita* basis and in 1971 the annual fee was fixed at 42.27 florins (£6.5) per registered patient when the doctors' list was under 1,800. For lists in excess of 1,800 a *per capita* fee of 29.22 florins (£4.5) was paid. These basic fees are supplemented by allowances for doctors working in thinly populated or remote areas and all fees include expense allowances and pension contributions. Also fixed fees are paid for certain types of care, e.g. obstetric services and travelling expenses. All the fees are related to price and wage indices and changed annually.

Treatment by specialist physicians can be acquired only with the authorisation of the patient's personal physician. In urgent cases authorisation can be made retrospectively. All such treatments are provided free of charge. The personal physician issues his patient with a transfer card (*verwijskaart*) which is valid for one month in one clinic. This card can be renewed a certain number of times by the specialist. The quantity of renewals varies from one specialism to another (there are eighteen specialisms) and is fixed by regulations. These renewal factors represent a certain monetary value (e.g. for an internal medicine specialist in 1971 the value was 27.38 florins [£4.2] which is higher than the value of the transfer card being 13.19 florins [£2.02]). If a specialist presents renewal cards (*herbalingskaarten*) in excess of the renewal factor the funds refuse to pay for the excess. The fees are agreed nationally by the funds and the specialists' medical organisation and vary with price and wage indices, because of which annual mark-ups are made. Specialist care in the home is limited to the payment of fixed amounts for the first and second home consultation. Subsequent home consultations connected with the same illness and provided in the same year are paid only on the express authorisation of the fund and on the presentation to the fund of a consultation card (*consult-kaart*).

An insured person who requires dental care can consult any dentist attached to the fund. Persons aged more than four years purchase a treatment certificate for 5.75 florins (£0.88). This is valid for six months, is renewable and entitles the holder to free and subsidised benefits. Children aged less than four years receive free treatment. Consultations and extractions are free of charge as are scalings, fillings and the extraction of nerves provided the insured person holds a valid treatment certificate, i.e. has been to the dentist in the last quarter. Other treatments and the provision of false teeth require a treatment certificate and the payment of supplementary contributions — sixty per cent of the cost of false teeth is met by the patient. If a patient does not have a certificate his payments are regulated by a scale of charges. The dentist is paid by item of service, e.g. in 1971 247.20 florins (£37.85) for a full set of false teeth.

Most (sixty per cent) pharmaceutical products and dressings provided outside the hospital are supplied by about 982 chemists (pharmacists) in 1972. The remainder, mostly in rural districts, are supplied by the physicians (about 1,349 in 1972), who are permitted to supply drugs but are not qualified pharmacists. Some sickness funds have their own pharmacies. Unless the insured member is required to use his own fund's pharmacy, he has to register with a pharmacy or with a GP — pharmacist attached to the fund. All drugs and dressings are provided free of charge. The pharmacist is paid an annual *per capita* fee (in 1973 this was fixed at 11.16 florins [£1.71] per registered person) and a fee for each supply of drugs (1.16 florins [£0.18]). The cost of drugs and dressings supplied are refunded on the basis of a periodically adjusted scale established by negotiations between the chemists' organisations and the funds. In 1973 physicians providing pharmaceutical supplies are paid 17.09 florins (£2.62) per registered person per year. The fee does not cover the cost of drugs and dressings which are the subject of a separate refund. This sum covered the supply of necessary drugs and dressings. The cost of certain unusual items is refunded to physicians according to a set fee scale. The physician receives an extra fee of 2.5 florins (£0.38) for certain categories of elderly person registered with them.

Hospital treatment (for periods of up to 365 days) has to be authorised in advance by the funds. The insured person can go to any hospital in his locality or a university hospital for treatment provided

65

that it is approved by the Ministry and by the Sickness Funds Council and that it has an agreement with the patient's fund. The funds pay for hospital services in various ways. The 'closed' clinics apply 'all-in' scales, i.e. their scales meet the cost of all types of service which are provided. These units have their own specialist staffs who treat those fund patients who are admitted and those private patients whom they admit themselves. The 'open clinics' take patients with the specialist of their choice. In this type of unit a distinction is made between clinical costs and medical costs. The costs of services administered in Class 3 Wards (i.e. wards with several beds) are paid by the funds. The individual can opt for better services (Class 1, 2a and 2b) and has to meet the cost of this by taking out voluntary complementary insurance. Most patients (ninety-eight per cent of the population) are insured to finance this type of expenditure.

All the population is insured by law (AWBZ) against the cost of treatment in nursing homes and hospital care after the 365th day; and, without time limit, nursing homes care for the elderly or chronic sick. The latter's cost of treatment was half covered prior to 1968. Now it is not covered by short-term sickness insurance but is fully covered from the first day by AWBZ. The treatment is provided in licensed and unlicensed institutions, treatment in the former being characterised by treatment by full-time doctors. These doctors are mostly general practitioners and they are assisted by nurses who are specifically trained for this type of work. Psychiatric care is provided after authorisation by the sickness fund. After authorisation the insured is then entitled to stay in a recognised institution.

About sixty per cent of confinements take place in the home where the mother is attended either by the GP physician (forty-five per cent of all cases) or the midwife. If necessary either the midwife or the physician can call in a specialist. Hospitalised confinements (forty per cent of the total) are not financed by the funds unless hospitalisation is due to medical advice. Hospital confinements at individual initiative have to be met in full by the mother unless the local office of the Department of Social Affairs is prepared to offer financial assistance.

Pre- and post-natal services are provided in the home or in one of the eighteen recognised district maternity centres. These centres are run by the Cross Associations. In 1973 the sickness funds paid – for a maximum of ten days – 69.00 florins (£10.56) per day for home services and 29.20 florins (£4.47) per day for district maternity care services. In the latter case any difference between the charges levied by the centre and the fund's payment has to be met from private sources. Every mother is required to register at her local maternity centre six months before the expected date of confinement.

Once a child is born its mother has access to numerous Cross child health services. There are 2,700 baby clinics in the Netherlands[12] most of which are directed by family physicians. About seventy per cent of children under one year of age attend these clinics. There are more than 2,000 infant clinics which are generally directed by family physicians and act as child guidance clinics. Generally these centres provide advice and check-ups only. Any cases of disease or sickness detected are reported to the individual child's physician who is responsible for examination and treatment.[13]

The school health service is largely provided by the municipalities. It is financed by the Sickness Funds (seventy-five per cent) and the municipalities (twenty-five per cent). Once again it is diagnostic rather than therapeutic.

The General Special Sickness Expenses Act (AWBZ) substantially increased the scope of social insurance and gave the insured the right to treatment in recognised institutions for the mentally handicapped, institutions for the physically handicapped, nursing homes (from the first day) and hospitals, sanatoria, and psychiatric institutions (from the 366th day of illness). Unmarried people aged more than sixty-five who have been resident in an institution for more than a year pay 355 florins (£54.36) a month (1973) from the 366th day of their stay. Married male insured persons have to pay a contribution of 468 florins (£71.67) a month (1973) if he and his wife are aged more than sixty-five years and have been resident for more than a year in a hospital or other institution.[14]

We have seen already that the provision of the Sickness Funds Act does not apply to thirty per cent of the population. These people — largely the more affluent — purchase insurance cover from a variety of funds — some private, some municipal and the some the sickness funds (described in section [1] above) which provide compulsory social insurance. The nature of these arrangements is very diverse. Most of these people appear to be uninsured for general practitioner care and dental treatment (in the latter case there is little chance to acquire insurance even of the demand is present).

(b)   Cash Benefits

Cash benefits in the short term are governed by the Sickness Act. This Act ensures employed persons against the loss of wages due to sickness, accident or infirmity. There are two waiting days (i.e. no benefit is paid for the first two days of sickness) and then benefit lasts for a maximum of fifty-two weeks. The level of benefit is eighty per cent of the daily wage but no benefit is paid on the 'uninsured wage' — in 1973 the uninsured wage was that above 125.91 florins (£19.3) per day.[15] Each industrial association can fix the benefit at a higher level or reduce or remove the 'waiting day' restriction if they so wish. For the preg-

nancy and confinement of an insured person, the benefit paid is equal
to one hundred per cent of the daily wage up to the above ceiling for
six weeks before the expected date of confinement and one hundred
per cent, for six weeks after the confinement.

Death benefits are paid at the rate of one hundred per cent of daily
earnings up to the ceiling for the month of the insured's death and for
the two subsequent months.

The Incapacity Insurance Act gives benefits to those who, after they
have received benefits under the above Act for fifty-two weeks, are
still at least fifteen per cent incapacitated for any type of work and
less than sixty-five years of age. The level of benefit depends on the
level of wage and on the degree of incapacity from which the worker
is suffering. The seven categories of incapacity are as follows:

Table 12

Incapacity for work	Percentage of benefit
Less than 15 per cent	No benefit.
15 to 25 per cent	10 per cent of 100/106 of the daily wage
25 to 35 per cent	20 per cent of 100/106 of the daily wage
35 to 45 per cent	30 per cent of 100/106 of the daily wage
45 to 55 per cent	40 per cent of 100/106 of the daily wage
55 to 65 per cent	50 per cent of 100/106 of the daily wage
65 to 80 per cent	65 per cent of 100/106 of the daily wage
80 per cent and over	80 per cent of 100/106 of the daily wage.

There are no increases in benefit for the marital partner or for dependent children. The usual ceiling on benefits applies. The benefit is
based, not on total earnings, but on a figure which is six per cent
lower. Benefits in the incapacity category of eighty per cent and more
can be raised to one hundred per cent of the patient's condition merits
it. All allowances are reviewed if the incapacity worsens. Substantial
efforts are made to rehabilitate the beneficiaries of this insurance.[16]

Private insurers (life and non-life companies) supplement compulsory cash benefits insurance. In 1972 the estimated premium income
of these companies was seventy-two million florins. Contributions are
related to age and result in the purchase of a hundred florin (£15.31)
annuity units. These units are paid to the insured person in relation to
the incapacity of the insured e.g. twenty-five per cent — thirty per
cent disablement entitles the insured to thirty per cent of the annuity.

7 Provision

In the previous section, some details of the nature of the employment and remuneration of doctors, dentists and pharmacists have already been given. In this section an attempt will be made to examine the supply (stock and flow) of medical personnel and the nature of hospital provision.

(a) Medical Personnel

There were approximately 18,000 active physicians in the Netherlands in 1972. The Dutch hope to expand this stock until a doctor patient ratio of 1.4 to 1.5 per thousand habitants is reached in 1980, (at present the ratio is about 1.3 doctors per thousand population). Of the present stock of doctors about thirty per cent are general practitioners and some thirty-five per cent are specialists. The rest are training to be specialists or are involved in 'social medicine'. The number of general practitioners was static for the period 1960 to 1970 whilst the number of specialists increased by 1,663.

An analysis by Stolte (1971) of the stocks of the other types of medical personnel is rather perfunctory — he claims that there is a 'shortage' of dentists with the number available unable to 'provide the services need'. The meaning of 'shortage' and 'needed' is not discussed. He notes that the stock of nurses has risen continually since the War despite higher entrance requirements and a longer period of training. Of the 68,000 nurses about ten per cent (7,000) are male. Nurses are trained in the hospital. Training can be undertaken with the aim of achieving one of two qualifications: the 'B' certificate (for the nursing of mental patients) is awarded after three years of successful study; the 'A' certificate is available for all those with a minimum of ten years general education (MAVO IV certificate) and takes three and a half years to complete. In 1971 there were 19,500 probationers and 20,500 qualified nurses employed in ordinary Dutch hospitals.[17] The training of nurses for the mentally handicapped takes three years during which the trainee is tied to the institution where she started. In the late 1960s there were 790 midwives and 4,500 maternity nurses. The latter have a fifteen month special training course. Taking account of all types of medical and para-medical personnel, it is estimated (Stolte, 1971) that the Dutch health service employ about 3.8 per cent of the labour force (175,000).

Additions to the stocks of the more skilled health service workers depend on the training facilities that are available. Medical training facilities (for physicians) are available at seven medical university faculties (Leiden, Utrecht, Groningen, Amsterdam [Municipal], Nijmegen, Amsterdam [Protestant] and Rotterdam). Entrance is possible for anyone with a school leaving certificate at an advanced level — this is usually awarded at the age of eighteen. The course takes six or seven years and the qualification permits its holder to practice medicine freely and without restriction. Specialists are trained by courses which last from four to eight years. The courses are supervised by the Royal Netherlands Medical Association and the Universities concerned. Stolte (1971) estimates that the faculties are producing about 350 new doctors per year.

Dental training is provided in the Universities of Utrecht, Nijmegen, Groningen and Amsterdam. Entrance requirements are the same as for medical students although the course only lasts six years. Pharmacists are trained over a period of eight years. Those qualified pharmacists seeking to work in hospital pharmacies undergo further training lasting two years.

Table 13 *Medical Personnel 1966-72*

	1966	1967	1968	1969	1970	1971	1972	percentage change 1966-72
Physicians	14550	14774	15128	15644	16292	17381	18142	+24.6
Dentists	3034	3133*	3243	3034	3364	3444	3648	+20.2
Pharmacists	1158	N.A.	1019	1019	1057	1084	1114	-3.7
Midwives	785	775	781	785	775	883	829	+ 5.6

Source: World Health Organisation (1971, 1972 and 1973) and
Statistical Yearbook, Central Bureau of Statistics.
* Change between 1966 and 1968 devided by two.

Table 13 shows stock figures for the period 1966-72. As can be seen from the table there has been a significant increase in the number of physicians and dentists practising in the Netherlands during the period.

The stock of physicians increased by nearly a quarter (24.6 per cent) whilst the stock of dentists increased by over a fifth (20.2 per cent). The number of pharmacists and midwives changed by much smaller amounts: a loss of 3.7 per cent and a gain of 5.6 per cent.

(b) Hospitals
Table 14 shows WHO figures for the number of hospital beds in the Netherlands over the period 1966-68.

Table 14   *Hospital Beds 1966-69*

		1966	1967	1968	1969	Annual average percentage change
(a)	General Hospitals	57559	58691	63415	61607	+6.9
(b)	Specialised Hospital					
i)	Maternity	669	455	551	360	-48.4
ii)	Paediatric	1166	927	820	659	-43.4
iii)	Asthma	279	443)		571	
iv)	Cancer	341	350)		371	
vi)	Neurology	485	474)		474	
vi)	Opthalmology	284	294)	4391	301	
vii)	Orthopaedics	190	176)		140	
viii)	Rheumatology	395	418)		420	
ix)	Epileptics	801	803)		944	
x)	Other (rehabilitation centres (1969=1461)	175	1268)		1633	
(c)	Total (excluding TB and mental)	62364	64289	69187	67480	+8.2

Source: World Health Organisation (1971, 1972 and 1973) *op. cit.*

Table 14 gives an indication of the trends in the movement in bed
stock in the late 1960s. From this limited data with its problems of
definition a growth rate of approximately 6.9 per cent can be seen in
the total number of beds. This data ignores psychiatric and TB hospital
bed facilities. In 1969 there were thirty-nine psychiatric hospitals with
some 27,500 beds.[18] There were ninety-four units for the mentally
handicapped with some 17,000 places. The decline of TB has reduced
the number of sanatoria substantially over the last two decades. In
1960 there were 9,100 beds for the care of tuberculosis sufferers. By
the beginning of the 1970s there were 700 beds. The provision of 190
nursing homes for the chronic sick (with about 23,000 beds) must also
be noted. In total the EEC (1973 (a) page 20) estimate that there are
139,832 hospital beds in the Netherlands. This level of provision,
10.52 per thousand population, (EEC 1973 (a) page 24) is similar
to the figures given by Stolte (1973). A breakdown of this estimate is
given in Table 15. On the basis of *ad hoc* bed patients objectives
Stolte argues that there is a need to increase general hospital beds by
0.2 per thousand and psychiatric beds by the same amount.

Table 15   *Hospital Bed Stock 1971*

	Units	Beds	Beds per 1000 population
General Hospitals	254	68,527	5.15
Psychiatric Hospitals	39	26,782	2.01
Mentally Handicapped	113	17,500	1.32
Epileptics Hospitals	6	1,400	0.11
TB Sanatoria	5	700	0.05
Nursing Homes	206	22,495	1.69
Other (blind, deaf, maladjusted children, etc.)	10	2,500	0.19
Total	633	139,904	10.52

EEC (1973 (a) p. 24 cites an overall bed population ratio of 11.9. This would appear to be erroneous given a population of 13.3 million.

Source: Stolte (1973) Table 1 p. 6.

Most of these hospitals are owned and operated by private non-profit making organisations, many of which are religious. In 1969 there were 327 hospital units, of which 290 were private. These 290 private hospitals provided 119,302 (eighty-six per cent) hospital beds whilst the various public establishments (thirty-seven) provided 20,529 beds (fourteen per cent). All hospitals enter into agreements with the sickness funds but the resultant bargaining is not unconstrained. The Hospital Tariffs Act 1964 (*Wet Ziekenhuistarieven*) placed the control of tariffs in the hands of the Council for Hospital Tariffs. The Council is made up of representatives of the sickness funds, the insurance companies, the National Hospital Council and three independent members.

As all general hospitals in the Netherlands are non-profit making bodies by law, the Council sanctions only those tariffs which are at a level approximately equal to costs plus some allowance for depreciation. In some cases, e.g. the municipally owned general hospitals (twenty per cent of the general hospital bed stock), subsidies are provided by the owners to cover an inadvertant annual deficit. Apart from this the only direct public aid to hospitals appears to be the guaranteeing by central and local government, of loans to private hospitals who submit their plans for approval, and the provision of investment finance to public and University hospitals. The former measure reduces the cost of investment finance to private hospitals. The basis of the tariffs is the hospital's annual budget. Each year all hospitals must submit their annual budget to the Hospital Tariff Commission. Costs are calculated on the basis of the number of days of hospitalisation with variations for the categories of cure. In most hospitals there are four classes of hospital care: classes 1, 2A, 2B and 3. Compulsory insurance covers the cost of only the cheapest (class 3) type of care. Many hospitals (about one in three) have only a single undivided 2nd class. The costs of bed provision rise about twenty per cent per class. Hospital fees for 3rd class were between 50 and 180 florins per day in 1972. Usually the more modern the hospital the more expensive it is. Class 2A provision varied in price from 82 to 256 florins per day (1972) and 1st class provision is still more expensive. The physicians' fee is additional to these costs and for higher class beds it is calculated by multiplying the rates levied on private patients in 3rd class beds by factors of 1½ for class 2B and 2 for class 2A. The fees for 1st class beds are not usually subject to any limit. We should note that the fees paid to physicians by private patients in 3rd class beds are approximately three times larger than the fees levied on social insurance beneficiaries on the same beds.

Compulsory social insurance pays hospital fees for 3rd class treatment only. The funds offer supplementary cover to meet the cost difference between hospital and treatment fees for any higher classes of care. The costs of the basic (3rd class) benefits are thought to be less than cost, i.e. the fees paid for higher classes of treatment appear to subsidise the 3rd class treatment of compulsorily insured beneficiaries. This cross-subsidisation exists not only for the provision of beds but also in the provision of physicians' care – the insurers believe that the fees charged by doctors to private patients (thirty per cent of the population) make up seventy per cent of specialists' income.

Although the financial burden of providing hospitals does not rest on the State it has interested itself in many aspects of hospital provision. Legislation providing for the control of the regional (eleven in number) contribution of hospital beds on the basis of 'real needs' has come into force (*Wet Ziekenhuisuoorzteningen* 1970). 'Real Needs' are translated into *ad hoc* guide lines, e.g. general hospital bed patient ratios of 4 per 1000 in rural areas, 4½ per 1000 in small towns, and 5 per 1000 in urban areas. These targets compare with the 1969 provision level of 5.63 per 1000 (EEC 1973 (a) page 26). This figure was the arithmetic mean of a regional distribution which ranged from 3.14 to 7.08 (Burkens [1973] and Stolte [1971]). It is intended to increase the scope of this legislation to control building and the purchase of expensive equipment and to harmonise accounting systems despite strong opposition. Also it is anticipated that the scope of the planning legislation will be extended to cover the entire health care system rather than only the hospital service.

The provision of care for the aged, the chronic sick and the mentally ill us undertaken in general hospitals and specialised institutions. The latter are quite important. Licensed nursing homes for the care of the chronic sick provide 15,000 beds. Most of these beds are provided in small units (average size 150 beds). Stolte [19] estimates that there is a 'need' for 7000 more beds in this category 'partly to replace the few non-licensed institutions that are run for profit'. The elderly who are mentally ill are cared for in licensed institutions and unlicensed institutions which provide about 8000 beds. Each category (licensed and non-licensed) provides about half of this total. Several thousand elderly persons who are mentally ill are resident in psychiatric hospitals, some of which are setting up specialised units for their care. Psychiatric care is provided in thirty-nine hospitals with 27,000 beds and the patients may be admitted on a voluntary basis or on certification (about twenty per cent of the total number of admissions).

The crude indicators that are available indicate that the Dutch hospital system is not very efficient. A high level of provision is complemented by a high average length of stay. The average length-of-stay statistic has changed little during the 1960s – 1960 = 20.13; 1969 = 20.7 (EEC 1973 (a) page 31). The bed occupation level is very high (92.03 per cent). These characteristics have been seen in other hospital systems (Feldstein 1965) and we can note that in the Netherlands hospital bed supply appears to create its own demand.

9 Conclusion

The Sickness Funds Insurance Act (*Ziedkfondswet* – ZFW) and the general Special Sickness Expenses Act (AWBZ) provide medical care insurance for wage earners complemented by a form of national insurance which provides long-term, serious illness cover. All those above the earnings ceiling (thirty per cent of the population) can register with a private insurance company if they wish to have protection from the cost of short-term illnesses. Cash benefits – the Sickness Act (*Ziekewet* – ZW) and the Incapacity Act (*Wet op Arbeidsongeschiktheidsverzekering* – WAO) – for wage earners cover both short (ZW) and long term (WAO) periods of illness.

As in many other West European countries the philosophy of egalitarianism or justice is resulting in the increasing involvement of the state in the provision of health care. It was said in the introduction that health care in the Netherlands is privately financed and provided. As a global view this is correct but this private organisation has been the subject of increasing control and supplementation in recent years. The reluctance of the market to provide insurance cover the chronic and long-term illness led to the 1967 legislation which, although continuing to use private sickness funds, has led to increasing state financial involvement. The guarantee of private hospital investment loans in exchange for prior building authorisation from the Government, was the first step in the road to planning the distribution of hospital beds. The planning controls aimed at a more equitable regional distribution of hospital beds, are to be extended in the near future to achieve a more equal distribution of all health care inputs.

These trends will no doubt continue largely as a result of the rapid cost inflation. Whether the present level of compulsory coverage will be maintained is an intriguing question. The result of the present organisation is that the rich are excluded from medical care and hence do not directly contribute to the cost of providing for the poor. The lack of significant explicit redistribution hides the fact that implicit redistribution takes place as a result of the physicians practising price discrimination. This reliance on physicians as an agent of redistribution does not appeal to all commentators. However, to replace this instrument could be costly because compulsory, comprehensive social insurance, even if agreed to by the representatives of the electorate, would result in the physicians demanding a sharp increase in social insurance fees to compensate for the loss of income due to the reduction of private practice. It is possible that progressive taxation and public subsidies might be a less costly and more effective method of redistributing resources from the rich to the poor.

A Commission has been appointed to propose a new financial structure for health care in the Netherlands. Four plans have been submitted to this body. The Trade Unions favour a considerable elevation in the ceiling to a level equal to the legal insurance ceiling for old age (24,300 florins [£3,721.28] per year). This would seriously curtail the activities of private insurance institutions. The latter have submitted plans which leave the insured free to choose between the funds and private insurers and which result in the public subsidisation of those opting for private insurance. This would enable the private insurer to offer coverage at a lower contribution rate. The employers favour the private insurers' scheme. The Commission has received this scheme, the trade union scheme and two other schemes which propose compromise solutions. They have not published their conclusions as yet.

NOTES

1. The health services ate the only sector of social security in which there are denominational organisations.
2. G. Spitaels *et al* (1971), Vol III.
3. I.e. those nursing services which are divorced from the hospitals. The Associations employed 3,845 nurses in 1971.
4. The Social Insurance Organisation Act divides trade and industry into twenty-six industrial associations (*bedrijfsverenigingen*). All are non-profit making and are governed by boards consisting of equal numbers of employers and employees. (See Ministry of Foreign Affairs [1968] *Digest of the Kingdom of the Netherlands – Social Aspects*, The Hague, p. 7). Civil servants and railway workers are not covered by this Act. They have their own arrangements.
5. The Social Insurance Council is made up of a chairman and eighteen other members. One third of the members come from the central employers' organisation, one third from the central employees' organisation and one third are appointed by the Minister. The Council supervises the organisations and advises the Government on technical aspects of social insurance problems. It can 'impose regulations designed to promote proper and coordinated enforcement of the social insurance laws on the executive bodies under its supervision' *op. cit.* p. 7.
6. 1971 = 17,050 florins (£2,611);
   1972 = 18,800 florins (£2,879);
   1973 = 20,900 florins (£3,200).
7. See Sickness Funds Act (updated 1971) sections 38 and 39.
8. The WAO data for 1967 is obtained by doubling the income and expenditure figures for the half year in which the scheme was in operation.
9. See note 8.
10. The patient may change his doctor every six months if the physician agrees (Sickness Funds Act – updated 1971 – Section 44).
11. See Section 1 Administration (above) for more details of the composition of these organisations.
12. Ministry of Social Affairs and Public Health, (1968), p. 16.
13. Ministry of Social Affairs and Public Health, (1972), p. 6.
14. Ministry of Social Affairs and the Social Security Information Centre (1971, 1972).
15. The ceiling and the daily earnings figure is adjusted whenever the Index of Wages changes by more than three per cent or at the beginning of the year when adjustment is necessary due to wages policy.
16. For details see e.g. Spitaels *et al* (1971) Vol III p. 672.
17. Ministry of Social Affairs and Public Health, (1972) [a].
18. Stolte (1971), p. 151.
19. Stolte *op. cit.* p. 152.

References

British Medical Association (1971), *Health Service Financing*, London.

Burkens, J.C.R. (1973) *Health Services in Holland,* mimeograph. Paper presented to a seminar at the Kings Fund Health Centre, London, May.

European Communities Commission (1971), *Comparative Tables of the Social Security Systems in the Member States of the European Community,* Sixth Edition Vol I, General System Brussels.

European Economic Commission (1973 (a)), *The Cost of Hospitalisation in Social Security,* Department of Social Affairs, Brussels.

European Economic Commission (1973 (b)), *Main Report Covering Three Investigations into the Principal Items of Expenditure in Sickness Insurance Covered by Social Security, Department of Social Affairs,* Brussels.

European Economic Community (1973) *Report on the Development of the Social Situation in the Community in 1972,* Brussels and Luxembourg.

Feldstein, M. (1965) 'Hospital Bed Scarcity', *Economica.*

Illuminati, F. (1972) 'The Cost of Health', *International Social Security Review* No 4.

Langendonck, J Van (1972) 'Social Health Insurance in the Six Countries of the European Economic Community', *International Journal of Health Services,* Vol 2, No 4.

Ministry of Foreign Affairs (1968) *Digest of the Kingdom of the Netherlands: Social Aspects,* 4th Edition, The Hague.

Ministry of Foreign Affairs (1970), *Facts and Figures,* Vol 8 (Public Health) and Vol 11 (Social Insurance).

Ministry of Social Affairs and Public Health (1968), *Public Health in the Netherlands,* The Hague.

Ministry of Social Affairs and Public Health (1972 (a)), *De Volksgzond,* (Public Health), The Hague.

Ministry of Social Affairs and the Social Security Information Centre (1971, 1972 (b)), *Social Security in the Netherlands – a short survey,* The Hague.

Ministry of Public Health and Environment Hygiene (1972), *Environmental Health in the Netherlands,* 3rd revised Edition, The Hague.

Spitaels, G. *et al* (1971) *Le Salaire Indirect et La Couverture des Besoins Sociaux,* Vols I, II and III, Universtite Libre de Bruxelles, Brussels.

Stolte, J.B. (1971) 'Health Services in the Netherlands', *World Hospitals.* Vol 6, pp 147-56.

Stolte, J.B. (1973) *Health Services in Holland* mimeograph. Paper presented to a seminar at the Kings Fund Health Centre, London, May.

US Department of Health, Education and Welfare (1972), *Social Security Programs throughout the World 1971,* Washington.

World Health Organisation (1971, 1972 and 1973), *World Health Statistics Annual,* Vol III.

4 BELGIUM

The Evolution of Health Care in Belgium

The complex system of health care in Belgium reflects the heterogeneous nature of the country. The geographical position of Belgium has led to her being the buffer between two 'cultures' — the Latin and Saxon — and the recipient of regular invasions for over 800 years. The heterogenity of the country with its three official languages[1] and sharp Walloon-Flemish division has, inevitably, affected its institutions. The administration of government is decentralised into regional and local units although most decision making is undertaken by the central government in Brussels. There are 2,000 local authorities, some of which are very small (300 population) and these organisations have an important role in the provision of health care. The Roman Catholic church has been involved in the provision of health care in Belgium for centuries and, like the local authorities, it continues to play a major role today.

The evolution of social security in Belgium can be traced back to the late Middle Ages when the corporations (guilds) undertook to provide a minimum level of subsistence for the aged and sick members of the local community. In 1791 (Le Chapelier Act) the role of the corporation was abolished (due to fears of subversion) and only charitable organisations were allowed to organise the finance and provision of health care. This legislation was not enforced in a rigorous manner and societies whose objects were essentially humanitarian were permitted to thrive and develop into mutalities. By the beginning of the nineteenth century, sickness funds (or mutualities) existed in several places and their number increased as the Belgian industrial revolution gained momentum. At this time the funds were largely involved in income maintenance rather than the direct reimbursement of the costs of medical care. Also they were basically neutral in their philosophy (i.e. neither Catholic or Socialist). It was not until after the publication of the Communist manifesto (1848) and the spread of Socialism that the funds began to ally themselves with the trade unions, both Catholic and Socialist. This development led to the present ideological pluralism of the sickness funds — some are Catholic, some are Socialist and some are neutral.

During the course of the nineteenth and twentieth century the development of the sickness funds has been encouraged by the State. Legislation in 1851 permitted the funds (of which there were 200) to become corporate bodies for the first time. Subsequent legislation (1894) allowed the funds to receive subsidies from local and central government, gifts and legacies from philanthropic bodies and exemption from certain forms of taxation. From 1900 the State granted an initial subsidy to all new sickness funds and subsequently, subsidies towards the operation of the funds were forthcoming. For twelve years this subsidisation of the operation of funds was dependent on the whim of the government and the treasury. However, after 1912 a system of systematic and continuing subsidisation was adopted which initially resulted in funds receiving a subsidy equal to sixty per cent of members' contributions. The period from 1906 to 1920 was one in which the organisation of the funds changed to a close resemblance of its present scale. By 1920 the funds had federated into five national unions.[2]

The inevitable transition from financial intervention to compulsory coverage culminated in the introduction of compulsory insurance in 1945. The financial vehicles for this scheme were the five national sickness funds federations and a Government auxiliary fund. Important subsequent legislation (1963) altered the relationship between the funds and the doctors, hospitals and other providers of care.[3] It also renewed the method of finance and improved the levels of reimbursement. Compulsory insurance was extended to cover the heavy risks of the self-employed (1964)[4], civil servants, the physically handicapped, the mentally handicapped, domestic servants, students, clergymen, members of religious orders and all other persons without compulsory insurance (all in 1969).

As a result of these changes ninety-nine per cent of the Belgian population is covered by compulsory health care insurance. However, the exact meaning of the word cover must be carefully defined as, for instance, over one and a half million people (the self-employed) are members of a scheme which provides only for heavy risk medical care.

1 Administration

The inherent complexity of the Belgian system of health care makes it rather difficult to describe the administrative organisation. As can be seen from Diagram 1 there are seven ministries involved in national policy making, guidance and control of health care. Of these seven ministries — Labour, Public Work, Defence, Agriculture, Education, Public Health and Social Welfare — it is the Ministry of Social Affairs which is of primary importance in the financial operation of the general scheme and the scheme for the self-employed. This ministry is responsible for social security and in this capacity it is responsible for national policy making and the guidance and control of health care insurance.

Diagram 1 *The Organisation of Health Insurance in Belgium*

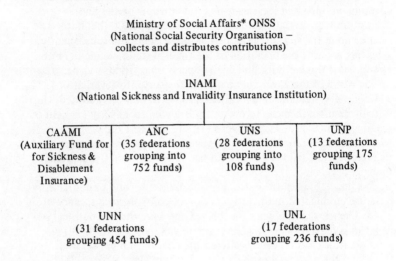

Ministry of Social Affairs* ONSS
(National Social Security Organisation –
collects and distributes contributions)

INAMI
(National Sickness and Invalidity Insurance Institution)

CAAMI	ANC	UNS	UNP
(Auxiliary Fund for for Sickness & Disablement Insurance)	(35 federations grouping into 752 funds)	(28 federations grouping into 108 funds)	(13 federations grouping 175 funds)

UNN
(31 federations
grouping 454 funds)

UNL
(17 federations
grouping 236 funds)

* The Ministries of Labour, Public Works, Defence, Agriculture and Education are involved also in national level policy making, guidance and control of health care. However, the role is slight in comparison with the Ministry of Social Affairs.

On the financial side all social security contributions are paid to an autonomous organ of this Ministry (ONSS – the National Social Security Organisation) which divides the revenue between the various types of Social Security (retirement and widows' pensions, sickness and disablement insurance, involuntary unemployment, family allowances and, for workers only, annual holidays) according to the pre-determined coefficients. The health care revenues are handed over to another autonomous institution INAMI (the National Sickness Insurance Institution) which distributes the resources amongst six organisations according to predetermined coefficients which are related to institutions' membership.[5] These six organisations are five confederations of sickness funds or *mutualités* and an auxiliary Fund:

(a)   The Confederations or *mutualités* of sickness funds:

(i)   the National Alliance of Christian Mutual Society (*l'Alliance Nationale des Mutualités Chretiennes* – ANC) covers about forty-five per cent of the insured population.

(ii)   the National Union of Belgian Non-Denominational Mutual Societies (*l'Union Nationale des Mutualités neutres de Belgique* – UNN) covers about ten per cent of the population.

(iii)   the National Union of Socialist Mutual Societies (*l'Union Nationale des Mutualités Socialistes* – UNS) covers about twenty-nine per cent of the population.
(iv)   the National Union of Belgian Liberal Mutual Societies (*l'Union Nationale des Mutualités Liberales de Belgique* – UNL) covers about five per cent of the population.
(v)   the National Union of Belgian Occupational Mutual Societies (*l'Union Nationale des Mutualités Professionelles de Belgique* – UNP) covers about ten per cent of the population.
(b)   the Auxiliary Fund CAAMI (*la caisse auxiliare de l'assurance maladie-invalidité*) covers the rest of the compulsorily insured population.[6]

The income received by the confederations and the Auxiliary Fund is divided amongst their constituent members. The sickness funds – 1745 in number – are the units which reimburse the insured and the institutions where health care is consumed. Except for supplementary insurance, the funds cannot determine benefits or contributions as these are determined by central government in consultation with the funds and other interested parties.

The employees of the Belgian railway and their dependents (233,991 people) together with seamen and their dependents (8,386 people) are insured under separate arrangemnets. The miners and the civil servants have a special (separate) scheme for invalidity.

Two types of voluntary insurance continue to be of some importance – compulsory-voluntary insurance and voluntary insurance. Both types of insurance are provided by the sickness funds. The former is voluntary in that it is not laid down by statute law but is compulsory in that the funds make contribution to such insurance a condition of membership. Voluntary insurance is taken out by those wishing to supplement their compulsory cover. Thus the beneficiary may have benefits deriving from compulsory insurance, compulsory-voluntary insurance and voluntary insurance. As we will see below (Section 6: benefits) the latter two forms of insurance serve the purpose of supplementing statutory benefit levels.

The financial administrative structure described in this section enables those in need to purchase medical care. This care is obtained from a variety of individuals and organisations, e.g. the physician, the hospital and the pharmacist. The organisation of these providers of care is referred to below (Section 7: provision, in particular).

The final administrative organ of which we must take account is the Cross Associations (Yellow and White). These organisations are similar to those existing in the Netherlands and provide social workers, home nursing, preventive care and propaganda (bi-weekly newspapers) to their members who contribute about 50 BF (£0.54) per month.

2 Coverage

Table 1 gives some details of the changes which have taken place in the coverage of compulsory health care insurance in Belgium in the period 1949 to 1972. Since 1960 the degree of coverage has increased from 56.48 per cent to 99.30 per cent of the population. This large increase has been largely due to legislation which has extended the scheme progressively and which was outlined in the introduction.

Table 1 *Coverage 1949-72*

Year	Total Number of beneficiaries	Total population	Total beneficiaries as a percentage of total population
1949	4,366,900	8,625,084	50.63
1960	5,183,836	9,178,154	56.48
1963	5,548,052	9,328,126	59.48
1964	7,495,450	9,428,100	79.50
1965	8,700,000	9,499,234	91.59
1966	8,890,898	9,556,380	93.04
1967	9,010,751	9,605,601	93.81
1968	9,083,007	9,631,910	94.30
1969	9,357,620	9,660,154	96.87
1970	9,479,766	9,650,944	98.23
1971	9,581,683	9,695,000	98.80
1972	9,666,661	9,727,000	99.30

Source: INAMI (1972) p 221 and ANC Research Department

The population statistics were estimates for each year of the period 1963-9. The 1970 figure is the census figure.

The data in Table 1 excludes seamen, railwaymen and their dependents, who are a very small portion of the total population.[7] Table 2 gives disaggregated statement of the number of people covered by compulsory health insurance in Belgium in 1972.

Table 2 *Coverage 1972*

1.	General Scheme	
(a)	Active workers	3,085,416
	Dependents of active workers	3,487,470
(b)	Old Age Pensioners	690,384

Table 2 *(Cont)*

Dependents of pensioners	327,329	
(c)Widows	343,808	
Dependents of Widows	51,541	
(d)Other beneficiaries*	5,161	
Total		7,991,109
2. Self-employed scheme		
(a)Active workers	543,904	
Dependents of active workers	864,174	
(b)Old Age Pensioners	97,955	
Dependents of pensioners	49,289	
(c)Widows	48,960	
Dependents of widows	2,977	
(d)Others†	26,113	
Total		1,633,372
Overall Total		9,606,661

Source: INAMI (1973) Note No 72/158.
  * Orphans (3671) and military dependents (1940).
  † Orphans (1283), clergy (24,815) and others (15).

The population of Belgium in 1972 was 9,727,000. So the coverage in 1972 was over ninety-nine per cent of the population. The small residue (120,400) are able to acquire help from the social aid programme (of which we will say more later) or are members of the railway or merchant shipping compulsory social insurance schemes.

In the case of the self-employed, compulsory cover is for large risks only. The self-employed supplement their cover by voluntary contributions. Some twenty per cent of the employers guarantee by insurance their employees subsidisation of heavy medical care costs in as far as they are not met by compulsory insurance (*ticket modérateur*). Many other employers offer similar benefits and fund them by special enterprise funds.

3 Qualifying Conditions

Health care benefits (both medical care and sickness insurance) are available to those individuals who fulfil certain qualifying conditions. The contributor must be a member of a mutual society of sickness fund chosen by him, or be registered with the Auxiliary Fund. Dependents are bound by the contributor's choice. The contributor must

83

have completed a qualifying period of 120 days of work, or its equivalent, during a six-month period. Also he must have submitted to his fund, for the qualifying period in question, quarterly contributions vouchers of a certain minimum value, or other contribution documents. These documents inform the fund of the situation of the contributor.

These qualifying conditions are relaxed for widows, pensioners or orphans and the handicapped. A certificate of retirement has to be submitted to the insurance organisation by the individual's pension fund. Orphans have no waiting period qualification and they are eligible to benefits provided a certificate of loss of parents or guardians is submitted to the insurance organisation by the family allowances fund. A handicapped person is eligible for medical benefits as soon as he is recognised as being handicapped. Recognition is made by the medical control department of the National Sickness and Invalidity Insurance Institute who sends the relevant certification evidence to the individual's insurance organisation.

The self-employed have to fulfil similar contribution requirements. Members of religious orders can apply to acquire heavy risk medical care coverage from a sickness fund. If they fail to make such an application they are not covered. Inactive (pensioners, invalids, etc.) self-employed persons have no waiting period and are covered by insurance provided a retirement certificate is sent to the sickness fund by the pension fund.

In all the above cases, the insured dependents have the same rights as the contributor.

4 Finance

(a)   Medical Care

The contribution rates for medical care insurance vary between various categories of workers and, as in the Netherlands, are of two types, general and heavy risk. The general contribution rates and ceilings for workers covered by the general scheme are related to a price index and are as follows: blue collar or manual workers pay two per cent of the wage up to a monthly earnings ceiling of BF 28,775 (£313), the employer of this type of labour pays 3.75 per cent of his wage up to the same ceiling; white collar workers or non-manual workers and their employers pay the same contribution rates up to the same ceiling as for manual workers. For heavy risks the overall contribution rate is three per cent up to the lower ceiling of BF 17,265 (£188). The employee pays two fifths (1.2 per cent) of this contribution and the employer pays the remainder.

Other groups pay varying contribution rates. The self-employed pay two per cent of the earnings between a yearly earnings floor of BF 84,896 (£924) and a ceiling of BF 445,704 (£4,855) (1973). As a consequence if any self-employed person earns less than BF 84,896 he will pay two per cent of BF 84,896, i.e. BF 1,697.92 (£18) each year to acquire medical care benefits for heavy risks only. If he wants to insure himself and his family for small risks he has to make further contributions. The Belgian seamen are covered by a special scheme. Here the contribution rate is 4.80 per cent of earnings up to the monthly earnings ceiling of BF 28,775. The employee pays 2.20 per cent and the employer pays 2.6 per cent. Most pensioners pay no contributions − and acquire one hundred per cent reimbursement of the costs of routine care. If the old person's pension is the result of less than fifteen years employment he has to pay a monthly premium of BF 50 (£0.54) if he was an employed person and BF 20 (£0.22) if he was self-employed.

(b) Sickness Insurance

The provision of sickness benefits to those in the general scheme is complex. First it is relevant to note that blue collar, or manual workers are paid directly (the guaranteed wage) by the employer during the first seven days in most cases (i.e. there are exemptions) at a rate equal to eighty per cent of full wage. White collar or non-manual workers have their wages paid by the employer for the first thirty days of sickness. This inequality of treatment and the greater incidence of sickness amongst manual workers has led to the result that the contribution rates of the two classes of workers differ. The blue collar or manual worker pays 1.20 per cent of his monthly wages up to a ceiling of BF 17,400 (£189).[8] His employer pays 1.8 per cent of his monthly wage up to the same ceiling. White collar or non-manual workers pay 0.80 per cent of their monthly wage up to the ceiling of BF 17,400. Their employers pay 1.8 per cent of the wage up to the ceiling.

The self-employed person pays 1.33 per cent of his annual income between a minimum (floor) of BF 84,896 (£924) and the first step maximum (ceiling) of BF 265,300 (£2,889). For annual income between BF 265,300 and BF 445,704 (£4,855) a contribution rate of 0.785 per cent is levied.

Sickness benefits of seamen and miners are governed by separate arrangements. For seamen the overall monthly contribution rate is 2.40 per cent up to a ceiling of BF 17,400 (£182). Of this 2.4 per cent, the employee pays 1.10 per cent and the employer pays 1.30 per cent. For miners the total contribution rate is 5.6 per cent of wages. The employee pays three per cent and the employer pays 2.6 per cent. There are no earnings floor or ceilings for this scheme. These contributions finance both medical care and sickness benefits for the miner.

5 Income and Expenditure

The income and expenditure data given in this section is the most recent that is available. Table 3 gives details of general scheme and self-employed scheme expenditure in medical care and sickness insurance during the period 1966-71. Two types of medical care are listed ('C' — ordinary medical care, and 'M' — social diseases) with their component parts. Total expenditure on medical care under the general and the self-employed schemes rose from BF 20,674.2 million (£225 million) in 1966 to BF 38,071.9 million (£414 million) in 1971. The general scheme medical care expenditure rose by eighty per cent in the period whilst that of the self-employed rose by 160 per cent. General scheme expenditure rose to BF 42,488,2 million (£462 million) in 1972 and the 1973 budget was 47,782.8 million (£520 million). The figures for the C (ordinary care) and M (social disease) categories was 40,236.5 (£438 million) and 45,207.9 (£492 million) for the former, and 2,251.7 (£24 million) and 2,577.9 (£28 million) for the latter.

General scheme sickness insurance expenditure rose from BF 7,907 million (£86 million) in 1966 to BF 14,045 million (£152 million) in 1971, i.e. by 77.6 per cent. Sickness insurance for the self-employed was not introduced until 1971 when the expenditure was relatively trivial (£0.118 million) and unrepresentative (see Table 3). The overall expenditure of both schemes rose from BF 31,895 million (£347 million) to BF 56,714 million (£617 million), i.e. by seventy-seven per cent.

The causes of this inflation are not too difficult to identify. A significant cause of expenditure inflation was the expansion of the coverage of the compulsory insurance schemes. To this must be added the increased *per capita* consumption of medical care and the rise in the price of inputs (e.g. medical salaries, pharmaceutical products and hospitalisation).

Table 3 *Medical Care Expenditure 1966-71 in BF million (and £m)*

(a) General Scheme	1966	1967	1968	1969	1970	1971
(i) Ordinary Medical Care (c)						
C1 Medical fees (doctors** dentists & nurses)	386	5768	6418	7357	8409	9337
C2 Pharmaceutical products	4634	5093	5869	6925	8315	8824

Table 3 *(Cont)*

		1966	1967	1968	1969	1970	1971
C3	Para-medical services	1059	916	1069	1275	1496	1648
C4	Special treatments†	2636	2788	3267	4255	4974	5804
C5	Surgery	950	989	1068	1218	1331	1549
C6	Maternity	330	333	340	374	399	427
C7	Hospitalisation (hotel costs only)	3052	3096	3707	4417	5119	5622
C8	Rehabilitation	39	43	48	64	74	90
C9	Tuberculosis	134	131	156	160	172	176
	Miscellaneous***	-25	-28	-51	-76	-91	-15
C10	Total (C1–C9)*	18196	19133	21895	25972	30202	33464
		(£198)	(£208)	(£238)	(£283)	(£329)	(£364)

(ii)	Social Medicine (M)						
M1	Cancer	221	245	291	312	339	393
M2	Tuberculosis	259	247	249	244	249	231
M3	Poliomyelitis	9	10	11	10	8	8
M4	Mental illness	708	765	885	1025	1203	1412
M5	Handicapped	50	66	88	101	112	121
M6	Total (M1-M5)	1248	1336	1525	1694	1912	2167
		(£13)	(£14)	(£16)	(£18)	(£21)	(£23)

(iii)	C and M Total and overall total						
C		18196.9	19133.7	21895.0	25972.9	30202.0	33464.9
M		1248.6	1366.1	1525.8	1694.4	1912.5	2167.6
Overall Total		19756	20820	23788	28130	32175	35632
(C, M and other)		(£215)	(£227)	(£259)	(£306)	(£350)	(£388)

(iv)	Sickness Insurance						
Short term		3901	3919	4237	4810	5524	6769
Invalidity		1532	1648	1693	1820	1952	2378
Invalidity		2227	2471	2975	3412	3798	4420
Death (funeral benefit)		245	258	289	303	377	464
Other		-	-	-	2	6	14
	Total	7907	8298	9195	10347	11653	14045
		(£86)	(£90)	(£100)	(£112)	(£126)	(£152)

(v)	Administrative cost	2882	2993	3255	3627	3960	4296
(vi)	Other†† (General Scheme)	310	352	369	486	105	NA
(vii)	Total expenditure	30855	32463	36607	42590	47893	53973
		(£336)	(£353)	(£398)	(£463)	(£521)	(£589)

Table 3 *(Cont)*

	1966	1967	1968	1969	1970	1971
(b) Self-employed's scheme						
(i) Ordinary medical care (C)						
C1 medical fees	0.7	0.9	4.1	6.8	9.2	13.2
C2 pharmaceutical products	52.5	59.2	81.7	110.4	154.4	181.5
C3 para-medical services	-	0.1	2.4	4.6	8.2	12.4
C4 special treatments †††	8.3	9.3	337.2	554.9	680.9	773.2
C5 surgery	154.7	158.4	171.3	194.9	212.1	234.6
C6 maternity	57.7	55.5	54.7	55.4	57.1	58.5
C7 hospitalisation (hotel only)	429.5	434.3	502.1	528.8	709.7	806.2
C8 rehabilitation	-	0.4	3.3	5.6	3.3	9.1
Miscellaneous	25.5	28.9	51.4	76.4	91.4	110.3
Total C (C1-C8)	729.2	747.5	1208.6	1592.9	1931.7	2198.8
	(£8)	(£8)	(£13)	(£17)	(£21)	(£23)
(ii) Social diseases (M)						
M1 cancer	47.1	51.3	60.3	65.3	71.6	76.4
M2 tuberculosis	18.6	18.0	18.5	15.8	19.1	16.4
M3 poliomyelitis	1.1	1.4	1.0	1.5	2.0	1.7
M4 mental illness	112.8	130.4	151.0	173.8	224.1	238.2
M5 handicapped	8.7	12.5	13.8	18.3	19.4	20.4
Other items	0.3	0.3	0.2	-2.7	-5.8	NA
Total M (M1-M5 & Other)	188.7	214.1	245.0	272.2	330.3	353.1
	(£2)	(£2)	(£3)	(£3)	(£3)	(£4)
(iii) Overall Total (C, M and Other)	918.0	961.7	1453.2	1864.3	2262.3	2551.8
	(£10)	(£10)	(£16)	(£20)	(£25)	(£27)
(iv) Sickness insurance †	-	-	-	-	-	10.9
(v) Administrative costs	121.6	114.0	118.1	172.1	179.2	178.5
(vi) Total Self-Employed Scheme	1039.6	1075.7	1571.3	2036.4	2441.5	2741.2
Overall Total (Both Schemes)	31895	33539	38178	44626	50335	56714
	(£347)	(£365)	(£415)	(£486)	(£548)	(£617)

Sources: (a)   Ministry of Social Affairs (1972) pp 180-83 and 264-5.
           (b)   ANC research department supplied 1971 figures.

***   Miscellaneous – transfers from the self-employed scheme to the general schemes.
†††   Special treatment – X-rays, radio therapy, internal medicine, urgent acute cases, dermatology, physiotherapy, dental surgery and general (undefined) special treatments.
**   Medical fees for doctors are surgery visits only. Other medical fees are disguised in C4 and C5.
*   All totals are derived from the source. Items may not sum to these totals because of the presentation of the data in millions rather than in thousands.
††   Other = international conventions, etc.
†   Sickness insurance for the self-employed has been in operation since 1971.

The relative rates of growth of expenditure can be seen from Table 4 which itemises general scheme expenditure in index form. With 1966 = 100 the most rapidly rising expenditure items up to 1971 were: rehabilitation which started from a small base (230.7), nursing expenditure (226.1), special treatments (220.7), pharmaceutical expenditure (190.5), and hospitalisation (hotel costs only) expenditure (185.0). Expenditure on medical fees for visits to doctors' surgeries grew relatively slowly. The main increase was 183.4 with that latter expenditure growing to 177.7. However, as is noted in the footnote to Table 3, this type of remuneration of physicians is only one of several. Others exist in disguised forms in items C4 and C5.

Table 4 *General Scheme Expenditure 1966-71 (1966=100)*

	1966	1967	1968	1969	1970	1971
C1 Doctors' surgery visits	100	107.7	121.4	139.8	160.7	177.7
dentists	100	98.8	100.8	111.9	122.6	138.7
nurses	100	125.2	147.9	172.3	202.3	226.1
C2 pharmaceutical	100	109.9	126.7	149.4	179.4	190.5
C3 para-medical	100	86.7	101.0	120.4	141.5	155.8
C4 special treatment	100	105.9	124.1	161.6	189.0	220.7
C5 surgery	100	104.2	112.6	128.5	140.5	163.6
C6 maternity	100	100.9	103.0	113.3	120.6	129.4
C7 hospitalisation	100	101.4	121.4	144.7	168.1	185.0
C8 rehabiltation	100	111.5	123.8	163.7	189.8	230.7
C9 TB	100	98.1	116.6	119.7	128.4	132.0
C10 Total	100	105.3	120.6	143.2	166.4	183.9
M (Social diseases)	100	108.7	124.1	136.0	152.7	176.2
C + M Overall Total	100	105.5	120.8	142.7	165.6	183.4

Source: ANC Research Department.

This expenditure was financed from revenue from three sources: contributions by employers and employees, state subsidies and other. As can be seen from Table 5, the latter category is relatively unimportant and we shall subsequently ignore it. The table shows the evolution of the income and expenditure of the general and the self-employed schemes during the period 1966-71 and differentiates between cash and in kind expenditure. It can be seen that in 1966 the general scheme's medical care programme was financed largely by contributions from the insured (sixty-six per cent) although the State subsidies were far from unimportant (thirty-one per cent of the total). By 1971 the share of the State in the total income of the scheme had risen to 33.9

per cent. The self-employed's medical care programme in 1966 was financed largely by contributions from the insured (sixty-two per cent). Once again the role of the State was large (thirty-seven per cent) but, as can be seen from the 1971 statistics, it declined marginally (to 26.8 per cent) over the period. With regard to sickness insurance the State provided 42.4 per cent of the general scheme's income in 1966 and slightly less in 1971 (forty-two per cent).

Table 5 *Income and Expenditure: General Scheme and Self-Employed's Scheme 1966-71 in BF million (and £m)* ***

(a) Medical Care	1966	1967	1968	1969	1970	1971
(i) General Scheme						
Income						
Contributions	15145.3	15216.4	16653.8	18321.4	22345.8	25478.2
State subsidies	7216.6	7964.9	8779.3	9404.9	11067.0	13351.0
Other †	312.5	472.4	437.4	419.1	470.0	457.9
Deficit	-	-	342.9	2620.1	1601.9	-
Total	22674.4	23653.7	26213.4	30765.5	35484.7	39287.1
Expenditure						
Ordinary medical care	18196.8	19132.1	21892.4	25930.8	30276.5	33464.8
Social diseases	1229.9	1336.4	1525.7	1663.0	1878.4	2167.6
Other**	2402.0	2477.8	2795.3	3171.7	3329.8	3572.4
Surplus	845.7	707.4	-	-	-	82.3
Total	22674.4	23653.7	26213.4	30765.5	35484.7	39287.1
	(£246)	(£257)	(£285)	(£335)	(£386)	(£427)
(ii) Self-Employed's Scheme						
Income						
Contributions	895.7	893.4	957.8	1000.3	1049.0	1151.2
State subsidies	545.9	467.1	318.6	703.3	860.4	1010.0
Other	1.5	2.1	2.0	-	2.8	-
Deficit	-	-	294.8	342.6	532.6	582.5
Total	1443.1	1362.6	1573.2	2046.2	2444.8	2743.7
Expenditure						
Ordinary medical care	729.5	748.0	1208.4	1592.9	1838.6	2086.3
Social diseases	205.9	213.7	244.8	273.1	330.5	353.1
Other	123.1	115.0	120.0	180.2	175.7	304.3
Surplus	384.6	285.9	-	-	-	-
Total	1443.1	1362.6	1573.2	2046.2	2444.8	2743.7
	(£15)	(£14)	(£17)	(£22)	(£26)	(£29)

Table 5 *(Cont)*

(b) Sickness Insurance

(i) General Scheme	1966	1967	1968	1969	1970	1971
Income						
Contributions	5015.7	5146.0	5471.5	6120.4	7555.6	9143.4
State subsidies	3707.9	4162.8	4781.7	5299.3	5810.4	6053.8
Other	8.9	22.9	36.5	45.4	38.0	43.6
Deficit	-	-	-	-	-	-
	8732.5	9331.4	10289.7	11465.1	13404.0	15840.8
Total Expenditure						
Sickness benefit*	3901.6	3919.9	4237.5	4810.6	5524.3	6768.9
Invalidity	3759.8	4119.8	4668.6	5233.0	5751.0	6797.9
Death (Funeral)	245.9	258.9	289.9	301.9	371.6	463.6
Other††	801.1	823.8	898.0	1012.4	1115.5	1299.5
Surplus	24.1	209.0	195.7	107.2	641.6	510.9
Total	8732.5	9331.4	10289.7	11465.1	13404.0	15840.8
	(£95)	(£101)	(£112)	(£124)	(£146)	(£172)

(ii) Self-Employed
Scheme †††

Income	
Contributions	111.1
State subsidies	6.6
Total	117.7
Expenditure	
Sickness benefit	2.0
Invalidity	8.8
Other	1.4
Surplus	105.5
Total	117.7
	(£1)

Source: Ministry of Social Affairs (1972) pp 72 and 236; and ANC (Christian Mutualites) Research Department.

* Sickness benefit is that benefit which is paid in the first year. After one year the insured will normally be eligible for invalidity benefits.
** Cost of administration, etc.
*** The differences between Tables 4 and 5 are due to *regularisations* which are unexplained.
† International conventions.
†† Costs of administration of INAMI and the sickness funds.
††† Sickness insurance of the self-employed began in 1971 and the figures are unrepresentative of the scheme in full operation.

During the period the medical care component for the general scheme was in deficit for three years (1968-70) but returned a small surplus BF 82.3 million (£0.89 million) in 1971. On the other hand, the self-employed medical care scheme went into 'deficit' at the same time as that of the general scheme but its 'deficit' was positive and increasing in 1971 — BF 582.5 million (£6 million). The sickness insurance component of the general scheme was in surplus throughout the period. Indeed it grew substantially from BF 24.1 million (£0.26 million) to BF 510 million (£5 million). Because of the fact that compulsory sickness insurance was extended to the self-employed in 1971 and that there is a substantial lag in the publication of Belgian statistics, there are not meaningful income and expenditure figures for this part of Belgian health care.

We can conclude this discussion of income by saying that the financial role of the State in these two schemes is substantial. This role is governed by a multitude of complex laws which define the legislative rationale of the subsidisation. State intervention is both general and specific. The State pays ninety-five per cent of the cost of social diseases (category M in Table 3 above). For ordinary medical care a State subsidy of twenty-seven per cent of the budget of the insurance institutions is paid to INAMI. Sickness benefits are subsidised also. The government finances half the cost of invalidity benefits during the second and third years of disability. From the fourth year of disability the government pays ninety-five per cent of disability benefits. Also the State meets seventy per cent of the cost of death (or burial) grants. Finally, the government pays contributions on behalf of unemployed workers. The amount contributed on the worker's behalf is equal to the average daily value of all contributions for all insurance organisations for each day of unemployment.

Despite this substantial State involvement in the finance of health care, State control of expenditure is limited. The income of the schemes is distributed by an autonomous agency to sickness funds which are autonomous and decentralised to a considerable degree.

State financial aid to the compulsory insurance programme is not the only form of Government involvement in the financial affairs of health care industry. Social aid programmes provide a floor to protect those without means or compulsory social insurance to finance illness. Expenditure under this head is relatively low: 1961 BF 301.9 million (£3 million), 1970 BF 519.7 million (£5 million), an annual growth of 7.5 per cent.

Before we leave this section it must be emphasised that the data presented here are the income and expenditure figures which flow through INAMI. They do not represent income and expenditure figures for all health care in Belgium. Such figures do not appear to exist and this fact can be explained in several ways. Firstly, there is the usual problem of private insurance. In Belgium private insurance can mean many things. When we described the contribution picture we noted that there were 'compulsory-voluntary' contributions made to the funds to finance supplementary benefits. These income flows are not included in the data set out above. Also there is 'voluntary-voluntary' insurance to supplement cover and health care expenditure which is financed out of private income and savings. This additional finance is difficult to quantify. Part of it pays the e.g. twenty-five per cent in some cases which is not covered by compulsory insurance or enables the insured person to acquire care in superior hospital accommodation (2nd or 1st class as opposed to regulation 3rd class). However it is not possible e.g. to multiply *'ticket'* (see Section 6 below) expenditure by 4/3 to take account of the twenty-five per cent self-financed element. One reason for this is that compulsory insurance finances only seventy-five per cent of e.g. agreed physicians' fees, and unfortunately many physicians charge fees in excess of 4/3 times the refund. Finally as was mentioned earlier (Section 2 − coverage) many employers run schemes of one sort or another which subsidises heavy medical bills of their employees. Part of this is financed by private insurance and part by special enterprise funds. The cost of this is not known (see Quaethoven [1973]).

Unfortunately the statistical picture of Belgian health care is not too clear. The above analysis fills in the substance of the income and expenditure characteristics of the Belgian system of health care.

6 Benefits

(a) Medical Care

The provision of medical care benefits is regulated by Article 23 of the 1963 Act. The general rule is that the insured person is free to choose his general practitioner provided that the physician is qualified to practice in Belgium and that he is registered by the Medical Council's List. The general practitioner will visit the patient or treat him at a surgery. The official tariffs affecting the remuneration for doctors are drawn up in agreements between the insurance organisations, the medical profession and the hospitals. For all types of general practice medical care the doctor is directly remunerated on a fees for service basis (or piece rate) by the patient who gets reimbursed from the sickness fund, if, and when, he presents a certificate issued by the doctor. For general medical care the rate of reimbursement is fixed at seventy-five per cent of the agreed tariffs. If the fee is greater than the agreed tariff, only seventy-five per cent of the latter is reimbursed. Another way of expressing this is that the *ticket modérateur* is twenty-five per cent, i.e. beneficiaries pay twenty-five per cent of agreed tariffs (plus any excess over and above agreed tariffs). This rule applies to all consumers except old age pensioners, orphans, widows and invalids. These people get reimbursed a hundred per cent of agreed fees, subject to a means test (see page 97). It is not known overall by how much fees charged generally exceed tariffs. No limits are placed on the duration of these benefits or on the frequency of application for benefits, e.g. in theory and practice on any one day a beneficiary may consult several different doctors whatever their qualifications and the nature of the illness. For more technical services carried out during consultations the refund is at the same rate of agreed fee

Fees, and consequently the absolute level of reimbursement, are higher for consultations with specialist physicians. Specialists care is provided by any doctor who is recognised as a specialist by a credentials committee of the Ministry of Public Health. This committee consists of members of the various professional organisations of specialists and representatives of the Belgian University Faculties of Medicine. Some of the services provided by specialists are only reimbursed if they are carried out in hospitals under the 'proper' conditions.

An insured person who requires dental care (both 'corrective' and 'preventive') has a free choice of dentist and can recoup from the insurance organisations seventy-five per cent of the cost of such care. Dental prosthesis (e.g. false teeth) is, in principle, impossible to acquire with reimbursement until after the age of fifty years. This is part of a deliberate attempt to encourage the population to keep their teeth in good condition.

Pharmaceutical products are supplied by 4,660 pharmacies (EEC [1973] c) and reimbursement is governed by 1966 legislation. The general rules about insurance benefits with regard to drugs, depends on the type of drug which is used and the type of beneficiary. All old age pensioners, orphans, widows and invalids are exempted from prescription charges. Those who have to pay a contribution towards the cost of their drugs pay amounts determined by the following rules. A distinction is made between drugs prescribed and made up in a pharmacy ('magistral preparations') and the products of the pharma-ceutical industry, (branded, proprietary products or 'pharmaceutical specialities'). Unlike the previous benefits where the *ticket modérateur* was a percentage of the total cost, with drugs the ticket is a fixed lump sum payment. For 'magistral preparations', the beneficiary has to pay BF 25 (1970) whilst the latter type of benefit, 'pharmaceutical specialities' the beneficiary has to pay BF 50 (£0.54). Generally the pharmacist is paid the residue of the cost by the insurance organisation. For certain 'specialities' required by the chronic sick the lump sum payment is reduced to BF 25. The costs of 'specialities' is reimbursed only if they are on the list of recognised products. A technical council of the medical care insurance system maintains a list of approved medicines. Approval is based on tests of 'effectiveness' and on their relative cost. The general rules also give an array of subsidiary benefits. Glasses and other prostheses for the eyes, hearing aids and ortho-paedic appliances are obtainable. One estimate (EEC [1973] C page 38) asserts that Belgian pharmaceutical expenditure in 1971 was BF 8720.5 million (£95 million) but it is not clear what this total includes and excludes. Over the period 1966 to 1971 pharmaceutical expenditure under compulsory social insurance rose from BF 4,634 million (£50 million) to BF 8,827.7 million (£96 million), i.e. by ninety per cent.

In the case of the costs of hospitalisation, the insurance organisations as a general rule, reimburse one hundred per cent of the cost provided it is of a specified type. (Of this one hundred per cent, twenty-five per cent is directly funded by the State. The rest comes out of the general revenues of the fund.) Since the 1st January 1964 an Act has been in force which regulates the daily maintenance cost which public and private hospitals are permitted to charge.[9] The daily maintenance charge varies according to the type of care which is provided. It includes all the relevant costs incurred by providing a public bed in a common ward for a patient (i.e. depreciation costs, administration, nursing and maintenance staff costs), but exclusive of the payments for physicians services and for drugs. The former cost is reimbursed in the way described above and the latter's reimbursement procedure is described below. If the insured person prefers a private ward he is charged a supplement. The hospitals are permitted to charge a supple-ment of up to BF 229 (£2.5) for care in a ward of two beds, and an unlimited supplement for care in a private room. These arrangements apply to public and privately owned clinics also. There is no limit to the suration of benefits provided that after a period of seven to ten days hospitalisation, the beneficiary's insurance organisation is informed informed of, and approves, continued care. For medical treatment in hospital supplements are limited to forty per cent of the tariffs if care is provided in a semi-private (two bedded) room. In 1974 this maximum percentage was reduced to twenty-five per cent and in 1975 it will be abolished. In private rooms (one bed) forty per cent supplements are permitted.

The benefits extend to care given by members of the para-medical professions, provided the skill is recognised by Medical Care Service of the National Sickness and Invalidity Insurance. These benefits cover nursing care in the home, physiotherapy treatments supplied in the home or in clinics and confinements in the home or in maternity clinics. The cost of these services is met in the now familiar ratio: seventy-five per cent (insurance), twenty-five per cent (patient), except for old age pensioners, widows, or orphans and invalids who get a hundred per cent reimbursements. Socio-medical services provide functional and vocational retraining, the cost of which is met wholly by medical care insurance.

Some examples of the levels of fees charged for different types of care are given below. The refunds are calculated on the assumption that the beneficiary is someone who is not self-employed, a widow, orphan, invalid or old age pensioner. All data is for 1973 (July).

Table 6

	Fee	Refund	Amount met from sources other than Social Insurance Refunds
Consultation with GP	133 (£1.45)	115	18
Specialist Consultation (first visit, thorough examination)	199 (£2.17)	156	43 (£0.47)
Dentistry			
1 Extraction (one canine)	175 (£1.90)	132	43 (£0.47)
2 Filling (one face)	287 (£3.13)	276	71 (£0.77)
3 Full set of false teeth			
i) aged less than 50	3144 (£34.25)	None	3144 (£34.25)
ii) aged more than 50	3144 (£34.25)	2358	786 (£8.56)
Surgery: tonsillectomy	2012 (£21.92)	2012	0

The exceptions to these general benefit rules are twofold. Firstly the self-employed are covered only for heavy risks. Secondly, certain groups are exempt from the rules concerning the *ticket moderateur*. The self-employed's heavy risk coverage includes the social diseases (mental illness, tuberculosis, cancer, poliomyelitis and the psysically handicapped), hospital care (including drugs), heavy surgery (from a certain money value upwards), deliveries, special care (e.g. X-rays), and, under certain conditions, rehabilitation. They may gain access to other benefits by making voluntary contributions. Indeed about sixty per cent do make some kind of supplementary contribution to acquire small risk coverage.

The second group who are exceptions to the general rules is comprised of that group of people who are exempt, in whole or in part, from paying the *ticket modérateur*. If widows, pensioners, invalids and orphans have an income not exceeding BF 121,004 (£1,318) (1974) plus BF 20,250 for each dependent they can get a higher rate of reimbursement from their insurance organisation. This rate is usually a hundred per cent of agreed tariff for all types of care including 'magistral preparations'. For branded drugs the lump payment is reduced to BF 25. The reimbursements for physicians' travelling expenses remains at the seventy-five per cent level. The means test is adjusted with changes in the cost of living.

(b) Cash Benefits

Sickness benefits under the general scheme vary according to the duration of disability. Primary disability benefits are paid during the first year of incapacity after the expiry of the guaranteed wage (see Section 4) and the passing of three waiting days, at the rate of sixty per cent of wages up to the relevant ceiling. After fifty-two weeks of this type of benefit the insured is eligible for inavlidity benefits. In this second period the insured gets benefits of sixty-five per cent or 43.5 per cent of previous earnings depending on whether he has dependents or not. The principal difference in the two periods of benefit is related to the financial aspects of the scheme and the participation of the State. As the insured passes through the years of incapacity the State's participation in the finance of the scheme increases as in Table 7.

The calculation of earnings prior to incapacity differs between categories or workers. The essential distinction is between regular and irregular workers. A regular worker is one who worked at least sixty days in at least three of the four quarters preceding the one in which the incapacity started. The former's previous earnings are calculated by dividing the wages cited on the contribution ticket by the number of working days on the same ticket. For irregular workers the same

Table 7 *Cash Benefits and State Finance*

Type of disability	Exchequer contribution (%)	Insurance organisation (%)
1. Primary disability	0	100
2. Invalidity — second and third years of disability	50	50
3. Invalidity — fourth year onwards	95	5

Source: Confederation of Christian Sickness Funds (1970) p 14.

calculation is made but fictitious wage allowances are added to the actual amount for every day of justified absence from work. From the second year of benefit a minimum benefit is guaranteed for regular workers. This minimum is equal to the retirement pension of manual workers with a complete contribution career. In September 1973, this minimum was BF 318 (£3.5) per day for workers with dependents and BF 183 for those without dependents. Since 1971 similar benefits have been available for the self-employed. However, benefits are not paid for the first six months of sickness (this — according to *Institut Belge d'Information et de Documentation* [1972] — was due to the demands of the self-employed who wished to avoid abuse). After this period primary incapacity benefits are paid for six months after which the insurance has the same characteristics as that of the general scheme.

Death (or funeral) benefits are paid by the insurance organisation at the death of an active or retired employee or domestic servant. The benefit is equal to thirty times the maximum benefit for primary disability. In September 1973 this amounted to BF 12,528 (£136.47). The money is paid to that person who can prove he paid the burial expenses.

7 Provision

(a) Medical Personnel

In the previous section some details of the nature of employment and remuneration of physicians, dentists and pharmacists were given. In this section an attempt is made to examine the supply (stock and flow) of medical personnel and the nature of hospital provision.

Table 8 shows the stock figures for physicians, dentists, pharmacists, midwives, physiotherapists and nurses during the period 1966 to 1970. In 1950 there were 8,122 physicians in Belgium.

Table 8 *Medical Personnel 1966-70*

	1966	1967	1968	1969	1970
Physicians					
i) absolute number	13,793	14,176	14,527	14,922	17,991
ii) number 1000 population	1.55	1.48	1.52	1.54	1.55
Dentists	1,230	1,305	1,406	1,702	1,341
Dental practitioners	473	464	463	524	503
(non-university level)					
Pharmacists	6,078	6,171	6,249	6,533	6,735
Midwives	3,815	3,843	3,563	3,615	3,593
Physiotherapists	2,812	3,222	3,677	4,249	4,847
Nurses	NA	NA	14,117	NA	NA

Source: *Statistisch Jaarboek van Belgie* 1971 page 77
Statistisch Jaarboek van volksgezondhuld 1970-71
Ministerie van volkesgezezondheid

By 1966 there were 13,793 and the latest figure for 1970 is 17,991. Thus in twenty years the doctor stock has more than doubled in Belgium. The stock of nurses has also increased. In 1968 there were 14,117 nurses in Belgium and although we have no data for the other years in the 1966-70 series we know that at the end of 1971 there were 15,952 nurses. During the period 1966-70 the stock of physiotherapists increased by over sevety-two per cent. The number of dentists of both types increased marginally (8.2 per cent) as did the number of pharmacists (10.8 per cent). The latter is an unusual trend by European standards whilst the trend in the stock of midwives is familiar: a decline of 5.8 per cent.

Some details of the types of physician-specialists are given in Table 9.

Table 9 *Specialist Physicians (end 1972)*

General medicines	7
Anaesthetics	441
General Surgery	918

Table 9 *(Cont)*

Abdomen surgery	14
Neurosurgery	33
Blood vessel surgery	6
Plastic surgery	27
Thoraic surgery	3
Obstetrics – gynaecology	548
Opthalmology	500
Urology	119
Orthopaedics	209
Stomatology	324
Dermato-vernerology	268
Internal medicines	909
Diseases of the chest	195
Stomach and intestinal diseases	97
Paediatrics	578
Cardiology˙	267
Neuro-psychiatry	629
Rheumatology	112
Physiotherapy	290
Clinical biology	420
Radio-diagnosis	571
Radio-radium therapy	144
Ear, nose and throat	385
Total	8,014

Source: Research Department, ANC.
Caution should be exercised in interpreting these figures.
There are not 8,014 specialist physicians in Belgium because
sometimes there is double counting e.g. a specialist in
internal medicine is also qualified in stomach diseases. It is
estimated that there were 7,450 specialists at the end of
1972 (Qualthoven 1973).

The total number of physicians in Belgium appeared to be growing
at an annual average rate of about five per cent and the number of
doctors (both inside and outside hospitals) per 1,000 population was
slightly greater than 1.5.

This growth would seem to be uncontrolled and unplanned.
Entrance to medical school is available as of right to all those who
fulfil certain minimal entrance requirements. Given the high monetary

rewards of the profession and this free entry it would seem likely that the stock of physicians in Belgium will continue to increase steadily. Indeed control is difficult if all the different groups (religious, political, etc.) are to be satisfied. At present there are 15,000 students enrolled at medical schools (a one hundred per cent increase over 1965: Blanpain 1973 page 6) and if this trend continues it is estimated that there will be 2.38 doctors per thousand population in 1980.

In general the physicians and the para-medical professions are paid on the basis of per item of service performed. The medical technical council sets out a complete list of types of care by category of benefit and assigns costs to each of these benefits. The cost of tariffs are determined annually by national commissions, consisting of equal numbers of the insurance organisations, the professions and the institutions providing care. When agreements are reached in these national level commissions they are disseminated to the grass roots by the Minister. Each member of a profession is free to accept or reject the agreement. If within thirty days they do not notify their objection in writing it is assumed that they agree. Any agreement can be imposed by the State in a region if more than sixty per cent of e.g. the physicians accept it. In the absence of an agreement fees may be imposed by the commission. These fees are the basis on which reimbursement is based but may be less than the fees charged by physicians. In the case of the professions other than the physicians (i.e. midwives, nurses, physiotherapists, orthopaedists, truss-makers, makers of hearing aids and opticians) national conventions have usually been agreed with ease at the local level. However, in the case of the physicians there have been numerous disputes and, on occasion, strikes and threats to withdraw labour.

(b) Hospitals

Belgian hospitals exhibit several interesting characteristics. The most important of these is the smallness of the hospital establishments. The average bed size of general hospitals increased from 118 to 136 during the period 1966 to 1971. Publicly owned hospitals tend to be larger. Most modern hospitals tend to be large but the majority of the existing stock is small and unable to exploit the economies of scale which are said to exist with larger units. Most establishments (sixty-seven per cent) and hospital beds (fifty-nine per cent) are owned by private bodies of which the Roman Catholic Church is, perhaps, the most important. This statement applies not only to general hospitals but also, usually, to mental and tuberculosis hospitals. Private organisations provided seventy-six per cent of mental hospital beds in 1971. The government owned hospitals are operated by local government in most cases. The general hospital and tuberculosis bed per thousand population statistic is the lowest of the original six of the EEC (EEC 1973 (a)). The total bed per thousand population statistic is 7.72.[10] However, this statistic appears to be correlated with a relatively low length of stay statistic because in 1968 the average length of stay for acute cases was between fourteen and 17.94 days (Blanpain 1973 Table 5 and EEC 1973 (a) page 28). Whilst the Netherlands has a large number of beds per thousand population (10.52) and a long length of stay (20.7) Belgium has a small number and length of stay which appears to be significantly less than her northern neighbour, if we take Blanpain's figure (1973).[11]

Table 10   *Hospital Beds 1966 and 1971*

	number of establishments		number of beds		beds per 1,000 population	
	1966	1971	1966	1971	1966	1971
1. General hospitals	367	334	43445	45828	4.56	4.74
2. Ownership of general hospitals						
(a) Government*	112	109	17401	18694		
(b) Private	225	225	26044	27134		
3. Average size of general hospitals (no of beds)						
(a) Government owned			155.36	†		
(b) Privately owned			102.13	†		
(c) All			118.37	136.00		
4. Specialised hospitals						
(i) Tuberculosis						
(a) Government owned	†	8	†	745		
(b) Privately owned	†	10	†	1545		
(c) Total	21	18	3636	2390		0.24
(ii) Mental						
(a) Government owned	†	†	†	6294		
(b) Privately owned	†		†	20259		
(c) Total	64		27389	26553		2.74

Source: World Health Organisation (1970, 1971).
         ANC Research Department.

* Government here means local authority.
† Not available.

Unlike the physician stock (and the increased flow) problem, the problem of hospital planning is being tackled. As in many other European countries (e.g. UK, France, the Netherlands) the problem of the inequitable distribution of hospital beds has been recognised as a problem which needs to be solved by policy changes leading to greater equity. There is a great density of hospital facilities in the North and in metropolitan areas. To correct this inequality the Ministry of Public Health has used the building subsidy as an instrument of persuasion. By granting or witholding the subsidy — which amounts to sixty per cent of building costs for local authorities and fifty per cent for private institutions — the Ministry has tried to execute a national hospital plan in which rural, semi-rural and urban bed population ratio targets have been established for various types of care (e.g. surgical — 1:2. internal — 1.), etc. See Schouwer [1970] page 95). Blanpain (1973 page 7) argues that the failure of this process was due to the small amount of funds available each year and the ability of frustrated applicants to use political persuasion to overrule negative decisions and so mitigate the efficiency of the process.

However, in July 1973, legislation was passed which radically alters the planning situation. Now the Minister of Health is directly responsible for the physical planning of hospitals. Any plan to create or change hospital facilities has to be approved by the Minister and be in line with the objectives of the hospital plan. A national planning council will advise the Minister and establish criteria for the adjustment of the plan over time. A Health Facilities Fund has been created (October 1973) to finance hospital construction by issuing bonds and by using State funds. Blanpain anticipates that this will lead to a more equitable distribution of facilities and the better provision of care for priority cases such as the mentally ill and the chronic sick.

8 Conclusion

The overall impression of the Belgium system of heath care is one of complexity and little coordination. Like every other country in this study, Belgium is suffering from rapidly escalating costs, uneven distribution of inputs (hospital beds, doctors, etc.) and an awareness of the 'inadequacy'[12] of care provided for e.g. geriatrics and the chronic sick. These problems are made worse in Belgium by the decentralised system of administration and the national/religious divisions. Blanpain (1973 page 8) summarises the health care problem in Belgium as follows:

Basically it comes down to a clash of diametrically opposed philosophies. The health authorities together with the hospital boards and the health insurance funds perceive health care as a social function and seek a more organised health care system with clearly defined objectives not only in the field of restorative care but also in the fields of preventive medicine, rehabilitation and health education. Organised medicine (the medical profession) fights a rearguard action seeing health care as the responsibility of the individual . . . Thus the profession opposes every move which increases the constraints binding its membership. The strong bargaining position of the medical profession has made moves towards a more even distribution of services and the containment of costs a very slow and sometimes distressing process.[13]

Blanpain's view that it is the medical profession which is the obstacle to progress may be received very sympathetically in other European countries where observers diagnose the same problems and the same obstruction.

NOTES

1. The three official languages are French, German and Flemish (Dutch). Flemish is the major form of communication in the north, whilst French is spoken in the southern (Walloon) portion of the country. German is the language of a small group in the east who occupy territory ceded to Belgium after the 1914-1918 War.
2. The five unions or confederations were, and still are:-
   (a) The National Alliance of Christian Mutual Societies (federated 1906);
   (b) The National Union of Belgian Non-Denominational Mutual Societies (federated 1908);
   (c) The National Union of Socialist Mutual Societies (federated 1913);
   (d) The National Union of Belgian Liberal Mutual Societies (federated 1914);
   and (e) The National Union of Belgian Occupational Mutual Societies (federated 1920).
3. The relationship between refunds and fees in Belgium is still a problem which causes concern to many consumers. At its initiation it led to the famous doctors' strike. When fees are renewed the conflicts between the funds, the Government and the doctors are renewed.
4. A definition of heavy risks (*gros risques*) will be found in the text below.
5. The determination of the coefficients has not proved to be a simple task. By relating them to membership little account was taken of the varying incidence of illness of members in the different funds. Consequently, in one year in the 1960s the Socialist Confederation was in deficit whilst the Catholic Confederation had a surplus. Mutual aid corrected the imbalances on that particular occasion. However, the Socialist Confederation continues to spend more *per capita* for demographic and industrial reasons.
   INAMI is managed by a General Council consisting of representatives of the employers, the employees (trade unions), the self-employed, the insurance organisations, the hospitals and all the medical professions

(the pharmacists, the midwives and the para-medical professions) except the physicians and the dentists who attend purely in an advisory capacity. This General Council is concerned with coordination and the distribution of the Institute's budget. The health care insurance is managed by a medical care department of the institute which is comprised of a similar spectrum of representatives as the Council. The benefits department manages cash benefits side of the institute and is governed by a board made up of representatives of the employers, the employees and the insurance organisations. In this board only the employers and the employees have voting rights in questions of the determination of contribution levels and the management of the reserves fund.

6. CAAMI — the Auxiliary Fund — was set up as an autonomous institution after the Second World War to provide an alternative (other than the confederations) vehicle of compulsory health care insurance.

7. The difficulties of acquiring substantive statistics about the Belgian health care system is illustrated by the fact that if we use the 1970 Statistical Survey of Social Security (*Annuaire Statistique 1970 de la Sécurité Sociale* [1972]) we derive membership statistics for 1970 of 6,567,552 for the general scheme (including seamen [8,386]) and 1,860,487 (*op. cit.* pages 118-19, 248) a total of 8,428,039. If we compare this with the data in Table 1 there is a deficit of 1,051,727. This deficit is due to the fact that these figures exclude special stature categories such as civil servants, students and the like.

8. All contributions ceiling data are that as at 1st October 1973.

9. This legislation complemented, but was separate from, the 1963 Act (6th August) which reorganised health care insurance.

10. EEC 1973 (a) 24 gives a figure of 7.45 beds per 1,000 population. This is for 1969. The data in Table 10 is of 1971.

11. Both the EEC and Blanpain's figure is for 1968.

12. 'Inadequacy' or 'adequacy' are inevitably terms derived from the observer's value judgement. There will never be adequate facilities in the sense that all 'medical need' (however defined) is met. The problem is to decide priorities and allocate resources towards the achievement of these priorities.

13. Blanpain (1973) p 8 with some minor linguistic alterations.

References

Belgian Embassy in London (Information Section) (1973) (i) *Social Security in Belgium*, (ii) *A Short Note on the Health Care Service in Belgium*, (iii) *National Insurance Contributions*, London.

Belgian Institute for Information and Documentation (1970) 'The National Social Security Office', *Belgian News* No 2, March 1970, Brussels.

Blanpain, J.E. (1973), Brussels. *Health Care in Belgium* mimeograph. Paper presented to a seminar at the Kings Fund Health Centre, London. September.

British Medical Association (1970) *Health Services Financing* Appendix L (Netherlands and Belgium by J. van Langendonck), London.

Confederation of Christian Science Sickness Funds (1970) *A Short Survey of Health and Sickness Benefits Insurance in Belgium*, Brussels.

References *(Cont)*

Confederation of Christian Sickness Funds (1972) *The Alliance Nationale des Mutualities Chretiennes – a short history,* Brussels.

Dejardin, J. (1968) *Monograph on the Organisation of Medical Care within the framework of Social Security – Belgium,* International Labour Office, Geneva.

European Economic Commission (1973 (a)), *The Cost of Hospitalisation in Social Security,* Department of Social Affairs, Brussels (in French).

European Economic Commission (173 (b)), *Main Report Covering Three Investigations into the Principal Items of Expenditure in Sickness Insurance Covered by Social Security,* Department of Social Affairs, Brussels (in French).

European Economic Commission (1973 (c)), *The Cost of Pharmaceutical Consumption in Social Security,* Department of Social Affairs, Brussels (in French).

European Economic Community (1973 (d)), *Report on the Development of the Social Situation in the Community in 1972,* Brussels and Luxembourg.

Illuminati, F (1972) 'The Cost of Health', *International Social Security Review,* No 4, Geneva.

Institut National d'Assurance Maladie-Invalidité, *Rapport General* 1970 (INAMI 1972) Institut Belge d'Information et de Documentation (1970-72) *Fiche Documentaire* No 331 and 368.

Langendonck, J. van (1972) 'Social Health Insurance in the Six Countries of the European Economic Community', *International Journal of Health Services,* Vol 2 No 4, New York.

Ministry of Social Affairs (1972), *Annuaire Statistique de la Sécurité Sociale 1970,* Brussels (in French).

Ministry of Social Affairs (1972), *Rapport General sur la Sécurité Sociale 1971* Brussels (in French).

Ministry of Public Health and the Family (undated), *Organisation Sanitaire de la Belgique – L'Aide Sociale,* Brussels (in French).

Rezschazy, R. (1957), *Histoire du Mouvement Mutualist Chretien en Belgique,* Brussels (in French).

Quaethoven, P. (1973), *Health Services in Belgium: Financing, Staffing, Training and Research,* mimeograph. Paper presented to a seminar at the Kings Fund Health Centre, London. September.

Schouwer, P. (1970) 'Post-War Development of the Belgian Hospital System', *World Hospitals,* Vol 6 pp 94-5 and 123-7.

Smout, M. (1973), 'L'evolution des depenses de l'assurance maladie,' *Orientation Mutualiste* Mai-Juin, pp 103-34.

US Department of Health, Education and Welfare (1972), *Social Security Programme throughout the World 1971,* Washington.

World Health Organisation (1971, 1972, 1973), *World Health Statistics Annual,* Vol III, Geneva.

5 FRANCE

The Evolution of Health Care in France

The first national law to affect the finance and provision of health care in France was enacted in 1928. This legislation was revised and expanded in 1945 and 1967. As a result of this legislation health care is regulated by a variety of schemes. The majority of the population — over seventy per cent — are compelled to be members of the general scheme (*régime général*). The rest of the population are covered by special schemes e.g. for miners, agricultural workers, seamen, civil servants and railway employees. However, these special schemes are not comprehensive vehicles of social security. Some special schemes omit coverage of particular types of risk and in this case the groups concerned may be members of the general scheme for this risk only. An example of this is the provision of medical care benefits for both ordinary sickness and maternity under the general scheme for civil servants[1], salaried agricultural employees and SNCF (the railways) since the beginning of 1971. Furthermore the coverage of these schemes has been extended considerably in the last decade. For instance it was as late as 1966 that legislation substantially extended the previously limited coverage of the four special schemes for the self-employed.

The general scheme is a unified system which operates on a geographical basis. Since 1967 sickness, maternity, invalidity, survivors, and occupational social insurance have been administered by an organisation which is separate from the administration of old age pensions and family allowances.[2] This move was prompted by a desire to avoid cross-subsidisation between the different types of social security provision.

The sickness funds which administer the health care service at the local level receive their finance from the central general fund and provide cash refunds to individual health care customers. These refunds do not always meet the full cost of health care. The *ticket modérateur* determines the insured's participation on the cost of care — in many cases they pay twenty-five per cent of agreed tariff out of their own resources. Individual members of the social sickness insurance schemes pay relatively low direct contributions as the employer pays over three times as much as the insured person.

As a result of the general and special scheme arrangements over ninety-nine per cent of the French population is covered by compulsory health care insurance. However, once again we must emphasise that this coverage is not complete — the general scheme, for instance, does not fully reimburse individual consumers. Consequently additional insurance and private incomes finance a significant proportion of the health care provided in France.

1 Administration

The administration of sickness, invalidity, maternity and death insurance in France is divided among several organisations. Under the general scheme the National Sickness Insurance Fund (*La Caisse Nationale d'Assurance Maladie*), which is directly supervised by the Ministry of Public Health and Social Security[3] and by the Ministry of Finance, covers most of the industrial work force. The National Sickness Insurance Fund, a public corporation with financial autonomy, supervises and promotes sickness insurance throughout France. Also, since the reforms of 1967, the Fund has been responsible for the financial solvency of sickness, maternity, invalidity and death insurance on the one hand, and for industrial accidents and occupational diseases on the other hand. No cross-subsidisation between these two systems and the systems of old age pensions and family benefits is permitted. At the regional level sixteen Regional Sickness Insurance Funds (*Les Caisses régionales d'Assurance Maladie*) carry out functions which reflect the need for local collective fund action e.g. the fixing of fee scales which the local funds will pay to local medical personnel. The grass-roots administrative functions are carried out by the local or primary funds (*Les Caisses primaires d'Assurance Maladie*) which are financially autonomous institutions. There are 121 local or primary sickness funds whose area, where convenient, coincides with that of the département. These funds are responsible for the initial registration of the insured person, they dispense benefits and they make agreements with the medical profession in order to facilitate the provision of these benefits. The local branches of the primary funds pay out benefits to claimants. Diagram 1 summarises this administrative organisation.

Diagram 1 *Sickness Insurance in France – The General Scheme*

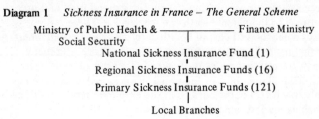

Ministry of Public Health & ——————— Finance Ministry
Social Security

National Sickness Insurance Fund (1)

Regional Sickness Insurance Funds (16)

Primary Sickness Insurance Funds (121)

Local Branches

The insurance scheme administered by the National Sickness Insurance Fund is the largest public fund in France. However, it is not the only one. Certain groups have managed to retain the privileges associated with their own particular funds. Such special funds cover civil servants, service men, miners, railway workers, seamen and the employees of the gas and electricity industries. Agricultural workers are members of another separately administered and financed scheme which generates benefits similar to those of the general scheme (Law of 25th January 1961). The self-employed have, since 1969, been compelled to join corporately based insurance schemes. The coverage of these schemes is being progressively increased to bring them into line with the provision of the general scheme. There are four such schemes for the self-employed: for farmers, for artisans, for the self-employed in industry and commerce, for the trades and for members of the liberal professions. The farmers have an independent organisation (in which a distinction is made between wage earners and non-wage earning (i.e. those farming their own land/employees), but the other three categories are catered for by one institution (CANAM: *Caisse Nationale d'Assurance Maladie et Maternité des Travailleurs non Salaires des Professions Non Agricoles*).

The general and special schemes are monitored by the political administration. At the national level the Ministry is involved, via the health map exercise (see below), in the central planning of medical care facilities and the subsidisation of schemes in deficit. Each of the sixteen regions and ninety-six *départements* of France are intimately related with the health care structure at the regional and local level. Each regional *préfet* is assisted in health matters by a *Directeur régional de la Santé* and a *Médicin Inspecteur régional* (MIR). The *Départemental Préfet* is assisted by a *Directeur départemental de la Santé* (DAS) and a *Medicin Inspecteur départemental*. These officials are involved in the finance and provision of public health service (*Santé Publique*) and public hospital services — the local Mayor is usually the chairman of the local health administrative committee.

In addition to the compulsory sickness insurance schemes, private associations, the Mutual Societies, provide additional health insurance cover. These societies provide insurance against risks which are ignored by the State system and against risks which are only partly covered by the State system. Thus membership of a Mutual Society can, as a result of agreements reached between the mutual societies and the Funds, ensure for its member complete freedom from any charge for medical benefits — this is particularly useful in the case of the *ticket modérateur*. It is generally estimated that nearly fifty per cent of compulsory members are registered with a mutual society. The number of mutual societies is large but, with the exception of the 800,000 member General Mutual Association for National Education, their size is small. The small mutuals tend to federate to operate joint hospital facilities. The compulsory system provides virtually uniform benefits and there is considerable scope for complementation and supplementation by the mutual societies.

2 Coverage

As we have noted, France, like many of her neighbours, does not have one system of sickness insurance. However, the coverage of the schemes is almost complete – Van den Heuvel states that ninety-nine per cent of the French population are covered either by one form of compulsory insurance or another.[4] All wage earners are directly insured. Recipients of an invalidity pension, recipients of industrial accident annuities where incapacity is greater than 66 per cent, recipients of old age pensions and the unemployed are also insured.

Table 1 *General Scheme Membership 1960, and 1968-71 (in thousands)*

Number Contributing	1960	1968	1969	1970	1971
General Scheme	11,761	12,000	12,315	12,645	12,875
Civil Servants*	970	1,840	1,980	2,040	2,130
Others†	540	840	855	895	935
Total contributing membership	13,371	14,680	15,150	15,580	15,950
Number Qualifying††					
General Scheme		16,240	16,670	17,160	17,550
Civil Servants		3,040	3,240	3,340	4,430
Others†		160	170	180	190
Total qualifying membership		19,440	20,170	20,680	21,170
Total Membership		34,120	35,320	26,260	37,110

Sources: i) 1960 data G. Spitaels, *et al.*

ii) *Ministeres de la Santé Publique et de la Sécurité Sociale* (1972) Bulletin de Statistiques No 6 Vol A. November-December.

* Civil Servants – this includes local authority employees and workers in the nationalised gas and electricity industries.

† Others include students, war wounded, 'conventioned' doctors and voluntarily insured people.

†† Number qualifying = those qualifying by virtue of others contributions e.g. children, spouses, old age pensioners, etc.

Table 1 shows the movement in the number contributing in 1960 and 1968-71, and the number qualifying for benefits under the general scheme in each of the years in the period 1968-71. It can be seen that over the period 1960-71 the total contributing membership has risen by 2,569,000 or sixteen per cent, i.e. 1.3 per cent per annum. Of its component parts, the civil servant category expanded the most rapidly. The number of people qualifying, but not contributing towards the cost of health care rose by 1,730,000 in the period 1960-71. All components in this aggregate increased. Perhaps the most noticeable characteristic about the number of non-contributing members is the increasing number of pensioners. For instance in the period 1968-71 the number of pensioners and qualifying dependents in the general scheme rose from 4,000,000 to 4,490,000 i.e. by 12.2 per cent. In the civil servants' scheme the numbers were 1,060,000 and 1,210,000 i.e. by 14.1 per cent in the same years. This marked increase in the number of pensioners eligible for health care benefits poses many familiar problems. Because of their relatively higher demand for health care the cost of providing care is greater than that of helping the younger. Increased pensioner coverage and demographic trends will tend to exacerbate the financial problems of the health care system in France.

Table 2 *General and Other Scheme Membership 1968-9 (in thousands)*

			Insured Persons*		Protected†† Persons
A. Wage earners & assimilated workers					
i)	general scheme (non agricultural)				
(a)	all risks		11,950	)	
(b)	part risks			)	
	- voluntarily insured		230	))	28,050
	- various		30	)	
ii)	assimilated schemes		2,440		5,770
		TOTAL	14,650		
iii)	special schemes**		1,969		7,466
		TOTAL	16,619		
B. Self-Employed					
i)	agricultural		1,869		5,400
ii)	industrial & commercial)				
iii)	trades)		1,375†		3,873
iv)	liberal professions)				
		TOTAL	3,242		
OVERALL TOTAL			19,861		50,559

Source: *Ministere de la Santé Publique et de la Sécurité Sociale (1971).*
There is some overlapping, with dual fund memberships.
Coverage percentage as in text.
With the exception of note † all data is for 1968.
* Excludes old age pensioners who benefit from cash sickness benefits.
† Estimated data for 30.10.1969.
** SNCF, Mines, Marine, Marchande, Clercs de notaires, etc.
†† Insured persons plus dependents.

Table 2 shows the overall membership of the general and specific social health care insurance schemes in 1968-9. The total coverage was ninety-eight per cent compared with ninety per cent in the previous year. The statistic for the self-employed category is an estimate for 30th October 1969. Previous to 1st January 1969 these people were not covered by compulsory insurance. *Santé et Sécurité Sociale* (1973 p.948) gives 1970 data for the number of insured persons only. The differences between the 1970 data and that in Table 2 are small. The total number of insured persons was 20,396,000. The self-employed category (B[i]-[iv]) in the 1970 data are smaller than the 1968-9 estimates — B(i) is 1,694,000 and B(ii)-(iv) is 1,321,000. Unfortunately the 1970 data source does not give any information about the total number of protected persons, and so for expositional purposes we present 1968-9 data in Table 2.

As will be shown below some benefits cover only part of the cost of medical care. Many people augment their social insurance by joining mutual societies. The number of mutual societies fell from 12,592 to 10,154 in the period 1961-9 i.e. by 19.4 per cent. The number of participating members on the other hand grew by 29.2 per cent from 24,274,000 to 31,306,000. Table 3 shows some characteristics of these societies and their members. The largest category is 'Other' and this shows the fragmented nature of the societies. The largest individual category is surgical (it provides a wide range of benefits from medical care to pensions) with nearly twenty per cent of total membership in 1969. Mutual accident societies have high average sizes and the largest share of total percentage membership. Despite their fragmented nature these societies have a substantial coverage. 61.4 per cent of the population are participating members and significantly augment the coverage of social insurance beneficiaries.

Table 3   *Mutual Societies – Membership Characteristics 1969*

Type of Society	Number	Number of members in	
		a) absolute terms	b) percentage terms
Surgical societies	142	6,139,929	19.6
Company societies	2111	2,400,271	7.7
Societies for artisans, the liberal professions and shopkeepers	175	286,649	0.9
War veterans societies	219	172,745	0.5
Sporting accident societies	2	2,065,399	6.6
Mutual accident societies	91	9,086,342	29.0
Civil servants and other central and local authority workers societies	444	3,397,565	10.8
Gas and electricity industries	102	419,974	1.3
Other	6868	7,396,652	23.6
TOTAL	10154	31,365,526	100.0

Source: *Ministère des Affaires Sociales* (1973) *op. cit.* page 630.

112

Those without social insurance cover were reduced considerably in
number by the 1966 legislation affecting the self-employed. Prior to
this legislation such people could have acquired health care finance
via the Social Aid legislation if they had been without means. Social
Aid is the safety net which guarantees French citizens assistance in
both cash and kind. Table 4 shows the number of Social Aid
beneficiaries in the categories which are of interest to us in this study.
This data can be complemented by 1970 statistics. In 1970 medical
aid beneficiaries numbered 878,983 for domiciliary care and 523,720
for hospital care (the Table 3 source does not give the data separately).
21,212 benefitted from medical aid to the tubercular and there were
74,184 beneficiaries of the medical aid to mental patients programme.
The data in the Table suggests that the number of recipients of
medical social aid declined in the late sixties, in part no doubt due to
the extension of compulsory social insurance to, e.g. the self-
employed, but had revived by 1970.

Table 4 *Social Aid Beneficiaries 1962-68 and 1970*

Categories of Social Aid	1961	1963	1964	1965	1966	1967	1968	1970
Medical aid	1114.5	1121.3	1085.3	1049.5	1011.7	987.5	771.2	878.9
Medical aid to the tubercular	18.9	21.5	20.3	19.7	20.6	19.2	17.8	21.2
Medical aid to mental patients	93.0	90.4	85.9	85.0	83.6	94.4	77.4	74.1
Total in receipt of Social Aid	1226.4	1233.2	1191.5	1154.2	1115.9	1101.1	866.4	974.2

Source: *Ministère de la Santé Publique et de la Sécurité Sociale* (1971).

1968 and 1970 data from *Ministère de la Santé Publique* (1972,
1973) and *Ministère des Affaires Sociales* (1972, 1973), editions
page 554 (1972).

The overall effect of this many faceted system of health care insurance
is that all the population has access to medical care. About ninety-
nine per cent of the population are compelled to indulge in social
insurance and the residual one per cent can acquire access to benefits
via the Social Aid programme.

3 Qualifying Conditions

Benefits in kind and cash benefits are paid if the contributor fulfills certain qualifications.

(a) Medical Care

Since 1968 to qualify for benefits in kind the member must have been in paid employment for either 200 hours during the three months preceding the date of the treatment for which benefits are claimed, or 120 hours during the month immediately preceding the benefit claim. When these conditions are met the worker is registered on the Fund's membership list. 'Dependent children' are carefully defined to include (i) all children under the age of sixteen years, (ii) those under eighteen years in apprenticeship schemes, (iii) those under twenty years in education, (iv) and those who, owing to infirmity or chronic illness, are permanently incapable of taking up paid employment. Other dependents can only benefit if two conditions are met. Firstly they must be living in the same residence as the insured and be exclusively employed in household work and the upbringing of at least two children who are not over fourteen years and who are maintained by the insured member.

(b) Cash Benefits

Cash benefits are paid only to the insured person who is certified (by his doctor) to be incapable of work. Since 1968 the insured has had to meet conditions:-

(1) for benefits during the first six months of illness: the insured must have been in remunerative employment for not less than 200 hours during the three months preceding the need for benefit;

(2) for benefits from the sixth to the thirty-sixth month (three years) of illness (long-term sickness): the insured must have been registered for twelve months prior to the first day of the month preceding the date of the cessation of work, and he must have worked for not less than 800 hours during the twelve months prior to the interruption of work, of which 200 hours must have been during the first three months of that year.

Cash sickness benefit may be continued, at the discretion of the fund, for a period not exceeding one year more than the three year period under (2) above, provided that work will tend to improve the insured member's state of health or if the insured member is being retrained or rehabilitated for employment compatible with his state of health.

Subject to these qualifying conditions cash sickness benefits are paid after three 'waiting days'.

114

The qualifying conditions for maternity benefits are as follows:
the insured person must have been in remunerative employment for not
less than 200 hours during the quarter year preceding the start of the
ninth month prior to the presumed date of confinement, or for 120
hours during the month preceding that date, and having been registered
for ten months prior to that date.

4 Finance

The system of sickness, maternity, invalidity and death insurance
administered by the National Sickness Insurance Fund (the general
scheme) is financed by contributions made by the employer and the
employee. Contributions are mainly based on earnings (see Table 5) or
pensions partly up to the limit of the earnings ceiling, and partly on
the whole income. The total rates are 13.95 per cent and 12.95 per
cent for the former, and three per cent for the latter. In both cases
the employer bears most of the costs. An additional charge was into-
duced in 1967 (Ordinance 21st August 1967) and is not related to
earnings. This is a contribution which is proportional to the premiums
for compulsory motor vehicle insurance and is payable wherever the
policy holder is a member of a compulsory sickness insurance scheme.
This contribution is levied at the rate of three per cent of the insurance
premium and is collected by the car insurance companies.

The earnings ceiling is fixed annually be Decree. It is related to the
ceiling applicable in 1962 (i.e. 9,600 NF − £912) using a coefficient
resulting from a comparison of the general index of earnings reported
by the Minister of Labour on 1st October of any year, and the same
index as at 1st October 1961.

Table 5 *Contributions to the National Sickness Insurance Fund*.*

Type of cover	On wages up to the ceiling			On total wages	
	Employer	Employee		Employer	Employee
		Under 65	Over 65 years		
Sickness, maternity disablement and death	10.45%	2.5%	1.5%	2%	1%
Old age insurance	5.7%	3.0%	-	-	-
Family Allowance	10.5%	-	-	-	-
Industrial accidents	Variable	-	· -	-	-

Source: *Ministere de la Santé Publique et de la Sécurité Sociale* (1971).

* The so called 'General Scheme' at 1st January 1974.

The amount so calculated has to be in multiples of 120 NF (£11.41). The earnings figure upon which contribution assessments are based cannot be less than the minimum wage applying at the time. The earnings ceiling at 1st January 1974 was 27,840 NF (£2,646) per annum or 2,040 NF(£193) per month.

These same platforms or earnings ceilings are applied in schemes other than that of the National Sickness Insurance Scheme (the general scheme). However, the rates of contribution differ. In the mineworkers' scheme there are two sets of contribution. The first is 13.75 per cent of earnings up to the ceiling. The employer pays 9.75 per cent and the employee four per cent. The second part is paid wholly by the employer at the rate of two per cent of all earnings. The agricultural self-employed pay contributions related to their annual income. Since October 1973 those earning less than 7,000 NF (£665) per year have been exempted from the payment of contributions and are automatically beneficiaries of the National Solidarity Fund. Those earning more than 7,000 NF pay contributions which rise in thirteen steps as income rises, e.g. those earning 7,000 to 8,999 NF (£885) pay 700 NF (£66) in contributions each year; those earning 9,000 to 10,999 NF pay 880 NF (£83) in contributions; those earning in excess of 59,999 NF (£5,703) pay 2,580 NF (£245) in contributions. It is important to remember that contribution rates vary from one category of workers to another. The non-agricultural self-employed contributed fifteen per cent of earnings up to the ceiling in 1972.[5]

5 Income and Expenditure

An attempt to discuss the income and expenditure characteristics of the French health care system is fraught with difficulties. To minimise these difficulties an attempt will be made to proceed in an orderly fashion. First the income and expenditure characteristics of the general scheme will be discussed. Unlike the analysis of other countries it is not possible to clearly differentiate between medical care and sickness benefits, i.e. in kind and cash benefits. Consequently where appropriate each scheme will be discussed in its totality without breaking this section up into (a) medical care and (b) cash benefits. Then an analysis of the income and expenditure details of other schemes of social health care insurance will be provided. To this discussion an analysis of the medical social aid programme will be added. Finally a discussion of health care consumption in France will be provided. It is to be noted that because of the nature of the funding operations of the general and other schemes it is not possible to differentiate between contributions for medical care and sickness insurance. However, where possible, the distinction between in kind and cash benefits is shown on the expenditure side.

Table 6 *General Scheme Income 1968-71 in millions of frances (£m).*

(a)	General Scheme	1968	1969	1970	1971
	Contributions				
i)	up to the ceiling	14,413	16,906	19,587	23,521
ii)	on total income	4,478	5,334	6,081	6,892
Total		18,891	22,240	25,668	30,413
		(£1795)	(£2114)	(£2441)	(£2891)
(b)	Associated Schemes				
i)	civil servants	1,747	2,406	2,553	3,016
ii)	local authority employers	512	583	675	873
iii)	nationalised gas and electricity industrues	182	217	225	267
iv)	voluntary insured	388	219	456	491
v)	students	61	79	98	91
vi)	war invalids	193	210	251	272
vii)	salaried farm employees	603	744	844	951
viii)	motor insurance surcharge	72	164	166	185
ix)	other	206	322	299	384
x)	SNCF				570
Overall Total		22,855	27,193	31,235	37,513
		(£2172)	(£2584)	(£2969)	(£3565)

Source: *Ministère des Affaires Sociales* (1973) *op. cit.* page 531

Table 6 shows the income of the general scheme for the provision of sickness insurance, maternity insurance, invalidity and death insurance for the years 1968-71. All the data is in millions of francs (£m). The total income of the general and associated schemes increased by 14,658 million francs (£1,393m) in the period 1968-71 (i.e. by over sixty-four per cent) to 37,513 million NF (£3,565m).

As was shown in Section (4) most of this income is derived from contributions by employers. *Santé et Sécurité Sociale* (1973) gives income source breakdown for all social security only. For all forms of social security the employers contribute 76.9 per cent of total income in the general scheme. 16.6 per cent comes from employees and the rest (6.5 per cent) is made up of transfers and a variety of other minor items. It is interesting to compare this rapid increase in income with

117

the expenditure under the same head by the general fund. Table 7 shows general scheme expenditure for the period 1968-71.

Table 7 *General Scheme Expenditure 1968-71 in millions of francs (£m).*

	1968	1969	1970	1971
Health Care	14,724	18,248	21,284	24,779
Sickness Insurance	2,822	3,094	3,413	3,737
Total	17,342	21,342	24,697	28,516
	(£1667)	(£2028)	(£2347)	(£2710)
Maternity outlays	961	1,172	1,364	1,976
Invalidity pensions	1,050	1,175	1,344	1,487
Death grants	125	146	172	191
Total	19,682	23,835	27,577	32,170
	(£1870)	(£2265)	(£2621)	(£3058)
Agricultural employees scheme outlays	1,034	1,343	1,497	1,789
Compensation to Overseas departments	64	58	63	94
Sanitary and Social Work	316	379	438	483
Medical control	166	209	241	269
Administration	1,303	1,537	1,771	1,977
Other	79	65	125	210
Overall Total	22,644	27,426	31,712	37,975
	(£2152)	(£2607)	(£3014)	(£3610)

Source: *op. cit.* page 532.

The increase in expenditure shown in Table 7 is very similar to the trend exhibited by the income series, i.e. a growth of over sixty-seven per cent in the period 1968 to 1971. This approximate balance in income and expenditure is shown clearly in Table 8 which shows general sceme income, expenditure and surplus/deficit for each of the years in the period 1968-71.

Table 8 *General Scheme Income and Expenditure 1968-71 in million of francs (£m)*

	1968	1969	1970	1971
Income	22,855	27,193	31,235	37,513
	(£2172)	(£2584)	(£2969)	(£3565)
Expenditure	22,644	27,426	31,712	37,925
	(£2152)	(£2607)	(£3014)	(£3610)
Balance	+ 211	-233	-477	-462
	(+ £20)	(- £23)	(- £45)	(- £45)

Source: *op. cit.* page 515.

Table 8 shows that only in one year – 1968 – has the income of the general fund health care insurance exceeded the expenditure. In both 1970 and 1971 the deficit was over 460 million francs (£45m). Such deficits are usually met by government grants. Indeed the French general and special health care systems seem to face a common problem of rapidly escalating expenditures which can be financed only by increased government aid or increased employee contributions. It is assumed that it is difficult to increase employer contributions because of its effect on prices. Whether this assumption is valid will be discussed below when an overall picture of French health care has been produced (see 8 – Conclusion).

Before presenting the income and expenditure data for some of the special schemes it is useful to analyse the breakdown of general scheme expenditure on medical care by type. Table 9 shows the breakdown in general scheme expenditure by type in 1971. In addition to breakdown by type of medical care there is a division into expenditure with and without the *ticket modérateur*. The *ticket* determines the degree of individual involvement in the payment of the cost of care. In most cases care is provided with *ticket modérateur* and the individual pays part of the cost unless he has supplementary (non-compulsory) insurance. For some types of care (e.g. hospitalisation over thirty days, where the beneficiary is chronically ill or in receipt of an old age pension, etc. – see Section (6) benefits for full details) free services are provided (i.e. without *ticket modérateur*) by the general scheme.

Table 9   *General Scheme Expenditure by Type and With or Without the* Ticket Modérateur *(1973) in million of francs (£m).*

Type of Expenditure	With ticket mod.		Without ticket mod.		Total	
	francs	%	francs	%	francs	%
Consultations	986.6 (£93m)					
Home Visits	602.9	9.24	244.8 (£23)	1.76	1231.4 (£117)	5.02
Fees for surveillance	6.1	5.65	210.2	1 51	813.2	3.31
Routine Surgery	420.1	0.06	25.7	0.19	31.8	0.13
X-rays	467.0	3.94	674.9	4.86	1095.1	4.46
		4.37	230.4	1.66	697.5	2.84
Laboratory Analysis	462.7	4.39	277.3	2.00	739.9	3.01
Dental treatment	1034.1 (£98m)	9.69	229.7 (£21m)	1.66	1263.8 (£210m)	5.15
Auxiliary staff expenditure	541.8	5.08	350.9	2.53	892.7	3.64
Other fees in the private sector	33.7	0.31	32.7	0.24	66.4	0.27

Hospitalisation						
(accommodation charges only)	1786.9	16.74	9083.2	65.46	10870.1	44.28
	(£168m)		(£863m)		(£1033m)	
Drugs	3728.5	34.93	1639.9	11.82	5368.4	21.87
	(£354m)		(£155m)		(£510m)	
Spectacles & appliances	160.8	1.51	98.1	0.71	258.9	1.05
Thermal Cures	64.7	0.61	26.7	0.19	91.4	0.37
Other	87.7	0.82	284.5	2.05	372.4	1.52
Total benefits	10674.7	100.00	13875.5	100.0	24550.2	100.00
	(£1014)		(£1318)		(£2333)	

Source: *Ministère de la Santé Publique* (1972) Bulletin de Statistiques No 6
tome A 1972 Novembre-Decembre page 15.

The most important single item of expenditure for medical care provided with *ticket modérateur* was drugs. This is perhaps not very surprising in the light of the price discrimination practiced by the drug companies[6] and the relatively high drug consumption levels in France. Hospitalisation in the 'with ticket' category of expenditure consumed only 16.4 per cent (£169m) of the total. However, in the 'without ticket' category hospitalisation took 65.46 per cent (£863) of the total. Overall hospitalisation, i.e. accommodation or hotel charges only, was the single most important expenditure item taking over forty-four per cent of the total expenditure in 1971 (£1,033m). Apart from hospitalisation (44.28 per cent) and drugs (21.87 per cent – £510m) only two items consumed more than five per cent of total expenditure: consultations (5.02 per cent – £117m) and dental treatment (5.15 per cent – £120m). As can be seen from the table over fifty-six per cent of expenditure was without *ticket modérateur* – the single most omportant item being hospitalisation which accounted for over sixty-five per cent of the without *ticket modérateur* expenditure. Thus although some treatments of the French health care system exphasise the importance of the *ticket* it is necessary to keep the importance of this policy instrument in perspective.

It is drug expenditure and hospitalisation expenditure which are the fastest growing items in the budget. With a base of 100 in 1959 the index of hospitalisation expenditure rose to 228.9 in 1965 and 475.0 in 1970. A similar index for drugs rose from 100 in 1959, to 211.5 in 1965, and to 384.0 in 1970. For medical services the index rose from 100 to 211.5 to 364.0 in the same years. Overall medical care consumption rose from 100 in 1959, to 245.1 in 1966, to 408.0 in 1970. This compares with a total consumption index series of 100 in 1959, 188.4 in 1965, and 281.2 in 1970. It appears that French medical care

120

expenditure is expanding at a very rapid rate. By 1972 (Bulletin de
Statistiques Sept-Oct 1973, p.XIV) the general scheme's expenditure
was 28,745 mNF (£2,732m) i.e. a growth of seventeen per cent
compared with 1971. Hospitalisation and drugs expenditure, by
increasing to 12,736 mNF (£1,210m) and 6,063 mNF (£576m)
respectively, grew at a rate less than that of the overall budget (i.e. by
seventeen per cent and thirteen per cent respectively) which in the
light of 1960s trends was unusual.

Table 10   *General Scheme Maternity Insurance Expenditure 1971
in millions of francs (£m)*

(a) Medical Care	Total	Percentage
Laboratory analysis	28.1	2.43
Confinement fees	121.7	10.50
Other private sector fees	214.0	18.47
Public sector fees	42.2	3.64
Hospitalisation (accommodation)	694.0	59.89
Health benefits	11.2	0.97
Breast feeding bonuses & milk coupons	26.1	2.25
Miscellaneous benefits	11.7	1.01
Other benefits	9.7	0.84
Total	1,158.8 (£110m)	100.00
(b) Cash Benefits	817.5 (£77m)	
Overall Total	1,976.4 (£187m)	

Source: *op. cit.* page 16.

Maternity insurance is an associated programme of the health care
system administered separately within the general regime. Table 10
shows the 1971 expenditure under this heading. Maternity benefits are
partially medical care and partly cash benefits. The latter takes up
approximately sixty-four per cent of total expenditure (817.5m NF −
£0.77m) with the average daily allowance (1971) being 28.12 NF. Of
the medical care benefits, medical fees account for over thirty per cent
of expenditure and hospital accommodation benefits consume a further
59.89 per cent. Total medical care expenditure was 1,158.8 million NF
(£110m) and the total cost of the general scheme maternity insurance
programme was 1,976.4 million NF (£187) in 1971.

    The final general scheme (Table 11) gives a clear picture of the distribution of health, maternity and death benefits[7] among the component parts of the general scheme. For all categories except the first and the sixth no cash sickness benefits are given by the general scheme. Of course this does not mean that e.g. civil servants get no sick pay. The social sickness insurance of some of the groups (e.g. civil servants) is arranged by separate institutions. The first column of the Table shows that most of the general regime expenditure is on medical care (eighty per cent of the total) and that the general scheme, rather than associated groups, receives most of the medical care expenditure (over eighty per cent of the total).

Table 11   *The Distribution of Health, Maternity and Death Benefits 1971 in millions of francs (£m)*

	Medical Care		Sickness Insurance		Death benefit	All
			Type of Insurance			
	Non-mat	Mat	Non-mat	Mat		
General scheme	20088.4	1014.6	3736.1	817.5	189.9	25846.6
Civil servants	3331.6	127.3	-	-	-	3459.0
Students	132.7	9.8	-	-	-	142.5
War wounded	251.1	0.4	-	-	-	251.6
Conventioned doctors	53.6	3.4	-	-	-	57.6
Voluntarily insured	919.2	3.1	0.9	0.05	0.05	923.8
Painters, sculptors & Engravers	1.6	0.02	-	-	0.03	1.7
Total	24778.4	1158.8	3737.0	817.5	190.0	30682.8
	(£2355)	(£110)	(£355)	(£77)	(£18)	(£2916)

Source: *Ministère de Affaires Sociales* (1973).

Note: Mat. and Non-mat refer maternity and non-maternity programmes

So far the concern of this Section has been the general scheme. Now an attempt must be made to analyse comparable statistics for the special schemes. The agricultural special scheme (operational since the beginning of 1969 for the self-employed farmer) is in two parts — wage earners employees and non-wage earners (i.e. farming their own land). In 1971 (1970)[8] the total contribution income of the salaried farm workers fund was 4,219 (3,710) million NF [£401m (£352m)], of this 518 (458) million NF [£49m (£43m)] was contributed by the employees (12.3 per cent) and 1,286 (1,162) million NF [£122m (£110m)] was paid by the employer (30.5 per cent). The largest income component, 2,035 (1,717) million NF [£193m (£163m)] was from transfers (48.2 per cent). Subsidies (8.6 per cent from the government) and other minor items accounted for the residual income flow. However, this income paid for benefits other than medical care and sickness benefit.[9] In 1971 (1970) the total expenditure of the salaried part of the agricultural special scheme was 1,607 (1,376) million NF [£152m (£130m)].

Table 12   *Agricultural Special Scheme – Expenditure on Health, Maternity and Death Benefits 1970 and 1971 in millions of francs (£m).*

	1970		1971	
	Self-Employed	Wage Earner	Self-Employed	Wage Earner
Medical Care	2168	1222	2510	1431
Cash Benefits	-	154	-	176
Totals	2168	1376	2510	1607
	(£206)	(£130)	(£238)	(£152)

Source: *op. cit.* (1973) page 504 and 510.

The other part of the agricultural special scheme (that for non-wage earners) provides benefits other than medical care and sickness benefits. The total 1971 (1970) income of this scheme was 9,917 (8,746) million NF [£942m (£831m)]. Of this over thirty-three per cent came from *impôts reçus* or dues received from the sales of output, over twenty three per cent 3,103 (2,720) million NF [£294m (£258m)] from the ETI (i.e. contribution income which is not paid by the individual farmer), and about eleven per cent – 1,103 (931) million NF [£104m (£88m)] – from transfers. The complex nature of this type of insurance is unavoidable because with the *exploitants* or self-employed growers there is the problem of income in kind and in-accurate declarations of money income. This makes it hard to collect contributions related to income.

Although it is impossible to separate health care income from social security income in general the agricultural schemes, it is possible to make a meaningful distinction on the expenditure side. The total expenditure [10] on cash and in kind benefits rose from 3,544 million NF (£336m) in 1970 to 4,117 million NF (£391m) in 1971, i.e. a growth of sixteen per cent. As can be seen from the data in Table 12, the wage earners had a sickness benefit scheme unlike the self-employed. Most expenditure 95.6 per cent in 1970 and 95.7 per cent in 1971 was to cover the cost of providing medical care.

Table 13   *Other Special Schemes − Total Income and Health Expenditure 1970 and 1971 in millions of francs (£m)*

	1970		1971	
Total Income				
Contributions: Employee	9218	(£876m)	10364	(£985m)
Employer	7517		8449	
Subsidies	4586		4897	
Transfers	1238		1816	
Others	306		299	
Expenditure on health, maternity and death benefits				
Medical Care	2444	(£232m)	2742	(£260m)
Cash Benefits	430	(£ 40m)	459	(£ 43m)
Total	2874	(£273m)	3201	(£304n)

Source: *op. cit.* (1973) pages 504 and 510.

The income and expenditure characteristics of the three other special schemes are shown in Table 13. This Table gives the 1971 and 1970 total incomes of these schemes, i.e. it looks at the incomes which financed health and other social security benefits (e.g. pensions) for the liberal professions, artisans and the self-employed industrial and commercial workers. In 1971 48.6 per cent of the total income of these schemes came from employer contributions. Of the rest of the schemes' income 28.2 per cent came in the form of subsidies, eleven per cent in employee contributions and 10.5 per cent in transfers. On the health care (only) side most expenditure (1970 − eighty-five per cent; 1971 − 85.6 per cent) was on benefits in kind, or medical care.

Table 14   *Mutual Societies − Expenditure by Type of Society 1969* in millions of francs (£m)*

Type of Society	Health Care†	Maternity Care†
Surgical Societies	297.055	0.845
Company Societies	291.998	5.943
Societies for artisans, the liberal professions and shopkeepers	117.011	0.596
War Veterans Societies	0.016	-
Sporting accident societies	3.336	-

Mutual accident societies	7.186	
Civil servant, etc. societies	465.230	7.979
Gas and electricity industries	75.500	1.415
Other	421.473	4.191
Total	1678.800	20,969
	(£159m)	(£2.0m)

Source: *op. cit.* (1973) page 633.
† Medical care and cash benefits are not differentiated.
* This data is for those mutual societies making statistical returns.

The remaining category of health care insurance income and expenditure characteristics which is to be discussed is the mutual society. At least thirty million French people are participating members of mutual societies (Section (2) above). Table 14 lists the societies by type [11] and shows the (1969) expenditure for each category. No income data is available. All the data in Table 14 refers to mutual societies producing statistics. Table 16 gives a different expenditure estimate whose source is not made clear in the original French government document.

Table 15 *Health Social Aid Expenditure 1963 and 1968-70 in millions millions of francs (£m).*

	1963	1968	1969	1970
Medical aid to the tubercular	90.8	110.9	119.7	115.6
Central Government subsidy	*60.1*	*75.2*	*81.5*	*80.1*
Medical aid to the mentally ill	561.2	735.8	817.5	492.0
Central Government subsidy	*362.2*	*485.1*	*537.1*	*336.5*
Medical Aid	686.4	842.0	1047.0	1190.5
Central Government subsidy	*256.8*	*340.7*	*419.8*	*483.8*
Total	1338.4	1688.7	1984.2	1798.1
Central Government subsidy	*679.1*	*901.0*	*38.4*	*900.4*
	(£127)	(£160)	(£188)	(£170)

Source: *op. cit.* (1973) page 641.

The total expenditure of the mutual societies in 1969 was over 1698 million NF (£161m). Nearly ninety-nine per cent of this expenditure was under the heading health care, but for both this expenditure category and the other, maternity, it is impossible to differentiate between medical care and cash benefits.

The final expenditure figures which are relevant to this study concern social aid. Table 15 shows some of the social aid expenditure in 1963, 1968, 1969, and 1970. This expenditure is jointly financed

125

by central government, the *départements* and the *communes*, and their relative contributions vary considerably from one area to another, e.g. in *Haute Normande* the central government finances 94.1 per cent of expenditure whilst in *Region Parisienne* the central government's share is only 49.4 per cent and the department finances 48.6 per cent of the total. (*Santé et Sécurité Sociale* [1973] p. 654) As can be seen from the Table over fifty per cent of total social aid expenditure is met out of central government grants. During the period 1963-70 total expenditure roase from 1,338.4 million NF (£127m) to 1,798.1 million NF (£170m), i.e. thirty-three per cent. However, in 1970 absolute expenditure was lower than in 1969 perhaps in part due to the expansion of social health insurance of the self-employed. The share of the central government in the finance of this expenditure was 50.7 per cent in 1963 and fifty per cent in 1970. Unfortunately these figures represent only part − although a large part − of social aid health expenditure. Other items of social aid such as aid to invalids, the blind and the chronic sick and social aid to the aged contain large components of health care expenditure. Thus a significant proportion of total social aid expenditure of 6,071.9 million NF (£577m) in 1970 financed the provision of health benefits in cash and kind (a 1969 estimate from CREDOC is in Table 16).

Table 16

	Millions of francs	(£m)
1. Social Insurance		
General and associated scheme	19645,544	
Agricultural scheme (i) Self-Employed	1786.058	
(ii) Wage Earners	1024.477	
Mining Scheme	568.920	
Railway Scheme	871.640	
Marine Invalids Scheme	154.854	
Other Schemes	905.589	
All Schemes (Total)	24957.082	(£2372.34)
2. Social Aid		
Medical Aid	916.967	
Aid to the tubercular	109.984	
Aid to the mentally ill	788.417	
Other Aid	418.571	
Total Social Aid	2233.939	(£ 212.26)
3. Other		
Article 115	274.424	
University & School Medicine	-	
Armed Forces	-	
Private Administration	-	
Mutualities and private insurance	2085.106	(£ 198.19)

Table 16 *(Cont)*

4. Total	29550.551	(£ 198.19)
5. Industrial Medicine		
Household consumption	6966.000	(£ 622.16)
Total Medical Consumption	36516.551	(£3471.104)

Source: *Centre De Recherches et de Documentation sur la Consommation*
(1971) 'Evaluation de la Consommation – Medicale en 1969' Paris.

What do all these components add up to? Some of the information in
this Section has, of necessity, been concerned with medical care and
cash sickness and death benefits. In Table 16 CREDOC (*Centre de
Racherches et de Documentation sur la Consommation*) figures are
used to show the level of medical consumption in France in 1969.
The official (CREDOC) view of this estimate is that it is too low
because household expenditure on physicians services is underestimated.
The degree of underestimation is not stated. The total expenditure
figure shown – 36,516,551 NF (£3471.102m) – is high and since that
date it has increased further as a result of the progressive extension of
social insurance to the self-employed group. From the data in Table
16 expenditure per head in 1969 was approximately 722 NF (£68.63).
The amount of consumption of medical care financed by means other
than social insurance was 11,558 million NF (£1,098.67m) i.e. 31.6 per
cent. The shares in this total were: social aid 6.1 per cent; mutualities
and private insurance 5.7. per cent; household consumption nineteen
per cent and other 0.8 per cent. The role of household consumption –
nearly one fifth of total expenditure – is very significant. CREDOC
estimate that 5.5 per cent of GNP was spent on medical care in 1971.

6 Benefits

Membership of most of the French social health insurance schemes
makes the member and his dependent eligible for benefits in cash and
in kind. In this Section we will look at the two types of benefit
separately whilst bearing in mind that usually one contribution may
yield medical care and cash benefits.

(a) Medical Care
The French general scheme of compulsory health insurance provides
a substantial range of subsidies to recompense the consumer of medical
care. No benefit can be granted unless its use is sanctioned by a doctor.
Benefits cover treatments of all kinds: general and special medical
operations, treatment by dental surgeons and auxiliary medical staff,
transport and hospitalisation, pharmaceutical and prescriptions, appliances, laboratory analyses, etc. The patient acquires the necessary
treatment and the insurance fund repays medical expenses at a rate of

seventy-five per cent of the cost based on the current scale of fees in the locality where the nearest doctor to the insured's home resides, e.g. 16.5 NF out of 22 NF (£2) for a GP consultation. The fee scales applicable to the payment of doctors and their staff for the treatment of the insured and their dependents are determined, since 1971, by a national agreement (see Section 7 below). The fee scales are set so that they cannot exceed the ceilings defined by ministerial order and are applicable only after they have been approved by an 'Inter-ministerial Commission on Tariffs' consisting of representatives of the Labour, Employment and Population, Finance, Economic Affairs and Agricultural Ministries.

Table 17 *Conventional Fee Scales 1972 (1970)*

		Tariff	Zone A Refund	Tariff	Zone B Refund
Consultations					
(i)	GP	22.00 (17.00)	16.5 (12.75)	21.00 (16.00)	15.75 (12.00)
(ii)	Specialist	33.00 (29.00)	24.75 (21.75)	35.00 (27.00)	26.25 (20.25)
Home Visits					
(i)	GP	29.00 (24.00)	21.75 (18.00)	27.00 (22.00)	20.25 (16.50)
(ii)	Specialist	40.00 (38.00)	30.00 (28.50)	36.00 (34.00)	27.00 (25.50)

Zone A: Seine, Seine-et-Oise (Zone 1) plus certain communes in Seine-et-Marne.

ZoneB: Other *départements* and districts.

Source: *op. cit.* (1973) page 520-1.

In addition to these convention scales there are also official tables. Such scales (Table 18) apply to any district where it is not possible to agree a convention or where the convention has been rescinded. If, within two months of notice to agree given by the Regional Director of Social Security to the Primary Funds and the professional organisations, no individual recognition scheme (see below) and no convention is in operation, the Inter-ministerial Commission on Tariff fixes the fee which, as can be seen, are much lower than conventional scales. As is noted below (Section 7. Provision.) most physicians are now parties to national agreements and, unlike the 1960s, only a minority (five per cent) are subject to official fee scales system.

128

Table 18 *Official Fee Scales*

	Zone A		Zone B		Zone C	
	Tariff	Refund	Tariff	Refund	Tarriff	Refund
Consultations						
(i) GP	4.00	3.00	3.50	2.625	3.20	2.40
(ii) Specialist	8.00	6.00	7.00	5.25	6.40	4.80
Home Visits						
(i) GP	5.20	3.90	4.40	3.30	4.00	3.00
(ii) Specialist	10.40	7.80	8.80	6.60	8.00	6.00

Zone A : Seine and Seine-et-Oise (Zone 1)
Zone B : Lyons and surrounding area; Marseilles and surrounding area.
Zone C : Urban areas with over 100,000 inhabitants, Seine-et-Oise (Zone 2) Seine-et-Marne and Nord.

Source: G. Spitaels *et al* (1971) page 585.

In order to avoid the official fee scales of payment individual doctors may recognise the standard convention and the conventional scales. This makes available to the insured the services of doctors who will not require their patients to pay fees higher than the scale of refunds. Where the official scales are not in operation the insured may have to pay fees higher than the scale for refunds, e.g. for a consulatation with a GP the insured may be charged a tariff of 12 NF (£1.14) but will be able to get a refund on only seventy-five per cent of the official 4NF (£0.38) fee, i.e. a refund of 3 NF (£0.28).

The conventional scales may be exceeded in certain cases. The consultation of a distinguished doctor — as established by registration on the list drawn up by a commission after consultation with the departmental council of othe Order of Doctors — which is necessitated by a special need results in a fee payment to that doctor in excess of the conventional scale. The size of this additional fee and the present number of doctors categorised as specialised is not known; in 1962 5.94 per cent of doctors with private patients (2.76 per cent of GPs and 12.4 per cent of specialists) were on the list of distinguished doctors. Another cause of remuneration in excess of the conventional fees is where the service has to be provided at the patient's home. In this case the doctor's travelling expenses (in general a lump sum up to 2 km and a time and distance allowance for journeys over 2 km) are repaid to the doctor in addition to the conventional treatment fee. Also where the patient requires treatment between 8 pm and 6 am or on a

129

Sunday, the fees (both for travelling and treatment) are subject to surcharges of five per cent to ten per cent.

Pharmaceutical services are covered to varying extents. All prescribed preparations made up by the pharmacist are refundable, but only those branded products listed by order of the Ministry on the recommendation of a special committee are refundable. The process of refunding is not subject to any special provisions in the case of made-up preparations. However, in the case of branded products a stamp contained in the packaging must be affixed by the insured person to the prescription. The price is entered by the pharmacist and this control supposedly assists the French authorities in controlling the use and refunding of the product. The insurance scheme covers seventy per cent of the cost of medicaments in general and ninety per cent for specially expensive or 'irreplaceable' items. Normally the patient pays the whole of the price and is then refunded by the sickness insurance fund after deducting the participation payment.

Benefits such as hospitalisation, orthopaedic services and appliances are covered by the compulsory sickness insurance scheme. The insured, or his dependents, is covered for part of the cost of necessary [12] hospitalisation provided by public establishments or those private units which are authorised to give treatment. Also with fund approval the insured can be refunded part of the costs of purchasing, repairing and replacing orthopaedic appliances. The refund is related to fund approved fees and the particular *ticket modérateur*.

The *ticket modérateur* determines the insured's participation in the cost of a treatment and varies from type to type of benefit and standard of benefit received. The rate is fixed by Order in Council and may be either proportional or lump sum. In 1970 the ticket rates in force were as follows:

(i)   pharmaceutical products – thirty per cent in general and ten per cent for 'irreplaceable' and particularly expensive drugs;

(ii)   twenty-five per cent for fees for home visits and consultations, and for various services performed by practitioners (doctors, dentists, surgeons and midwives) and auxiliary medical staff (nurses, etc.) outside the hospital;

(iii)   twenty per cent for medical services provided by practitioners auxiliaries medical staff during hospitalisation in a public or approved private institution, and for the costs of laboratory analyses during such hospitalisation;

(iv)   twenty per cent of the fee scale for the costs of hospitalisation for short periods in public or approved private institutions.

An Ordinance of 21st August 1967 made it illegal for any institution (private insurer or public fund) to cover the complete cost of the *ticket modérateur*. Indeed the Ordinance laid down that the amount paid be fixed by decree and should not be less than one-fifth of the amount of the *ticket modérateur*. However an agreement in 1968 (23rd November) between the National Sickness Insurance Fund for Employees and the National Federation of French Mutual Societies permitted mutual societies to ignore the 1967 Ordinance and refund the whole of the *ticket*. Consequently some French men and women pay nothing for their medical care as the *ticket modérateur* is fully covered by supplementary insurance of one kind or another.

Free services (i.e. the *ticket modérateur* is zero) are provided by the general scheme as stated in the Act of 21st July 1968. This legislation abolishes or limits the participation of the insured person in the following circumstances:

(i)   if the cost of hospitalisation exceeds a certain sum or if the insured or his dependents are hospitalised for more than thirty days.

(ii)   when the insured person is receiving a supplementary allowance from the National Solidarity Fund rather than an old age benefit.

(iii)   if the insured obtains orthopaedic appliance of a nature specified in a decree.

(iv)   if the person is in receipt of a benefit for a prolonged or expensive illness which is included in the list established by decree on the advice of the Medical High Committee. In 1969 there were twenty-one conditions of this type.

(v)   recipients of an invalidity pension or old age pension paid to an invalid after his sixtieth birthday.

(vi)   those in receipt of industrial accident benefits who are certified as not less than $66^2/3$ incapable of work. This complete exemption applies even if the person is in work and extends to his dependents.[13]

Before terminating the discussion of the normal benefits in kind mention must be made of the 'third party pays' system. This system guarantees that the share guaranteed by social security cover is paid direct to the hospital or individual practitioner. The insured person pays only his part of the total cost. This 'third party pays' system applies only to hospitalisation and treatment in hospitals. For benefits other than this the patient pays one hundred per cent of the cost and is then refunded.

Maternity medical care insurance covers pre-natal treatment, the costs of confinement and post-natal examinations. To qualify for pre-natal benefits the mother-to-be must be examined before the end of the third, sixth and eighth months of pregnancy. The mother can opt for a home or hospital delivery. The costs of delivery are met by a lump sum payment. For an ordinary confinement the grant in 1972 was 320 NF (£30.42) in Zone A and 300 NF (£28.50) in Zone B. If the confinement takes place in the home an extra sum is paid to meet the cost of drugs (the amount of this is determined by the individual fund). A confinement in a public hospital entitles the mother to fourteen days treatment in the hospital at zero cost. After the fourteenth day she is required to pay the *ticket modérateur*. A confinement in a private clinic entitles the mother to the same grant as in a public hospital provided the fund has an agreement with the relevant clinic. If the clinic charges more than the conventional funds this excess has to be paid by the mother.

So far the examination of medical care benefits has been with reference to the general scheme only. For the schemes covering the self-employed medical care benefits consist of basic benefits (common to all groups), and supplementary benefits (applicable to one or more groups) resulting from supplementary contributions. The basic benefits cover general and special medical expenses, pharmaceutical expenditure and the costs of hospitalisation. The refund rate for *petits risques* (i.e. common illnesses) is fifty per cent for adults and sixty per cent for retired people and children below the age of sixteen. For *gros risques* (i.e. hospitalisation, surgical operations, pregnancy, confinements, postnatal care and chronic illnesses) the refund rate is one hundred per cent.

For those people who are outside the scope of social insurance, Social Aid provides a medical safety net in the form of Medical Aid. This is given to those people who are without resources and ineligible for other social security benefits. The person has free choice of a doctor who accepts the conditions of payment fixed by the department for medical aid — similarly for dental and midwifery care. All these medical personnel are directly controlled and remunerated by the central government. These services together with prescribed drugs are given of charge. In the case of hospitalisation part or all of the fees are paid by the local authority provided the hospital is public and in the patient's home area. The medical aid service is organised at the *département* level and the rules governing its operation have to conform to national standards and be approved by the Ministry. Special arrangements have been made to treat mental and tubercular patients in respect of hospitalisation.

(b) Cash Benefits

The general scheme pays out cash benefits to those claimants who fulfill the necessary qualification (see above (3) Qualifying Conditions). The amount of day compensation paid is based on the basic daily earnings of the insured and cannot be more than one sixtieth of the monthly contribution ceiling, i.e. (1st January 1971) 1,650/60 NF = 27.25 NF. This maximum is matched with a minimum equal to one three-hundred and sixty-fifth of the minimum invalidity pension, i.e. (1st January 1973) 1,750/365 NF = 4.79 NF (£0.55). Within these limits and assuming the insured is not hospitalised, the day compensation payment is equal usually to fifty per cent of the basic daily earnings. In the event of hospitalisation this level of benefits is maintained only if the insured has two or more children. If he is married with no children benefits are reduced by one fifth and the single man or woman gets his/her benefits reduced by three-fifths. If the insured is married with three or more dependent children the normal maximum day compensation is increased (1st January 1971) to 36.37 NF (£3.46) after the thirty-first day of sickness (i.e. two thirds of the basic daily earnings). However this increased benefit level must not exceed one forty-fifth of the monthly contribution ceilings (i.e. 1,650/45 = 34.74 NF [£3.30]) and cannot be less than four-thirds of the minimum day compensation (i.e. 4.79 x 4/3 = 6.28 NF [£0.59]).

These benefits are payable after three waiting days and are paid for every day of inactivity including otherwise non-working days (e.g. Saturdays and Sundays). The duration of the benefit is dependent on the claimants condition. An insured patient who is chronically ill can obtain day compensation for up to three years provided he meets the following requirements:

(i)   He must accept the treatments prescribed by his doctor and/ or his consultant.

(ii) He must attend medical consultation sessions and medical examinations.

(iii) He must abstain from any banned activities.

(iv) He must carry out exercises and/or work prescribed for him as necessary.

Those people who are not chronically ill can, in any period of three years, receive up to a maximum 360 days of compensation payments.

French maternity cash benefits have some novel features. Those women who are full insured 'compulsory' members and who give up work due to an impending confinement receive day compensation equivalent to fifty per cent of their basic daily earnings as in sickness insurance. Hospitalisation does not reduce these benefits which are paid from the first day of absence from work for fourteen weeks (six weeks legal absence prior to confinement plus eight weeks after). Various bonuses are paid. The mother is required to undergo a post-natal examination within six weeks of the birth of her child. This examination entitles her to a bonus varying in amount between the funds. Also mothers who breast-feed their babies can receive various bonuses and allowances.

In France the worker pays a joint contribution for sickness (cash and in kind benefits), maternity and invalidity. Consequently we must add to our usual coverage of cash sickness and maternity benefits, cash invalidity benefits. Invalids, or the disabled, are categorised into three groups depending on the magnitude of their condition. Group 1 consists of those invalids who are capable of paid employment. Group 2 consists of those who are incapable of certain activities or a certain activity. Group 3 invalids are those who are incapable of work and who need assistance to carry out normal everyday functions such as washing and using the toilet. The amount of invalidity pension paid is based on the average annual earnings corresponding to contributions paid during the ten years of insurance cover prior to:

(i)   the interruption of work and ensuing invalidity; or
(ii)   the accident causing invalidity; or
(iii)   medical confirmation of invalidity.

The rate of pension paid was as follows (1st January 1971) subject to a minimum payment (equal to the Old Wage Eearner's Grant) of 1,750 NF per annum:

Group 1 thirty per cent of basic earnings up to a maximum of 5,940 NF (£564.64) per annum (thirty per cent of the annual earning's ceiling).

Group 2 fifty per cent of basic earnings up to a maximum of 9,900 NF (£941.06) (fifty per cent of the annual earning's ceiling).

Group 3 As per Group 2 plus forty per cent (where the plus forty per cent cannot be less than 9,357.10 NF [£889.45] per annum) – this extra forty per cent is not paid if the person is hospitalised.

No allowances are paid for dependents. Each year the Labour Minister and the Finance Minister fix reassessment coefficients to pensions which have already been granted. Invalidity pensions terminate at sixty years of age and are replaced by old age pensions which cannot be less than the invalidity pension paid previous to this age. In the event of hospitalisation invalidity pensions are reduced in a similar manner to that applied to sickness insurance.

7 Provision

(a)   The Medical Professions

The French medical professions have been carefully regulated by the State for many years. The three principles which are allegedly inherent in this regulation are: that of granting the right to carry out their functions only to those able to guarantee their competence by presenting certified diplomas; that of maintaining a constant scrutiny of their morals (a job usually carried out by their peers); and that of providing sufficient supply to meet the 'needs' of public health.

The French physician is a good example of the extent and nature this regulation. The conditions under which physicians are permitted to practice is carefully controlled: professional capacity has to be certified by the possession of a State diploma received after the completion of seven years successful training; doctors must have French nationality (or have the right to practice in France by virtue, e.g. of EEC regulations) and be prepared to submit themselves to the surveillance of the Order of Medical Practitioners: this Order, together with the Order of Dental Surgeons and the Order of Midwives, was created in 1945. Membership is compulsory unless the physician, dentist or midwife is performing an administrative function. The function of the Order is to guarantee and enforce moral standards, to defend the independence of the professions and to implement the fundamental principle of the Deontological Code (Decree of 28th November 1955). This code laid down the 'basic' principles of 'liberal' medicine: freedom of the patient to choose his doctor, freedom of the doctor to prescribe, and direct negotiation of fees between patient and doctor and direct payment of fees by the patient to the doctor.

The result of the Code and social insurance legislation is that the great majority of doctors practise on a private basis. Doctors working in public hospitals are increasingly being paid by salary. Their salary is fixed by inter-ministerial decree and varies according to qualifications, seniority and type of work done. In hospitals full-time practitioners may hold private consultations twice weekly at the hospital and admit and treat private patients. In private hospitals the doctor's pay is determined by agreements between the patient and the doctor. The latter is paid directly by the patient.

Doctors practising in the community used to be remunerated by fees or conventions negotiated between the funds or the local representatives of the medical Orders. They are paid directly by the patient who gets his refund from the local social insurance office. It was estimated [14] in the late 1960s that fifty per cent of doctors in Paris, seventy-five per cent of doctors in Lyons and a third of doctors in ten other departments were not covered by these conventions. In these cases the lower official scales applied and the individual doctor was free to determine his own rates in excess of these. Thus the patient got a seventy-five per cent refund of the official rate only and might have had to pay a substantial fee out of his own resources. Overall Spitaels *et al* estimate that about eighty-seven per cent of all doctors are covered by conventions of one kind and another (*cf* 1962 = eighty per cent). This situation has been replaced by a national agreement made in October 1971 which replaced the system of compulsory agreement by a new definition of relations between the primary sickness funds· and the physicians. This agreement reiterated the principles of liberal medicine and fixed the rates for the various forms of treatment. Each treatment was assigned a key letter and a coefficient which determined the payment level. These rates are to be observed by the physicians except in special cases (e.g. where the work load in increased by hospital work, etc.). The rates are monitored by regional and national consultative bodies consisting of physicians and the social insurance institutions. The medical profession is to bar from the agreement any doctors who charge higher fees than those agreed. It is estimated that ninety-five per cent of all doctors are covered by this agreement. In exchange for their participation physicians receive a contribution from the sickness funds towards the cost of their sickness and old age insurance. For dentists the number of departments with conventions is extremely small.

As a consequence of the conventions the physician is paid by performance. The conventional case against payment by performance is that piece-rates provide a direct link between the level of health consumption and the level of the individual doctor's remuneration. Each 'piece' increases the doctor's pay and if he is bent on income maximisation the effect on the overall cost of the health service can be unfortunate as prescribing analyses, medicines, hospitalisations, etc. increases income but may be medically 'unnecessary'. The French are well aware of these drawbacks and recognise that there may well be a clash between the desire for economy and the desire of the doctors for 'freedom'. It is possible that capitation payments may be introduced.

The total number of doctors in France in 1972 (1969) was 68,778 (62,300). Some 49,825 (45,000) of these were treating private patients during at least part of their working year. This large stock of doctors (1.335 per 1,000 population) is being augmented by an increased supply. Table 19 gives some data on medical school intake and output in the 1960s.

Table 19   *The Flow of Medical Students*

	1961	1966	1967	1968	1969
Total Number	32,600	45,000	48,000	55,000	70,800
1st Year	8,000	13,000	14,000	19,250	26,000
Graduates	2,376	2,561	2,717	3,034	

Source: *La Ministère de la Santé Publique et de la Sécurité Sociale*,
        p. 36.

The conditions regulating the dental and midwifery professions are very similar to those affecting the medical profession. Dentists are trained in schools attached to Medical Faculties and spend five years

learning their skills. Midwives are produced after three years training
and acquire a State diploma. Both categories have programmes which
are aimed at increasing the flow of practitioners. In 1972 there were
21,914[15] dental surgeons, i.e. 0.426 per 1,000 population. The much
respected midwife [16] is a member of a profession whose size in 1972
was 9,132, i.e. 0.177 per thousand population. Table 20 shows an
increased flow of students but the output of graduates may not be so
significant due to the high failure rate.

Table 20   *The Flow of Dental and Midwifery Students*

	1965	1967
Dentists		
Students	5,802	7,000
Graduates	732	910
Midwifery		
Students	930	1,173
Graduates	308	308

Source: *Op. cit.* page 40.

The paramedical professions[17] are expanding rapidly from substantial
bases. The total number of nurses in France in 1972 was 162,703. Of
these 104,248 (sixty-four per cent) held State Diplomas (twenty-four
months study), 22,810 (fourteen per cent) were auxiliaries and 35,645
(21.8 per cent) were trained (for twenty-eight months) psychiatric
nurses. There were 2.025 trained non-psychiatric nurses per thousand
population. The total number of physiotherapists (three years training
for a State Diploma) in 1972 was 23,112, or 0.449 per thousand
population. There were 5,886 chiropodists (two years training for a
State Diploma) in 1972, i.e. 0.114 per thousand population.

Table 21   *The Flow of Paramedical Students*

Number of Schools		1965	1966	1967	1968	1969
i)	Nurses	227	233	251	261	263
ii)	Physitherapists	27	30	51	32	32
iii)	Chiropodists	7	7	9	9	9
Number of Students						
i)	Nurses	21,176	23,176	24,022	25,793	25,644
ii)	Physiotherapists	4,496	5,899	5,836	6,097	5,733
iii)	Chiropodists	477	614	770	876	1,051
Number of Diplomas Issued						
i)	Nurses	7,037	7,814	9,915	11,119	11,273
ii)	Physiotherapists	1,302	1,551	1,778	1,927	2,374
iii)	Chiropodists	240	245	435	435	447

Source: *Op. cit.* page 41.

The flow of paramedical positions for the professions is given in Table 21. All exhibit rapid expansion during the late 1960s in terms of graduates or numbers of diplomas issued. However the authorities are having difficulty, particularly with respect to training nurses, in filling their training places in professions whose 'image' and relative wage is seen to be poor.

(b)   The Hospitals

The organisation and finance of the French system of hospitals is complex. Table 22 gives details of the number of beds in particular specialisms for the private and public sectors in 1972.

Table 22   *Hospital Bed Provision 1972 (as at 1st January 1972)*

	Public Hospitals	Assimilated Private units*	Private clinics	Total beds per 1000 pop.
Non-specialised units				
Medicine, surgery and maternity	210,500	-	100,300	310,800 (6.05)
Rest cure, convalescence and chronic ill	21,300	-	20,100	41,400 (0.80)
Sub-Total	231,800	-	120,400	352,200 (6.86)
Specialised units				
Psychiatry	87,000	21,300	10,200	118,900 (2.31)
Cancer Units	-	3,800	-	3,800 (0.07)
Tuberculosis	12,400	13,000	21,300	46,700 (0.91)
Functional Readaption	2,600	-	9,300	11,900 (0.23)
Sub-Total	102,400	38,100	40,800	181,300 (3.53)
Overall Total	334,200	38,100	161,200	533,500(10.39)

Source: *La Revue Française Des Affaires Sociale* (1973).
* Private establishments operating as public hospitals or assimilated with public hospitals.

Of the 533,500 beds avaialbe in 1972 (10.39 beds per thousand population), thirty per cent were owned by private establishments. The importance of the private provision varied from sector to sector. Of the total number of medical, surgical and maternity beds thrity-two per cent were privately owned. However, private participation in the provision of psychiatric beds was small: 8.5 per cent. Private units provided 48.8 per cent and 45.6 per cent respectively of the beds available for the categories cure, convalescence, chronic illness and tuberculosis. If assimilated private units are included in the latter category public provision was a mere 26.5 per cent of the total.
    It is important to distinguish between two types of private hospital.

The first type are non-profit making and represent some twenty-seven per cent of private units. The second type of private hospital is the profit-making establishment. These are owned by individuals (e.g. groups of physicians) or, more often, companies. The latter control over seventy-seven per cent of short-stay private beds and tend to be located in the more affluent areas of France, i.e. Paris and Provence Cote d'Azur. The non-profit making hospitals tend to be concentrated in Nord, Lorraine and Alsace and have an average size of about a hundred beds, twice that of profit making hospitals.

Since the Revolution public hospitals have been associated with the local authorities, usually the *commune*. Of the 902 general public hospital units in 1972 twenty eight were *centres hospitaliers regionaux,* (CHRs with an average size of 3189 beds), ninety-nine were *centres hospitaliers* (CHs with an average size of 633 beds), 404 were hospitals (with an average size of 175 beds) and 371 were rural hospitals (with an average size of 31 beds). The rural hospital has a medical and maternity department. The hospital has a general surgical, general medical, maternity, radiology, paediatrics, laboratory and out-patient facilities. The CH has those units possessed by the hospital plus ENT facilities, a larger paediatrics unit and facilities for the care of the chronic ill and those in need of rehabilitation. The CHR has even more specialised facilities.

Table 23   *Average length of Stay by Categories, Public Sector Beds 1961-71 (in days)*

Category	1961	1968	1969	1970	1971*
Medicine	28.0	22.4	21.1	20.2	18.8
Surgery	15.7	13.6	13.2	12.7	12.3
Maternity	9.2	8.0	8.0	7.9	7.9
Specialities	13.4	11.8	11.1	10.6	10.2
Total	21.4	18.7	18.0	17.3	15.7

Source: *Ministère des Affaires Sociale* (1973) page 252.
    *   Provisional data.

Table 23 shows average length of stay data for French public hospitals in the period 1961-71. If we discount the 1971 because it is provisional we can see that the average total length of stay fell from 21.4 days to 17.3 days, i.e. by nineteen per cent in the period 1961-70. The most significant reduction in the average length of stay was in the category 'medicine' where there was a fall of twenty-eight per cent to 20.2 days.

As can be seen hospital treatment is not the monopoly of the public hospital – the private sector accounts for a third of the total bed capacity. The partnership has given rise to numerous problems (coordination of the two sectors, disparities in the rates charged for treatment and accommodation in hospitals) which recent legislation, it is hoped, will mitigate. The Hospital Reform Law of 31st December 1970 made considerable changes in the existing organisation by setting up a public hospital service with the participation of certain private establishments. The legislation appears to have three main aims: to create a national public hospital structure; to establish rules to govern the coordination of the activities of the private and public hospital sectors; and to reform the management of the public hospitals.

These aims are to be met by creating a public hospital service provided by local authority hospitals and by private establishments which meet certain strictly defined criteria. A health map for France, showing all facilities and their utilisation rates, is to be used to establish a pattern of health 'needs'. Approval will be given only to those projects that correspond to the needs revealed by this health map exercise. Private hospitals are to be more carefully regulated. New rules are to be devised regarding permission for the opening of private establishments and for their participation in the public hospital service. Authorisation to open will be granted only if the establishment meets the health 'needs' of the area and complies with regulations affecting its operation, e.g. the qualifications of staff employed. Private hospitals that are permitted to open and those already open can participate in the public hospital service in three ways. Non-profit making establishments can take part in public hospital activities quite freely and will receive the same advantages as public hospitals (subsidies, medical, personnel, etc). Other private hospitals may acquire permission to perform as a public service hospital. However, they cannot receive equipment subsidies and the only public aid which is offered is that if they operate in a public capacity no competing public or private establishments will be opened in their area. Finally those private units which already have concluded agreements with the funds can make agreements of association with the public hospital service which permits them to use the joint services of the public sector. Two final points are noteworthy about the 1970 reform. Firstly an attempt is to be made to bring the prices per day of public and private hospitals into line. Secondly the board of governors of public hospitals is to be replaced by an administrative council with precisely defined functions. Now public hospitals units are financed jointly by Central Government (forty per cent) and the social insurance institutions (thirty per cent) and the local authorities (thirty per cent).

This recent legislation completes the transformation of the role of public hospitals. It was only in 1941 that these institutions ceased to be for the poor and needy only and were opened to all the population.

The 1970 legislation, if successful, will provide a comprehensive system for diagnosis and treatment. However, it leaves the actual organisation of the individual public hospital unaltered. Public hospitals have the legal status of corporate bodies and are financially autonomous. They are attached to the local authorities and on the financial side they are operated in such a way as to maintain a balance of income (from charges per day) and expenditure, without profit. Operating expenditure includes a depreciation item but there appears to be no built-in method of generating funds for expansion. The 1970 reform permits open market borrowing in some circumstances. Otherwise the public hospitals which wish to expand)or where there is a demand for new public hospitals) must be dependent on public subsidies.

So far no mention has been made of the psychiatric and tuberculosis hospitals. The provision of psychiatric hospitals takes many forms. There are autonomous psyciatric hospitals governed by the Decrees of 1948 and 1961. There are *département* psychiatric hospitals (about seventy-nine) administered by the *Département* to which they belong. In the *départements* with no psyciatric hospitals (about fifteen) private psychiatric hospitals (twenty-five in all) are sanctioned by the *Département* to discharge the functions of a public establishment. Lastly, there are psychiatric wards in general hospitals. In all there were 132 psychiatric hospitals (including general hospitals with psychiatric wards) in January 1972 with a bed capacity of 107,832. This represents a large increase in capacity over 1953 (77,200) but a decrease compared with 1964 (121,500) (see Table 24). In the early 1970s the bed capacity of psychiatric units was falling by about 3,500 per year. Public policy now demands the integration of psychiatric hospitals and general hospital units. (Aurousseau [1973] page 6)

Table 24   *Psychiatric Bed Provision*

Type of Establishment	Beds as at 31.12.1964	Beds as at 1.1.1968	Beds as at 1.1.1972
Public psychiatric hospitals	86,300	75,800	74,886
Private psychiatric hospitals performing public duties	23,800	30,100	21,694
Psychiatric wards in general hospitals	11,400	8,600	11,252
TOTAL	121,500	114,500	107,832

Source: *Ministère de la Santé Publique et de la Sécurité Sociale* (1971) page 68 and *Santé et Sécurité Sociale* (1973) page 341.

141

Table 25   *Tuberculosis Bed Provision*

Category	31st December 1965 Nos. of Estabs.	31st December 1965 Nos. of Beds	1st January 1968 Nos. of Estabs.	1st January 1968 Nos. of Beds	1st Jan. 1972 Nos. of Beds
Sanatoriums	209	34,351	201	34,172	27,018
Preventoriums	104	13,359	97	12,187	6,764
Aeriums	155	13,695	143	13,444	8,917
After Care	51	3,570	42	3,460	3,272
Residential Clinics	47	1,271	40	1,044	705
TOTAL	566	66,246	523	64,907	46,676

Source: *Ministère de la Santé Publique et de la Sécurité Sociale* (1971)
page 69 and *Santé et Sécurité Sociale* (1973) page 351.

(c)   Regional Inequalities

It is apparent from the dicussion of hospital planning (see above) and
the use of the 'health map' that the French authorities recognise as one
of their priorities the reduction in the geographical inequalities in the
provision of medical care. This magnitude of the problem is indicated
in Table 26, which shows the distribution of nurses, physicians and
hospital beds in 1968. The variation in the number of physicians
(both general practitioners and specialists) is quite large — from a low
of eighty-three per 100,000 people in the Pays de la Loire to 197 per
100,000 people in the Paris region; a variation of 137 per cent). For
nurses the low is 132 per 100,000 people in Lorraine to 317 per
100,000 in the Rhône-Alps region; a variation of 140 per cent. Bed
provision per 100,000 population was lowest in the Nord region (415)
and highest in the Alsace region (875); a variation of 110 per cent. As
in many countries the area surrounding the national capital does
relatively well on most provision indicators. The 'health map' exercise
of the French government has severe inequalities to ameliorate.

Table 26   *The Distribution of Medical Care Inputs 1968 (per 100,000
population)*

Région	Physicians	Nurses	Beds
Région Parisienne	197	286	686
Champagne — Ardenne	92	157	631
Picardie	99	239	450
Haute-Normandie	90	133	540

Table 26 *(Cont)*

Centre	100	155	530
Basse-Normandie	119	185	593
Bourgogne	113	147	576
Nord	85	140	415
Lorraine	98	132	605
Alsace	94	203	875
Franche-Compte	110	176	460
Pays de la Loire	83	180	479
Bretagne	94	203	504
Poitou-Charentes	137	141	442
Acquitaine	133	155	506
Midi-Pyrenees	99	205	531
Limousin	96	152	486
Rhône-Alps	112	317	650
Au vergue	93	204	565
Languedoc-Roussillon	169	185	650
Provence – Cote d'Azur	122	297	675
All France	128	214	580

Source: *Ministère de la Santé Publique et de la Sécurité Sociale* (1973) *op. cit.* No. 3 Mai-Juin pages 44-7.

8 Conclusions

Of the two main health care problems in France – those of rising expenditure and regional inequalities – the former is the most formidable. The absolute and relative sizes, and the rates of growth of hospital accommodation and drugs are the two most obvious symptoms of this malaise. No doubt the high expenditure on drugs is helped by the differential *ticket modérateur* on 'general' and irreplaceable drugs – the latter have a hundred per cent *ticket* and doctors apparently prescribe more expensive drugs to reduce the outlays of their patients. These problems are being exacerbated by political pressures. At present the degree of direct patient participation in the cost of medical care (via the *ticket modérateur*) is the largest in Europe. This position is being criticised by the French political left whose aim is to achieve one hundred per cent refunds. Despite the *ticket* and the dynamic earnings ceiling associated with the contribution system the French are predicting vast deficits in 1975.

Basically the French seem to be reluctant to move towards a

financing system which significantly redistributes the cost of medical care. Contributions to the sickness schemes, in the general scheme in particular, are heavily weighted towards the employer and to increase their role further may bring with it industrial price-increases which would be very unwelcome politically. It is possible that increased employee contributions would have the same effect. It is quite probable that the *ticket* has suppressed demand and if this is removed, increased demand could further worsen the health cost spiral. However, the removal of the *ticket* could make the system more redistributive, especially if employee contributions were raised and the ceiling removed. The choice is a nice one. If the system is made more equitable medical care resources will be subjected to greater demand pressure. If the system remains as it is it would become insolvent. It seems almost inevitable that the role of State finance will increase during the 1970s and beyond.[18]

The degree of central government planning of provision is, as yet, limited. A start has been made with the 'health map' exercise for hospital bed provision. The recognition of inequalities in bed provision and many other areas of provision may lead to more careful regulation of the geographical distribution of resources.

The French health care system is expensive and its cost is escalating rapidly. Like all other countries in Western Europe, the French people face the prospect of having to make difficult decisions about the findamental characteristics of the finance and provision of health care.

NOTES

1. See Commission of the European Communities (1973) page 15. Note the text (p 15) is different to the data in Table 1 (p 11) with respect to this item.
2. This tripartite structure of French Social security is not involved with the provision of unemployment insurance. This type of insurance is operated through communal or departmental agencies for unemployed workers, and a supplementary unemployment insurance scheme, dating from 1958, which organises cover on an occupational basis in industry and commerce.
3. The name of the Ministry responsible for health tends to change with political administration. The Ministry of Health and Social Security used to be called the Ministry of Social Affairs a few years ago, and prior to that it was the Ministry of Labour and Health.
4. R. van den Heuvel (1972).
5. Caisse Nationale D'Assurance Maladie et Maternité des Travailleurs non Salaires des Professions Non Agricoles (CANAM) (1973).
6. See A.J. and M.H. Cooper (1972).
7. When comparing this data with earlier data (e.g. Table 6) note that invalidity expenditures are omitted and the data refers to the general scheme

only.

8. Santé et Sécurité Sociale (1973) *op. cit.* p 500.
9. I.e. in addition to medical care, sickness, benefit, maternity and death benefit.
10. I.E. both components of the Agricultural Scheme.
11. For membership see Table 3 which shows membership by groups which are the same as those in Table 14.
12. I.e. certified as necessary by the general practitioner or hospital specialist.
13. The relative importance of benefits with and without the *ticket modérateur* can be deduced from Table 9 above.
14. See G. Spitaels *et al* (1971) p 604.
15. See *Bulletin de Statistiques* (1973), *op. cit.* Mars-Avril, p 7.
16. This social respect for the role of the *sage-femme* (midwife) is shown in the fact that recruitment to the midwife profession is easy compared with the 'less illustrious' job of a nurse where there is a reluctance on the part of young men and women to enter training.
17. As for note 15 and *Bulletin de Statistiques* (1973) *op. cit.* Jan-Fev p 4.
18. Aurousseau (1973) p 15 says that an increased role of the State in the finance of health care is currently rumoured. Indeed he argues that nationalisation may be imminent.

References

Aurousseau, M. (1973). Paper presented to the Kings Fund Health Centre Seminar, London, November.
Caisse Nationale D'Assurance Maladie et Maternité des Travailleurs Non Salaires des Professions Non Agricoles (CANAM) (1971 and 1973 various) *Rapport Annuel (1971 and 1972) du Directeur* (two volumes) *Statistiques* 1970, 1971 and 1972 (three volumes), Paris.
Centre de Recherches et de Documentation sur la Consommation, (various 1970-71) *Evaluation de la Consommation Medicale en 1969 et L'Evolution de la Consommation Medicale 1966, 1967 et 1969*, Paris.
European Communities Commission (1973), *Comparative Tables of Social Security Systems in the Member States of the European Communities*, Seventh Edition, Luxembourg.
La Revue Française Des Affaires Sociales (1973), L'Hospitalisation publique en France, Paris.
Ministère d'Etat Chargé des Affaires Sociale et Ministère de la Santé Publique (1972 and 1973), *Santé et Sécurité Sociale – Tableaux*, 1971 Edition, Paris.
Ministère de la Santé Publique et de la Sécurité Sociale (1971), *La Protection Sanitaire et Sociale in France*, La Documentation Francaise, Paris.
Ministère de la Santé Publique et de la Sécurité Sociale (1972 and 1973 various) *Bulletin de Statistiques*, 1972 No 6, 1973 Nos 1-5, Paris.
Spitaels, G., Klaric D., Lambert, S., and Lefevre, G., (Spitaels *et al*) (1971) *Le Salaire Indirect et la Couverture des Besoins Sociaux*, Vol III, Brussels.
US Department of Health, Education and Welfare (various), *Social Security Programs Throughout the World*, Washington.
Van den Heuvel, R. (1972), *Report on Health Care Organisation and Insurance in Continental Europe*. Paper presented to the Conference of the International Federation of Voluntary Health Service Funds, September, London.

6 LUXEMBOURG

The Evolution of Health Care in Luxembourg

Luxembourg is a small country in terms of geographical area and population size. The 350,000 people of Luxembourg are served, as far as health care is concerned, by a system of sickness funds whose activities have been regulated by legislation since 1901. The extension of the coverage of the funds to all wage earners was completed in two stages in 1925 and 1954. Salaried employees were brought within the system of compulsory coverage in 1951.

One of the greater difficulties facing any analyst of the Luxembourg health care system is a lack of comprehensive information. Whilst it is relatively easy to acquire information concerning the provision of hospital beds and physicians, it is relatively difficult to get a comprehensive and modern statement of the affairs of the sickness funds.[1] This problem is recognised by the institutions concerned as in 1973 a common data centre was set up to service all insurance institutions. The establishment of this centre has been accompanied by the creation of a general inspectorate for social security. The account of Luxembourg health care system below is short because of the size of the country. The lack of data, comparable in its modernity with that given in other chapters, is regretable but unavoidable.

1.   Administration

The Ministry of Labour and Social Security is concerned with the general supervision of the finance and provision of health care in Luxembourg. The institutional vehicle which delivers health care is the system of sickness funds. There are eleven sickness funds in Luxembourg which provide compulsory health care insurance, and they can be divided into four groups. The insurance of blue collar employees is governed by the legislation of 1961 and is provided by three funds: the regional funds of Diekirch, Greuenmacher and Luxembourg which, since 1969, have constituted the Workmans' National Insurance Fund, and two contract sickness funds[2], one for ARBED (Steel Industry) workmen and one for the workmen of the Societe Miniere et Metallurgique de Rodange. The group of funds have formed a joint association — the Sickness Fund Union — in order to further their

146

objectives. The second group of funds is those with responsibilities concerned with the health care insurance of civil servants and white collar employees, and their activity is governed by 1951 legislation. In this group there are funds which cover civil servants, local authority employees and private employees. Also there are the contract funds for ARBED employees, and the employees of the Luxembourg railway system and the Societe Miniere et Metallurgique de Rodange. Like the first group the members of this group have joint forces to form one association to further their ends: the Association of Civil Servants and Employee Funds. The last two groups of funds have one member each. The self-employed are covered by a fund established as a result of legislation in 1957. The farmers are covered by a fund established in 1962. The funds which cover wage earners[3] are governed by management boards consisting of representatives of the employees and the work force. In the contract funds the chairman is appointed by the employer and the vice-chairman is elected by the work force.

There is a complex system of procedures to deal with any disputes which arise. Any disputes between the funds are settled in the first instance by the Minister. Any ministerial decision can be appealed against and the case is then judged by the Council of State. Disputes Committee whose decision is usually implemented. Conflicts between the funds and their members are dealt with by the Social Insurance Arbitration Council whose decisions can be revoked by the Social Insurance Council on appeal. The decision of the latter two bodies can be reversed by the Luxembourg Supreme Court. Relations between the funds and suppliers of medical care are governed by collective agreements. If such agreements cannot be concluded the Commission for Conciliation and Arbitration has powers to attempt to get a reconciliation between the two sides. If reconciliation is impossible the Commission can file a report which states a solution to the argument. This solution, after approval by the Minister, can be implemented.

The four groups of funds which provide compulsory health care insurance for active (working) insured people, for those in receipt of a pension or an annuity, and for dependents, are augmented by a complementary voluntary insurance system which operates through a variety of bodies. Perhaps the most important of these bodies is the system of mutual aid funds. In the late 1960s there were sixty such funds with 110,000 members. The principal benefits to the insured and their dependents were financial aid in the cases of death and long-stay hospitalisation. The Mutual Surgical Fund of Luxembourg provides benefits to its members which meet the costs of surgery and stays in clinics both in Luxembourg and abroad. This fund is attached to the Mutual Dental Fund which provides financial assistance to those members needing to meet dental care expenses.

2.   Coverage

All active workers, all those in receipt of a pension or an annuity, and all dependents of insured members are covered by compulsory health care insurance. In 1970 these groups amounted to 98.9 per cent of the population; a growth of 13.8 per cent points since 1962.[4] By the late 1960s over 170,000 of contributing members were in funds for active workers. The most important of these was the Workmans' National Insurance Fund which had over thirty-six per cent of total contributing members within its ranks. The next most important groups were the Workers' Contract Funds (about nineteen per cent), the Employees Contract Funds (about nine per cent) and the other Employee Funds (about twenty-one per cent). The rest of the contributing members were divided almost equally between the self-employed's Fund and the Agricultural Fund. Those in receipt of pensions usually remain members of the funds which they joined during their working life. Their contributions are paid by the fund responsible for the payment of pensions and pensioners.

3.   Qualifying Conditions

If a worker is a fund member there is, in principle, no period of work or membership required before a member can claim benefits for himself, or his co-insured dependents. The duration of benefits in kind is unlimited except for hospitalisation where a maximum of twenty-six weeks care is provided. Cash benefits are paid for a period of twenty-six weeks after three waiting days of the worker is incapable of work. The funds may require six months of membership before they pay benefits in excess of the statutory minimum of fifty per cent of earnings. Maternity benefits are provided so long as a minimum period of fund membership has been fulfilled. This minimum is ten months during the preceding twenty-four months, of which six months have to have been during the year preceding the confinement.

4.   Finance

The contribution rate of blue collar (manual) wage earners in industry and commerce is up to 4.5 per cent of earnings up to an annual ceiling (end 1972) of LF 292,000 (£3173) or LF 800 (£8.6) per calendar day. The employer pays up to 2.25 per cent of earnings making an overall contribution total of up to 6.75 per cent of earnings up to the ceiling. Special rates and ceilings apply to salary earning (white collar) staff. In this category the total contribution is 3.9 per cent, consisting of an employer contribution of 1.3 per cent of earnings and an employee contribution of 2.6 per cent of earnings up to a ceiling of LF 292,000. One reason why the (white collar) contribution rates are lower for non-manual workers is that the employer meets the cost of cash sickness benefits for the first three months of illness. This reduces the expenditure on this item by white collar funds and hence their contributions. Pensioners pay 2.6 per cent of their pensions and their pension institutions contribute a further 1.3 per cent of the pension to give an overall pensioner contribution rate of 3.9 per cent. One aspect of these financial arrangements merit some comment. Luxembourg is unusual in that the employee or wage earner contribution rates exceed those of the employer. The usual employee-employer contribution ratio is two to one.

5. Income and Expenditure

Table 1 *Income and Expenditure 1967*

	a	b	c	d	e	Total
Income						
Contributions	333.918	254.006	169.327	77.972	66.964	902.189
State Intervention*	14,999	0	5.631	0	25.331	45.961
Other	16,013	9.370	2.649	8.807	1.319	38.158
Total	364.930	263.376	177.609	86.779	93.614	986.308
Expenditure						
Physicians' fees	73.358	63.375	44.028	23.895	26.367	231.023
Pharmaceutical expenses	82.120	73.451	53.342	29.704	33.918	272.353
Cash Incapacity benefit	74.772	73.450	1.229	880	0	150.331
Hospital (hotel) expenses	32.430	20.007	21.287	11.066	13.887	98.677
'Curative and therapeutic treatment'	26.107	15.864	27.345	11.493	13.848	94.657
Other	77.447	23.021	40.630	14.025	21.083	176.926
Total	366.234	269.168	187.861	91.063	109.823	1023.967

Key: a = Workmens' National Insurance Fund
b = Wage Earners Contract Funds
c = Sickness Fund of Employees
d = Employees Contract Funds
e = Others, i.e. Sickness Funds of the Independent Professions and Agricultural Sickness Fund

Source: *Health Services Financing*, (1971) p 438.

* Administrative aid plus the direct subsidy to the Agricultural Sickness Fund of 49.6 per cent of its total income.

Income and expenditure data for the health services of the Grand
Duchy of Luxembourg is limited. The most recent comprehensive data
available at the time of writing is that in Ahlboun's appendix to the
British Medical Association (1971) publication.

Table 2 *Income and Expenditure 1967 (percentage terms)*

	a	b	c	d	e	f
Income						
Contributions	91.50	96.45	95.33	89.85	71.53	91.47
State Intervention	4.11	0.00	3.17	0.00	27.05	4.65
Other	4.38	3.55	1.49	10.14[1]	1.40	3.86
Total	100.00	100.00	100.00	100.00	100.00	100.00
Expenditure						
Physicians' fees	20.03	23.54	23.43	26.24	24.00	22.56
Pharmaceutical expenses	22.42	27.28	28.39	32.61	30.88	26.59
Cash sickness benefits	20.41	27.28	0.65	0.96	0.00	14.68
Hospital (hotel) expenses	8.85	7.43	11.33	12.15	12.64	9.63
Curative and therapeutic treatment	7.12	5.89	14.55	12.62	12.60	9.24
Other	21.14	8.55	21.62	15.40	19.85	17.27
Total	100.00	100.00	100.00	100.00	100.00	100.00

Key: a = Workmens' National Insurance Fund
      b = Wage Earners Contract Funds
      c = Sickness Fund of Employees
      d = Employees Contract Funds
      e = Others. Employer subsidies are the main source of this item.
      f = Overall Average.

Source: *British Medical Association* (1971) p 438.

The involvement of the State in Luxembourg health care is relatively
small. Tables 1 and 2 show the absolute and relative contributions of

150

the State. The State contribution, LF 45,461 million (£0.494m) represented 4.65 per cent of total income. This contribution was made up of four component parts. The Grand Duchy contributes a subsidy equal, in the year under consideration, to twenty-seven per cent of the income of the Agricultural Sickness Fund. The State meets fifteen per cent of the cost of medical care for those in receipt of pensions and annuities. These resources are paid over to the funds *via* the fund which administers old age pensions. The third source of State support for the activities of the funds is that it meets fifty per cent of their administrative costs. The exceptions to this subsidy are the contract funds operated by the employers. These bear all their own administrative costs. The final subsidy takes the form of meeting two thirds of the pay and pensions costs of the physicians and one hundred per cent of the cost of auxiliary staff employed in the medical department of the Workmens' Sickness Insurance Fund.

Over ninety-one per cent of the total income of the funds was derived from contribution income. The manner in which this income was spent is shown in absolute and relative terms in Tables 1 and 2. Total expenditure of the funds was LF 1,023.967 million (£11.010m) and exceeded income by LF 37.59 million (£0.408m). The largest single expenditure category was the result of the purchase of pharmaceutical products (26.54 per cent). The next two largest items were physicians' fees (22.56 per cent) and cash sickness benefit (14.68 per cent). The relative importance of hospital expenses is low (9.63 per cent) for two reasons. Firstly the item is concerned with hotel (or accommodation) costs only, i.e. the cost of using drugs and the services of physicians is included under those items. The other reason is that not all the cost of hospitalisation is reimbursed by the funds and the cost is met by the funds only for the first twenty-six weeks of treatment in a hospital.

6.   Benefits

Throughout the discussion of benefits in this section it is to be remembered that the sickness funds differ from each other both in size of contributions[5] and in the amount of benefits they give. It is impossible to go into the minutiae of each scheme so the discussion of benefits will be in general terms.

(a)   Medical Care

Physicians' services may be provided by all those doctors who are approved by the Grand Duchy. Their fees are regulated by collective agreements following, if necessary, arbitration by the Commission for Conciliation and Arbitration. The outcome of arbitration, once approved by the Ministry determines the fee level for the following year, subject to any relevant change in the cost of living index to which the fees are related. The patient is free to seek treatment from the physician of his choice who is registered in the locality. The insured person pays the fees directly to the physician and is refunded by his insurance organisation. The size of the refund varies from one fund to another. Only in the case of industrial staff is the refund one hundred per cent.

The patient is also free to choose whichever hospital he prefers. Hospitalisation is completely free for those insured by the industrial staff sickness funds. However the other funds do not provide free treatment coverage and some refunds exclude dependents from eligibility for these benefits. Even in those cases where treatment is free the duration of the benefit is only twenty-six weeks. The fees charged by the hospitals are determined by negotiations between association of hospitals and the sickness funds.

Dental treatment is divided into two categories. Standard benefits – preservative treatment, extractions, etc. – may be eligible for refunds according to an official scale provided the fund's constitution provides for such refunds. The costs of supplementary benefits – false teeth, plates, etc. – are met by the fund in accordance with various individual regulations.

There is an official scale of prices for pharmaceutical products and an official list of refundable patent medicines. The official price scale can be undercut by sickness funds for made-up preparations. The funds' share of the cost of pharmaceutical products must be at least seventy-five per cent.

Regulations vary for other benefits. Hospital treatment of tuberculosis in sanatoria is provided according to the same regulations as those which apply to hospital treatment. Spectacles, hearing aids and artificial limbs are provided subject to the prior approval of the sickness fund. For approved items the fund contributes an amount within limits fixed by its regulations.

(b) Cash Benefits

Cash sickness benefits for white collar workers and civil servants are paid by the employers for at least the first three months of illness. Short-term cash health benefits are paid to the blue collar (manual) insured person or, in the event of hospitalisation, to his dependents on proof of incapacity to work. The benefits are payable, after a three day waiting period, for twenty-six weeks, with the possible extension for benefits of a further thirteen weeks if it is probable that the insured person will be able to regain his ability to work in that period. The benefit level without hospitalisation is a minimum of fifty per cent of maximum earnings, defined as the earnings on which the social security contribution is assessed.[5] The actual level of benefit paid varies from fund to fund in the range of fifty-five per cent to seventy-five per cent of earnings. If the insured person is hospitalised and single an allowance of 17.5 per cent to twenty-five per cent of previous earnings is paid. The family of a hospitalised beneficiary receive a standard minimum of twenty-five per cent of previous earnings plus other benefits provided for in the regulations up to a statutory maximum of seventy-five per cent. This results in benefits in the range of fifty per cent to seventy per cent of earnings depending on the particular fund and the size of the family.

If the incapacity proves to be a long-term problem and if the insured fulfills the contribution requirements he may be eligible for an invalidity pension. This is paid in the case of any person who loses more than two thirds of his earning capacity provided the wage earner has contributed for five years and the salary earner has contributed for forty months (with an average of eight months per year). The annual invalidity pension level (1971) is LF 24,000 (£261) plus an increment equal to 1.6 per cent of life time insured earnings subject to a minimum constraint of LF 3120 (£34) per month of LF 4158 (£45) if the recipient was insured before the age of twenty-five and for two-thirds of the period thereafter up to sixty-five years of age. For each child aged less than sixteen years a supplement of 415 LF (£4.5) per month is paid.

Maternity benefits are payable to those members who have been contributors for the last two years. The funds provide finance for the maternity services of a midwife, or doctor if necessary plus a nursing allowance of LF 5 per day (some variations according to fund). Cash benefits to the mother are paid at the rate of seventy per cent of earnings up to the ceiling for six weeks before, and after the confinement.

7. Provision

(a) Medical Personnel

The setting of fees is the subject of negotiation between the funds and the medical professions. The changes in the numbers of people practising various medical skills in Luxembourg over the period 1960 to 1972 is shown in Table 3.

Table 3 *Medical Personnel*

	1960	1965	1967	1969	1970	1971	1972	No per 1000 pop
Physicians	318	338	349	365	384	397	403	1.15

153

Table 3 *(Cont)*

	1960	1965	1967	1969	1970	1971	1972	No. per 1000 pop.
Dentists	117	117	114	118	117	120	121	0.34
Pharmacists	171	173	172	172	181	179	183	0.52
Midwives	63	53	96	100	98	93	91	0.26
Nurses	-	-	-	790	-	-	-	2.32

All data refers to number per 1000 population in 1972 except for nurses (1969).

Source: *World Health Organisation* (1970,1971) and *La Direction de la Sante Publique* (1974) Table 4.1.3. and 4.1.4.

The stock of physicians increased by eight-five over the period 1960-72 to 403, i.e. an increase of over twenty-six per cent. The stocks of pharmacists and dentists were relatively static, increasing by twelve to 183 in the former profession, and by four to 121 in the latter. The number of midwives changed dramatically during the twelve-year period. The stock fell until 1965 when there were only fifty-three midwives in Luxembourg. Between 1965 and 1967 the stock increased to ninety-six and ended the period at ninety-one. The only data available about nurses is provided by the World Health Organisation.[6] This shows that there were 790 nurses in Luxembourg in 1969. The number of personnel per 1000 population is given in the final column of Table 3. The figures for physicians, dentists, pharmacists, midwives and nurses are 1.15, 0.34, 0.52, 0.26 and 2.32 respectively.

(b)   Hospital Provision
In 1972 there were thirty-four hospitals in Luxembourg and these establishments had 4,274 beds, i.e. 12.21 per 1000 population (see Table 4). The general hospitals sector had 2,078 beds in twenty units. The average size of general hospitals was 103.9 beds and there were 5.93 such beds per 1000 population. The two psychiatric units in Luxembourg had 1,330 beds, the majority of which were in one unit owned by the government. The majority of general hospital beds — fifty-three per cent — are situated in units owned by private bodies. Only one of these private units operates for profit. It is argued that the diverse ownership pattern hinders the establishment of a national hospital plan.[7]

Table 4 *Hospital Provision in Luxembourg*

	General Hospitals a	General Hospitals b	Tuberculosis a	Tuberculosis b	Psychiatric a	Psychiatric b	Other a	Other b	Total a	Total b
1960	19	1851	2	201	2	1175	18	502	41	3729
1965	20	1982	2	200	2	1372	15	572	39	4126
1967	20	1974	2	200	2	1420	12	660	36	4254
1969	20†	2021††	2	178	2	1383	11	724	35	4306
1970	20†	2067††	2	170	2	1343	11	709	35	4289
1971	20†	2065††	2	171	2	1304	10	706	34	4246
1972	20†††	2078††	2	156	2**	1330	10	710	34	4274

a = number of units; b = number of beds

Source: *La Direction de la Santé Publique* (1974) Table 4.1.

*	Includes convalescent homes, centres for cures, isolation hospitals, specialist maternity homes and geriatric clinics.
†	11 of these units had maternity facilities.
†††	10 of these units had maternity facilities.
**	Of which one is owned by the Government and one is a voluntary hospital. The latter has about a quarter of the total beds.
††	The number of maternity beds in these hospitals was 151 in 1969, 146 in 1970, 143 in 1971 and 134 in 1972.

Such a plan would be useful if the Luxembourg government wishes to pursue the objective of greater regional equality in the distribution of hospital beds, length of stay and utilisation. Regional inequality is of less importance in so small a state. Even so the Nord area is relatively underprovided with 5.78 general hospital beds per 1000 population in 1967, compared with a Luxembourg average of 6.30 beds. The average length of stay in 1967[8] was 14.1 days in general hospitals. This was identical to the 1953 figure. Regionally the average length of stay varied from 13.7 days in Centre, to 13.9 in Sud and 15.9 in Nord. Utilisation rates for general hospital units varied from 79.2 per cent in Nord, to 74.2 per cent in the Centre and 70.2 per cent in Sud. In specialised units the utilisation rate was eighty-one per cent.

8.   Conclusion

The intricacies of the Luxembourg system of health care are similar to those of some of the other nine members of the European Economic Community. The Luxembourg government is aware of the defects and has introduced draft legislation to reform the sickness insurance schemes for wage earners. When these proposals are implemented the period of coverage for cash sickness benefits and hospitalisation will be extended and the finances and management of the health care system will be reorganised.

NOTES

1. Evidence of the paucity of the data can be seen from EEC (1972). Appendix 5 of this report gives social security expenditure data. The most modern data given for Luxembourg is 1968.
2. Contract funds cover these workers or employees contracted (i.e. working for) particular industries.
3. Wage earners are blue collar and white collar employees.
4. See EEC (1972) p 302.
5. See Section (4) Finance above.
6. The World Health Organisation (1970, 1971).
7. Ministere de la Sante Publique (1973) December p 2.
8. 1967 is the latest available data available from the Luxembourg Ministry of Public Health.

References

British Medical Association (1971) *Health Services Financing*, Appendix K by H. Ahlboun, pp 431-8.
European Economic Community (1972, 1973 (a), 1974), *Report on the Development of the Social Situation in the Community in 1971, 1972 and 1973*, Brussels and Luxembourg.
European Economic Community (1973 (b)), *Comparative Tables of the Social Security System in the Member States of the European Communities: General System 1972*, Brussels.
Luxembourg Embassy (1973), *Social Services in the Grand Duchy of Luxembourg*, London.
Ministere de la Sante Publique de Grand Duche de Luxembourg (1969, 1970, 1972, 1973), *Bulletin d'information et d'action sanitaires*, Mai 1969, Janvier 1970, Juillet 1972, Mars, Aout et Decembre 1973.
US Department of Health, Education and Welfare (1970), *Social Security Programs Throughout the World 1971*, Washington.
World Health Organisation (1971, 1972, 1973), *World Health Statistics Annual 1967, 1968, 1969*, Geneva.

7 ITALY

The Evolution of Health Care in Italy

The Italian health care system is the heterogeneous product of social, political, religious and economic forces. Historically Italy has existed as a single entity for only a little over one hundred years. Durung this time her politicians have attempted, with some limited success in the period of rapid economic growth since the last war, to reduce the inequality between the relatively affluent North and the relatively poor South. The divergences between the levels of economic development in these two areas continue to be large and it is not without reason that, for instance, Naples is referred to as the 'Calcutta of Europe'. Many of the problems associated with this inequality are recognised by Italian politicians. However, by and large they have been unable to adopt radical palliatives due to the basic weaknesses of post-war governments. Most of the administrations since the war have been coalitions consisting of centre elements (e.g. Christian Democrats who have links with the Church) or centre-left elements (e.g. the Christian Democrats and the Socialists). Italy's second largest political party — the Communists — have not, as yet, been part of any post-war administration. These coalitions have been unable to carry out many far-reaching reforms because of the lack of support of members of one coalition group or another. Measures that are to be translated into law usually take two years to progress through the Italian Parliament.

This failure to reform can be seen clearly in the field of health care. Although post-war reform legislation has affected some areas of care (e.g. hospital provision and staffing) the finance of the system is carried out by institutions created in the early 1940s. The largest single financing agency — *Institute Nazionale per L'Assicuraxione contro le Malattie* (the National Sickness Insurance Institution — INAM) — was created in 1943 to finance and, in part, provide health care for agricultural, commercial and insurance workers in the private sector. Prior to the creation of INAM the health care arrangements of workers in these categories had been regulated by collective bargaining procedures in each of the sectors. Care for State employees (civil servants) prior to 1942 was regulated by the Umberto I. Institute which provided medical care for blue collar workers employed by the State, and the Insurance Institute for State, civilian and military personnel. Since 1942 ENPAS — *Ente Nazionale di Previdenza e Assitenza per i Dipendenti Statali*

(National Provident and Mutual Benefit Institution for State Employees) – has provided health care for both categories of workers. INAM, ENPAS and five other funds provide compulsory insurance coverage for eighty-nine per cent of the population. (Vetere [1973] page 4.) Another three per cent of the population are covered by about 200 other insurance funds, many of which are very small. These funds have differing contribution rates and the levels and scope of benefits vary.

Health care is provided by the funds (INAM employs physicians to provide general and specialist services in clinics owned by the fund), the varying levels of government (regional, provincial and municipal), and private institutions and private individuals. Some physicians are contracted to the funds but many operate as private practitioners, charging fees which are sometimes met wholly out of the private income of their clients, but usually refunded by the insurance institutions. Hospitals are owned by private bodies, many of which are religious, but some of which are partnerships, a high proportion of whose partners are physicians, and independent public institutions. The latter are governed by boards drawn from the regional, provincial and municipal governments and financed out of revenues from the insurance institutions, the consumers, and local government and central government.

This heterogeneous, if not slightly chaotic, system of financing and providing health care has been the subject of various recent reforms. Some of these have been successful in that legislation has been passed by Parliament (e.g. the 1968 Hospital Law). However a good deal of effort has been stillborn in that it has made little progress as yet. A good example of this was the 1973 Health Reform Bill which proposes to establish a National Health Service provided by local authorities and financed by a progressive income tax. This piece of legislation was to have been introduced into Parliament in mid-1974 subject to the support for it from transient political coalitions. This proposal was the product of substantial efforts by some civil servants and may be the basis of future attempts to reform the Italian health care system.

At present ninety-two per cent of the Italian population are compelled to be members of insurance institutions. This flow of health care finance is augmented by budget expenditures by central, regional and local government, and by private expenditures whose magnitude is difficult to assess. On the provision side medical care is provided by private and publicly owned institutions whose activities are often poorly coordinated. Many observers realise that the potential for economy by reorganisation of both finance and provision is substantial. But it is far from easy for the Italian body politic to carry out reforms which are contrary to the objectives of powerful pressure groups capable of precipitating the collapse of, often, all to delicate governments.

1. Administration

The Italian system of compulsory sickness insurance is, like many of her institutions, very complex in nature. Indeed some unkind observers might view its nature as chaotic rather than complex. The largest single fund is INAM which covers about fifty-three per cent of the Italian population. The next six largest funds, ENPAS, ENPDEDP, INADEL and three funds for the self-employed [1] provide insurance cover for another thirty-five per cent of the population. Another four per cent of the population are covered by approximately two hundred private funds which are run by local authorities, professional groups and private firms, e.g. there is a fund in the provinces of Blazano and Trento [2] and a fund for the entertainment industry.[3] Most of the funds provide medical care and sickness insurance although in the case of ENPAS the latter are not funded by contributions but paid as of right by the employer. Insurance against the risks of industrial accidents is the perogative of a special Institute which also deals with compensation for occupational diseases. Tuberculosis is insured by INPS[4] which provides old age pensions and invalidity pensions. The tuberculosis insurance is financed by an ear-marked contribution.

The structure of many of these institutions is typified by INAM, the single most important insurance agency. INAM is a public corporation which is regulated by the Treasury Ministry and the Ministries of Labour and Social Affairs, and Health. INAM's work is controlled by by a board of thirty-four members. These members are appointed by the President of the Republic on the basis of eleven trade union representatives, seven emplyers' representatives, two retired persons' representatives, two delegates from the staff of INAM, two physicians to represent the medical profession, seven officials of the Labour and Social Security, Treasury, Health, Interior, Agriculture and Forestry Industry and Trade Ministeries, the President of INAM and the Presidents of the two agencies which grant industrial accident compensation, incapacity pensions and old age pensions. Thirteen members are selected from this Board to constitute the Executive Committee which supervises the Institute's operations.

At the local level INAM's administration is in the hands of twenty-six provincial offices − one for each of the provincial capitals with the exception of the provinces of Trento and Bolzano, which have separate funds which are linked to INAM and give similar coverage. These offices administer the sickness insurance scheme, particpate in public health activities and collect contributions except in certain sections of industry and banking and insurance where the contributions are paid direct to INAM's head office.

Health care provision has been the subject of change in recent years as the Italians have taken the first tentative steps along the road to more formal planning of their facilities. During the period 1970-72 fifteen regions were created which, when added to the five post-war regional creations, made a total of twenty. These bodies have had power devolved to them from the Ministry of Health. The Regions have the power to create and implement laws provided these do not contravene the Constitution or the 'fundamental laws' of central government: the Hospital Law 1968 appears to be the only relevant fundamental law in health care to date although there is considerable debate about it. The problem inherent in this structure is that the Regions could attempt to create their own National Health Service with differing levels of contribution and provision. Such an outcome is not welcomed by some observers (e.g. Vetere [1974] page 1) who seem to prefer a movement towards greater national uniformity by the implementation of a National Health Service.

Of the twenty Regions, the oldest five have minor powers because as yet the devolutionary trend has not affected them. The fifteen new Regions have control over hospitals and medical care but no influence over the financing institutions (e.g. INAM) which are regulated by central government. The Regions have boundaries whose logic lies in history rather than present socio-economic efficiency. Consequently their population varies enormously: from 100,000 to eight million. They finance (but do not provide) from local taxation and central subsidies, preventative health care services (school medical service, vaccination, the training of auxiliary health personnel). They distribute central government funds to the local hospitals. Many other functions are devolved from regional to provincial and municipal government. There are ninety-four Provinces in Italy and all have little political power. Their main function is to ensure that the municipalities are able to provide health and welfare services. Their direct functions include the care of psychiatric patients, the management of public health laboratories, the care of illegitimate babies, and the care of the un- insured who suffer from TB. In many ways their role is duplicated by the municipalities which act together in consort, but it is not possible to eradicate them as such action requires a change in the constitution.

As far as the delivery of medical care is concerned an important tier of non-central government is the municipality. There are about 8,900 municipalities in Italy and they deliver preventative services (e.g. vacci- nation and school health services which are in part financed by the province). Also they provide clinics for municipal physicians (9,500) and midwives (3,000). The municipal physician is salaried (about

250,000 lire per month [£166]) to ensure that those registered as poor get some services from a physician.[5] Despite the fact that the municipal doctor can work for the school health service and the local public health authority[6] he is relatively poorly paid in comparison with his peers. The inevitable result is relative lack of such personnel.

Public hospitals are independent public agencies which are governed by boards made up of representatives of municipal, provincial and regional government in accordance with the proportional political representation of the parties in these assemblies. In the event of it being impossible to form a board, the Regional administration has the power to appoint a temporary commissioner to administer the hospital. The board's members are not salaried but receive a modest fee. Being politicians they are responsive to local pressures and are known to have increased employment in the hospitals for political reasons. The hospitals are divided into three categories (regional, provincial and municipal) according to the extent of the functions. The municipal hospitals, which can be quite large, are relatively limited in the scope of the care they provide. Provincial hospitals and regional hospitals are progressively more specialised.

Private hospitals are partnerships or owned by religious orders. The partnerships include physicians generally. The standard of provision is not regulated by the central government although plans are being formulated by which some of the staffing provision of the 1968 Hospital Act can be extended to cover private sector hospitalisation.

This complex network of institutions is regulated by an equally complex network of central government ministries. The single most important ministry is that of Health but important health care powers lie outside its jurisdiction. The Ministry of Health is responsible for general health care planning, for the distribution of funds for hospital equipment and junior hospital physician payment and for a myriad of other supervisory roles.[7] The Ministry of Public Works is responsible for the finance of new hospitals; in the South there is a special agency for this function. The Ministry of Labour regulates the activities of the Insurance Institutions (INAM, INPAS, etc.). Finally government subsidies for health care are the product of the interaction of this ministry and a dichotomised Financial Ministry; the Italian government is very unusual in that it has separate spending and financing ministries: the Treasury Ministry and the Ministry of Finance. The spread of health care functions amongst so many central government ministries exacerbates political strife[8] and ensures inefficiency. When viewed from abroad perhaps it is most surprising that the Italian system of health care works as well as it does!

Figure 1   *The Organisation of Italian Health Care 1974*

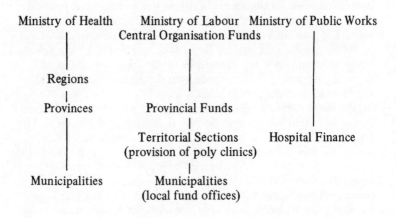

Figure 1 summarises this structure. The first column is concerned with provision. The Ministry of Health regulates decentralised provision whose level can vary because of history and because regions can extend provision autonomously provided they not infringe 'fundamental laws' (see above). The Ministry of Labour regulates the funds who channel their funds finance provision by regional and local government of private hospitals and private individuals (e.g. the physicians). Also the funds provide care *via* polyclinics at the 'territorial section' level, i.e. a geographical area larger than the municipality but smaller than the province. Finally the Ministry of Public Works controls the finance of new public hospital construction except in the South where there is a special agency.

The Health Reform Bill proposes to change this structure radically. Article 29 the Bill proposes to amalgamate all the insurance institutions and finance future health care from one fund financed by a proportional or progressive income tax which would be ear-marked for health care. The quantity and quality of all types of care would be standardised. The provision of health care would remain devolved on the regions. The central authorities would distribute the financial resources to the regions. The regional fund so created would be used to finance the delivery of health care by the local health units. The units would receive budgets from the regions which relate to their population and the level of benefit they are to provide. Each unit will have a population size between 50,000 and 200,000 usually[9] and its boundary will be conterminous with its constituent municipalities.

Figure 2 *The Future Organisation of Italian Health Care: a National Health Service*

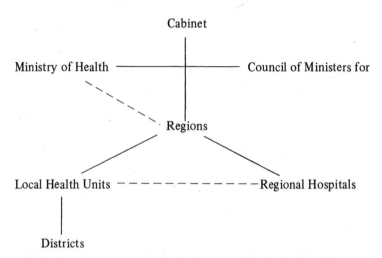

This organisation is summarised in Figure 2. The Ministry of Health's relationship with the regions will be indirect (dotted line) because the regions are political entities with direct links to the Cabinet. The Cabinet and the Council of Ministers for economic planning will decide how the funds will be allocated and what policies will be pursued after consultation with the Ministry of Health and the regions. The regions will provide regional hospital (large units with many specialities) but most provision will be by the local health units. This structure will bring finance and provision into one structure which, it is hoped, will lead to greater efficiency and uniformity. Whether this framework will be adopted depends on whether the central government is able to push through the relevant legislation. It is possible that if they fail some regions will act autonomously and implement their own versions of the national health service in 1975-6.

2. Coverage

Compulsory health care insurance covers over ninety per cent of the Italian population. The benefits derived from this coverage differ from one fund to another but, by and large, cover most medical care and some sickness insurance. Each sickness scheme has a particular clientele. For instance, INAM gives medical care coverage to the following groups: ministers of religion, people working in their own homes. orphans up to the age of eighteen years, apprentices, domestic staff, labourers and tenant farmers in the agricultural sector [10], blue and white collar staff in industrial, trading, banking and insurance sectors, old age pensioners, and the recipients of incapacity pensions (including those in receipt of annuities as a result of industrial accidents or occupational diseases) whose permanent incapacity is greater than eighty per cent. The dependents of the insured are also entitled to benefits in kind. The unemployed are not covered and have to have recourse to public assistance in time of need.[11]

Sickness insurance benefits are paid by INAM to all the categories listed above except for the following: tenant farmers in agriculture, white collar workers in industry, employees in the banking and insurance industries, domestic staff, orphans, apprentices and fishermen. Staff employees are exempted because by law employers are compelled to pay full salary to the sick worker for three months. In addition to this legal requirement some employers give benefits for a longer duration.

INAM's Maternity insurance scheme covers those sections of the community listed under medical care provision with the exception of the following categories: tenant farmers, staff employees in agriculture, domestic workers[12], persons who work in their own homes, orphans, apprentices and pensioners. The benefits are paid only to those workers who are in employment: dependents are not compulsorily insured for membership.

INAM and the other schemes covered nearly ninety-two per cent in 1971 although the extent of coverage in terms of benefits varies as is shown in Section 6 below. For instance, ENPAS appears to provide no sickness benefit but unlike INAM provides dental care benefits. However this statement is slightly misleading as the government pays sickness insurance benefits for at least three months to all civil servants. This benefit is not part of ENPAS and the insured person makes no contribution to its finance. These differences in the scope of schemes must be borne in mind when health care insurance coverage statistics are discussed. The benefits accruing to individual members of the compulsorily insured population can differ quite significantly.

Table 1 divides the compulsorily insured population into three major groups. The first group is insured workers, both wage earners and self-employed, whose numbers exceeded eighteen million (or thirty-three per cent of the population) in 1971. The number of pensioners with health care insurance was slightly in excess of seven

Table 1 *Health Care Insurance Coverage 1970 and 1971*

Category			1970	1971
I -	Insured workers			
	A)	Wage-earners	13,365,468	13,571,240
	B)	Independent workers		
	i)	self-employed ('direct farmers', artisans and traders	4,354,950	4,338,036
	ii)	liberal professions	150,515	150,669
	Total number of insured workers		17,870,933	18,059,945
II -	Insured pensioners			
	A)	Wage-earners	5,829,758	5,991,488
	B)	Independent workers		
	i)	self-employed (as above)	970,087	1,089,307
	ii)	liberal professions	8,777	8,945
	Total number of insured pensioners		6,808,622	7,089,740
III -	Qualifying dependents			
		of wage-earners	15,783,333	15,985,110
		of self-employed workers	5,709,208	5,667,196
		of persons registered with professional *albi*	144,382	146,785
		of pensioners who are ex-wage earners	2,436,451	2,503,707
		of pensioners who are ex-self employed	77,481	83,060
		of pensioners ex-liberal professions	11,483	11,542
		Total number of qualifying relatives	24,162,338	24,397,400
TOTAL QUALIFYING POPULATION			48,841,893	49,547,085

Source: *Relazione Generale sulla Situazione Economica Del Paese 1971* (1972) Appendici Tabella 12, p 490, Rome.

million (thirteen per cent of the population in 1971). The largest group is that of dependents: over twenty-four million (or forty-five per cent of the population in 1971). Total membership of all the funds in 1971 was equal to 91.92 per cent of the total population

Table 2 shows the coverage of the various categories of fund in 1971. It can be seen that INAM was by far the largest fund with 58.4 per cent of total membership and covering 53.7 per cent of the population. The three public sector schemes (ENPAS, ENPDEDP and INADEL) had a combined membership of over eight million people which represented 16.3 per cent of total membership in 1971 (fifteen per cent of the total population). The three self-employed's schemes had over eleven million members, i.e. 22.5 per cent of the total membership (20.7 per cent of the population). Taken together with INAM these six other

Table 2 *Coverage by Type of Funds 1971 (in thousands)*

Category and Administering Institution	Workers	Workers' Families	Pensioners	Pensioners Families	Total qualifying††
1. Wage earners					
General Scheme					
a) Workers in the private sector INAM	10,478	11,801	4,823	1,861	28,963
Special Schemes					
b) Public services* ENPAS	1,628	2,118	833	496	5,076
ENPDEDP	382	535	63	40	1,021
INADEL	764	996	173	69	2,002
c) seamen	81	230	- †	- †	311
d) other private sector funds	89	151	24	15	280
e) workers in Trento & Bolzano	147	151	74	22	395
2. Self-employed -					
farmers	1,315	2,572	898	21	4,806
artisans	1,500	1,900	139	55	3,595
traders	1,522	1,194	51	6	2,775
4. Liberal professions	150	146	8	11	317
TOTAL	18,095	21,779	7,089	2,598	49,547††

Source: *op. cit.* Tabella 14, p 492.

* ENPAS, ENPDEDP and INADEL and terms explained in Note 1 to this Chapter.
† These groups are covered by INAM.
†† Rows and columns may not sum to the final column total due to small rounding errors.

funds had 97.3 per cent of the total membership in 1971 (89.5 per cent of the population). Some of the other funds are very small, e.g. one liberal profession scheme, that of midwifery, had a total membership of 16,336 in 1971.

The number of people who are compulsorily insured, as a percentage of the population, has increased steadily during the last decade. For instance in 1960 INAM's membership was just over twenty-three million (23,747,764); in 1965 INAM's membership of over twenty-five million was equal to forty-seven per cent of the total population; and in 1971 INAM's membership was over twenty-four million, i.e. 53.7 per cent of the population. By 1971 ninety-two out of every hundred Italian citizens were covered by compulsory health care insurance, compared with eighty in every hundred in 1961. However it must be noted once again that the cover varied from one group to another.

In addition to those compulsorily insured about another four per cent of the Italian population have access to free medical care. These are people who are registered as poor and who are cared for by the municipalities.

3. Qualifications

The general qualification for coverage is that the insured person works in a particular sector or occupation and is by virtue of his work eligible for membership of a particular fund. Usually entitlement to benefit begins as soon as the worker takes up work. Entitlement can cease when the employment contract is suspended or dissolved although schemes such as INAM give medical care benefits, with the exception of hospitalisation, to those ex-members who have been out of work for less than six months. Tuberculosis benefits are derived from membership of INPS and the sick person must have at least two years insurance to be eligible for benefits. Once qualified the member can receive benefits for as long as he has medical need, unlike the other schemes' benefits which are limited to a period of twenty-six weeks (180 days).

4. Finance

The most important point to grasp in relation to the finance of compulsorily insured health care in Italy is that the rates vary within schemes and between schemes. The unusual feature of INAM is that the employers bear the largest part (about ninety-eight per cent) of the contribution cost. Table 3 shows the contribution rates of various non-agricultural categories of workers who are members of INAM. The individual employee pays 0.15 per cent of his wage on all his earnings, i.e. there is no earnings ceiling. The employer pays contribution rates which vary from one sector to another, e.g. he pays 12.46 per cent[13] of the earnings of a manual worker in industry and 9.24 per cent of the earnings of a travelling salesman in commerce. The rates vary between manual workers and staff employees largely because the latter claim no sickness insurance benefits from their health care insurance as the employer funds these benefits directly out of his current resources for three months. These total employer contribution rates are made up of four components: a health care contribution, a contribution to finance the benefits of old age (retirement) pensioners, a contribution to subsidise benefits to agricultural workers and a maternity element.

The foregoing discussion and Table 3 are concerned solely with the contribution rates of non-agricultural workers.

Table 3 *Non-Agricultural Contribution Rates INAM 1973**

Category	Employee	Health care	Employer OAPs	Agricultural Solidarity	Maternity	Total
1. Industry						
a) Manual workers	0.15	7.70	3.80	0.58	0.53	12.61
b) Staff	0.15	5.70	3.80	0.58	0.53	10.61
2. Commerce						
a) Manual workers and staff	0.15	6.20	3.80	0.58	0.31	11.66
b) Travelling salesmen & representatives	0.15	4.70	3.80	0.58	0.31	9.39
3. Banking & Insurance						
a) Staff	0.15	4.70	3.80	0.58	0.20	9.28

Source: *Instituto Nazionale Per L'Assicur aziono contro le Malattie* (1973) pp 88-91.

* There is no earnings ceiling.

Table 4 gives some details of the contributions paid by agricultural workers who are members of INAM. Wage earners in agriculture are insured as a result of payment of a fixed daily contribution all of which is paid by the employer. For male wage earners a contribution of 48.76 lire (£0.03) per day of employment (plus 2.43 lire of maternity cover is included) is paid. The female wage earner's contribution is 43.37 lire per day (plus 1.95 lire for maternity cover) and the young person's contribution is 40.37 lire per day (plus 1.95 lire per day for maternity). The contribution rates for transient 'helpers' are higher as can be seen from Table 4. Tenant farmers pay an annual contribution for each member of the family over twelve years old. However only part of the total costs of this contribution is met by the farmers concerned. In 1970 the total contribution was 12,094 lire per year made up of 8842 lire to acquire pharmaceutical benefits and 3252 lire for other benefits. Also they paid part of 28.8 lire per year to give sickness insurance to pensioners. Further complexity is added to the agricultural contribution picture by a series of blanket exemptions. Since 1952 farms over 700 meters above sea level (the equivalent of the British 'hill farmer') have been exempt. Farms with contributions of less than 3000 lire per year have been able to obtain a hundred per cent exemption from contributions whilst certain other cases have been eligible for forty per cent to sixty per cent exemptions The INAM picture is very complex.

168

Table 4 *Agricultural Contribution Rates INAM 1973*

Type of Care	Wage Earners			Permanent, casual and 'exceptional' helpers		
	Men	Women	Young People	Men	Women	Young people
Health care insurance	48.76	43.37	40.37	54.73	47.53	44.53
Maternity insurance	2.43	1.95	1.95	2.95	2.32	2.32
Total	51.19	45.32	42.32	57.68	49.85	46.85

Source: INAM (1973) *op. cit.* p 88.

Further complexities are added to the picture by the recognition of the
fact that INAM is only one, admittedly the biggest, fund. It would be
beyond the scope of the present book to analyse each scheme indi-
vidually. However to make the point about diversity one other scheme's
contribution arrangements will be discussed. A law of 1970 set the
present ENPAS contribution rates (ENPAS [1973]). The civil servant
pays 1.6 per cent of his earnings as contributions. In January 1974 the
State as the employer paid five per cent of his earnings as contribution.
The State's contribution rises by 0.5 per cent every other year starting
from a base of four per cent in 1972. This escalator clause is limited by
legislation which prevents the total rate (employer plus employee
contribution) rising above 8.60 per cent. The contributions are calculated on eighty per cent of salary: salary includes Christmas bonuses
and family allowances. Retired civil servants pay one per cent of their
pensions and the State pays 3.5 per cent of this pension to make a
total contribution of 4.5 per cent.

The provision of insurance for tuberculosis risks is administered
separately by INPS. Here the contribution rate is two per cent of
earnings and is wholly paid by the employer. This contribution rate
has to be added to the rates given above as most of the compulsorily
insured population are members of INPS.

The most important lesson that can be derived from this section is
that statistics can be misleading. The EEC state that as at 1st January
1973 the contribution rate for sickness (EEC 1973 p 153) and
maternity insurance in Italy was 14.61 per cent in total, of which 0.15
per cent was paid by the employee and 14.46 per cent by the employer.
This figure is the sum of the INAM and INPS contributions. It is to be
remembered that only fifty-three per cent of the Italian population
are members of INAM and not all of these people pay the cited rate
(see Table 3 above).

5 Finance and Expenditure

Total health care income in Italy is the sum of three streams. Firstly the funds, which are annually and chronically in deficit, meet about fifty-three per cent of the total. The central government meets the funds' deficit — equivalent to about sixteen per cent of total expenditure in 1971 — and the central Government, the Regions and the local authorities finance a further fifteen per cent of expenditure, i.e. the total government participation is equivalent to about thirty-one per cent of total expenditure. The remaining sixteen per cent of expenditure is financed by the consumer who purchases private medical care. This final category is at best subject to large errors and at worst purely hypothetical because of the lack of adequate data from which estimates can be derived. These facts must be borne in mind whenever the accounts of the funds are analysed. If they are not, serious errors can arise as when a recent survey (Spitaels *et al* 1971) analysed INAM's income and concluded that the degree of State financial involvement in Italian health care was small. The conclusion was derived from taking the income of account of INAM at face value and ignoring the fund's deficit and the involvement of various levels of government in the finance of all types of care.

Caution must be exercised in generalising about the Italian health care expenditure pattern also. Table 5 gives a breakdown of the medical care expenditure patterns of wage earners' funds, the funds of the self-employed and the funds of the liberal professions.

The wage earners funds are by far the largest spenders: they spend over eighty-seven per cent of the total expenditure by the funds. Of these institutions INAM is the largest allocating nearly eighty per cent of expenditure in this category and nearly seventy per cent of total funds expenditure. The services purchased by this expenditure are shown in the columns. Taking all the first category together it can be seen that nearly forty-five per cent of total expenditure finances hospital care. The second most important item is pharmaceutical products (26.1 per cent), followed by physicians' fees (18.8 per cent), outpatient treatment (seven per cent) and other (1.8 per cent). The variations in expenditure patterns between the funds reflect the differing benefit levels that are available to members.

This factor explains the differences between the expenditure pattern of the wage earners, the self employed scheme and the scheme of the liberal professions. Most expenditure by the self-employed schemes finances hospital care (75.2 per cent). Pharmaceutical expenses have to be met out of the patients' pockets and physicians fees are partly financed this way. The liberal profession schemes are concerned mainly with the finance of hospital care

170

Table 5 *Medical Care Expenditure by Categories 1971 in hundreds of millions of lire**

	Hospital Care	Outpatients	Physicians	Pharmaceutical expenses	Other	Total
1. Wage Earners						
INAM	770.0 (46.0)	108.9 (6.5)	344.8 (20.6)	434.5 (25.9)	14.1 (0.8)	1672.3
ENPAS	92.6 (46.9)	22.5 (11.4)	14.9 (7.5)	42.4 (21.5)	24.6 (12.4)	197.1
ENPDEDP	22.2 (39.5)	6.6 (11.7)	11.5 (20.4)	14.0 (24.9)	1.8 (3.2)	56.2
INADEL	35.0 (28.2)	16.9 (13.6)	18.6 (0.15)	47.9 (38.6)	5.3 (4.2)	124.0
Seamens' funds	3.7 (27.2)	4.9 (36.0)	2.0 (14.7)	2.6 (19.1)	0.2 (0.1)	13.6
Other private sector funds	3.4 (27.8)	4.7 (38.5)	0.8 (0.6)	1.4 (11.4)	1.7 (13.9)	12.2
Trento and Bolzano funds	11.2 (52.3)	1.5 (7.0)	3.5 (16.3)	4.6 (21.4)	0.4 (1.8)	21.4
Total	983.3 (44.7)	166.3 (7.9)	396.3 (18.8)	547.7 (26.1)	48.3 (2.3)	2097.1
2. Self-employed						
farmers	122.1	13.8	11.5	-	0.2	147.8
artisans	61.4	16.4	6.6	-	0.2	84.8
traders	44.0	25.8	0.1	-	-	70.0
Total	227.6 (75.2)	56.2 (18.5)	18.3 (6.0)	-	0.4 (0.1)	302.6
3. Liberal professions						
Total	4.6 (80.7)	0.3 (5.2)	0.1 (1.7)	0.2 (3.5)	0.3 (5.2)	5.7
4. TOTAL (1+2+3) [£m]	1170.5 (48.6) [£780m]	222.8 (9.2) [£148m]	414.7 (17.2) [£276m]	547.9 (22.7) [£365m]	49.0 (2.0) [£32m]	2405.4 [£1603m]

Source: *Relazione Generale sulla Situazione Economica Del Paese 1971* , (1972) Appendici Tabella 15-17 pp 493-6.

* The figure in brackets is the expenditure figure expressed as a percentage of total expenditure of the particular category (row total).

The total expenditure of the medical care funds in 1971 was 2405,400 million lire (£1603m). Of this total 1170,500 million lire (£780m) was spent on hospital care, 547,900 million lire (£365m) on pharmaceutical purchases and 414,700 million lire (£276m) on physicians' fees. If the expenditure of INPS on tuberculosis medical care is included in health care fund expenditure 100,000 million lire (£66.6m) extra has to be included to make a total of 2505,400 million lire (£1670m).

Sickness insurance expenditure by the funds was relatively large despite the payment of wages to the sick employee by the employer for the first three months of illness. In 1971 the wage earners funds spent 255,022 million lire (£170m) in financing cash sickness and maternity benefits. INPS (for tuberculosis victoms) spent an additional 41,995 million lire (£27m). Sickness expenditure by the self-employed funds was 302,648 million lire (£201m) and that by the liberal professions 6,595 million lire (£4m). The total sickness insurance expenditure in 1971 was 606,260 million lire (£404m), i.e. 24.1 per cent of expenditure on medical care and 19.4 per cent of total health care expenditure by the funds. The overall health care expenditure of the funds in 1971 was 3111,600 million lire (£2074m).

If medical care alone is analysed the expenditure of the funds be added to the expenditure of two other groups before an overall total can be estimated. In 1971 the Government paid about 738,000 million lire (£492m) to eradicate the chronic deficits of the funds. The substantial flow was augmented by central and local government expenditures of about 700,000 million lire (£466m).[14] All these expenditures were financed out of general taxation. Total medical care expenditure in 1971 was about 4695,500 million lire (£3130m). So far government and fund expenditure together have amounted to only 3,943,000 million lire (£2628m). The remainder – about 751,900 million lire (£501m) – is an estimate of private medical care expenditure. The estimate – in reality a 'guestimate' – is taken from Vetere (1974) and like all its peers must be viewed with some scepticism due to ignorance and the paucity of the data which is available. If this estimate is taken as approximate it can be seen that about six per cent of Italian GNP in 1971 was spent on medical care.

Table 6   *Average Cost per Insured Person INAM 1970 and 1971 in hundreds of lire*

	Hospital Care	Outpatients Care	Physicians fees	Pharmaceutical costs	Other	Total
1970	35.3	9.3	18.6	26.7	0.6	90.7
1971	50.3	10.1	19.5	28.3	0.8	109.1
Percentage change 1970-71	42.4	8.6	4.8	2.2	33.3	20.2

Source: *op. cit.* Tabella 18, page 496.

Table 7 *Percentage of Total Expenditure of INAM by Type 1960-71 (selected years)*

Year	Hospital care	Outpatient care	Physicians fees	Pharmaceutical costs	Other
1960	3.15	9.5	21.5	36.3	1.2
1964	33.30	9.5	21.6	34.4	1.2
1968	38.10	9.5	18.5	33.1	0.8
1971	46.00	6.5	20.6	25.9	1.0

Source: *op. cit.* Tabella 15, and Spitaels (1971) page 636.

So far the analysis has presented a static picture of expenditure in one year. The data in Table 6 enables us to acquire a picture of the outlay in terms of average cost per active insured person with INAM. The total average cost between 1970 and 1971 rose by over twenty per cent. The main cause of this rise was hospital care where average costs rose by over foty-two per cent according to the data in Table 6. The *per capita* average costs varied from fund to fund. The average cost of hospital care given by ENPAS rose from 21.8 to 36.7 hundred lire between 1970 and 1971, i.e. by over sixty-eight per cent. The identification of the chief cause of cost inflation as being hospital care is substantiated by the data in Table 7 which shows the percentages of total expenditure spent on particular types of care by INAM in 1960, 1964, 1968 and 1971. The share of hospital care as a percentage of total expenditure rose from 31.5 per cent in 1960 to forty-six per cent in 1971. To enable this increase to take place the share of outpatient care and pharmaceuticals fell sharply and the expenditure share of physicians fell slightly. In absolute terms INAM's expenditure on hospital care rose by twenty-three per cent per year between 1966 and 1970. Pharmaceutical costs rose by ten per cent per year and medical fees rose by thirteen per cent. The causes of the increased hospital expenditure were increased unit costs (sixty-one per cent of the total increase), increased frequency of hospitalisation (twenty-eight per cent) and more insured people (ten per cent). The causes of increased expenditure of medical fees were increased unit costs (fifty-nine per cent), increased frequency of visits (twenty-nine per cent) and increased membership (twelve per cent). The causes of increased pharmaceutical expenditure were increased unit costs (twenty-seven per cent), increased consumption per head (forty-three per cent) and increased membership (thirty per cent). Overall the increase appears to have been caused by three main factors. Firstly over the period 1960-71 the coverage of compulsory health insurance increased from eighty per cent of the population to ninety per cent. Secondly unit costs

173

increased and finally consumption rose.

The sharp rise in costs shown in Table 6 could be exacerbated by health reform. If reform led to a greater uniformity, or the levelling up of benefits, and had been implemented in 1973 when the average cost of local health unit care alone was estimated to have been 23,570 (£15), the total medical care expenditure would have been of the order of 5,580,000 million lire (£3720m). In the light of recent Italian history it is to be doubted whether such a large sum could have been financed out of direct taxation as is proposed in the Bill. The spectacle of the rapid escalation in costs is similar to the phenomenon precipitated by the Medicare legislation in the United States. As in the United States the problems associated with tackling this problem are immense, and, some might argue, beyond the power of the present weak central government in Italy. If such pessimism is justified the Regions may take over but this course may not lead to greater uniformity on the finance and provision of Italian health care.

6. Benefits

Once again the analysis must be prefaced by the fact that the characteristics of the schemes vary. Hence the scope and quality of benefits between schemes vary. The discussion which follows is divided into separate sections for medical care and cash benefits, and is largely concerned with the benefits derived from membership of INAM.

(a) Medical Care

All INAM's medical care benefits are granted for a maximum period of 180 days in any one year only. The majority of physicians, midwives and hospitals in Italy have entered into agreements with INAM. The insured person has a free choice of physician, provided that the latter has an agreement with INAM and is registered on the municipal medical list. The standard of treatment is governed by an agreement between INAM and the physicians in 1966 (amended 1969). The individual physician has the right to decline to register a particular patient unless he is the only physician on the local register. The doctor/patient ratio is limited to one to 1500 except under exceptional circumstances where it can be raised or lowered by twenty per cent. In the late 1960s the average list size was 677 and less than one doctor in eight had lists with more than 1500 patients on them. These characteristics are unlikely to alter due to the rapid increase in the output of medical schools which is discussed in Section 7 below.

Under the INAM arrangements the physician is paid directly by the fund and the patient does not participate in his finance. Some other schemes — e.g. ENPAS — merely refund according to a predetermined

174

scale. Any difference is paid by the insured. Payment to the physician can be in one of four ways: per item of service, *per capita*, a mixture of per item of service and *per capita* payment, and a fee per hour (ENPAS specialist care). Until recently the system of payment was the result of negotiation between the funds and the profession at the provincial level. Now the funds are trying to negotiate at the national level to achieve greater uniformity in the rates of payment. Most non-specialist physicians are paid per item of service and the usual result can be noted: compared with the other payment systems the number of visits is almost double (twelve against seven) and the number of pharmaceutical prescriptions is over sixty per cent greater (sixteen against nine).

It is a commonly held opinion that these payment systems result in large salaries being paid. This is a matter of much debate. Vetere (1974) cites 1971 average income received from the funds by non-specialist physicians of 6,500,000 lire (£4333). Such figures are viewed with some scepticism. The trade unions in particular have argued that medical salaries are high and rising rapidly due to the spread of social insurance. There is no central register of physicians and their activities so it is impossible to get an accurate figure of list sizes. Physicians can work for more than one fund, and the extent of private practice supplementation is unknown. It is possible that the mean income sickness fund in 1971 was near Vetere's figure but the distribution is skewed and it is likely that the median income is above the mean. This abnormal distribution, the possibility of private practice supplementation and the inadequacy of the data makes it difficult to improve on Vetere's estimate.

Specialist treatment by physicians is available after 'certification of need' by the general practitioner. Once again the details of the physician/fund/patient relationship is regulated by a fund/physician agreement (1966). Treatment can be provided in INAM's polyclinics, in specialised units in the hospitals or in the specialists' own premises. The 1966 agreement provided for specialist care in the home but to date this has been limited to paediatric care of children below the age of six. Specialists to whom patients are referred must be registered on the local list and special authorisation by the fund is required of a patient seeks treatment from a non-locally registered specialist. Payment is on a per item of service basis, and is paid in full, directly by the fund.

Pharmaceutical products and all dressings are supplied free of charge on presentation of a physicians' prescription. The details of the provision procedures are regulated by an agreement of 1959 (modified in 1964). Prescriptions are valid for five days and the pharmacist is reimbursed by INAM only if the prescription is sent with the product's packing. 'Made-up' prescriptions result in reimbursement in accordance with agreed figures.

Domiciliary midwife services are provided by registered midwives and regulated by an agreement in 1956. The level of payment is related to the population of the municipality in which the midwife works. In urgent and exceptional cases a mother can be delivered by the family doctor who is paid extra fees, the level of which are fixed by prior agreement between the funds and the physicians' organisations.

Insured persons and their dependents acquire access to free hospital treatment in all hospitals, both private and public, which have entered into an agreement with INAM. If they choose to enter establishments which have no agreement with the funds they are reimbursed according to fixed scales usually. Before admission the local office of INAM must grant its approval of the doctor's recommendation of hospitalisation. Urgent cases can be admitted by the hospital duty physician and provided the admission is medically approved the fund will accept responsibility for the financing of the treatment. INAM pays the hospital according to a fixed scale of agreed charges depending on the type of treatment given. In 1971 the average fee was 23,000 lire (£15) a day.[15] In addition to these charges payments are made to finance the services of the hospital doctor. These fees vary from one item to another. These fees and those paid by other funds and private patients do not cover the full costs of hospitalisation. The deficits of the public hospitals are met by local government subsidies.

The hospital physician works either full or part time. The former type of contract implies a forty-hour week and no private practice. Any work in excess of forty hours is remunerated at generous overtime rates. Part-time employment is for thirty-six hours with the possibility of using hospital facilities for private patient care. The promotion ladder involves movement from assistant posts, to first assistant posts and, finally, to consultant posts. Progress is by examination and free competition with one's peers and once the physician is an established consultant he is tenured for the rest of his working life. Table 8 gives an indication of the level of remuneration of public hospital doctors in 1971. They receive thirteen monthly payments per year. The higher paid full time consultant received 1,427,450 lire a month (£951), i.e. 18,556,850 lire a year (£12,371) for a forty-hour week and in common with many other Italian income recipients is able to avoid paying much direct taxation. The part-time consultant could earn 11,651,600 lire (£7767) per year and supplement this with private practice income. Public hospital stipends are regulated by regional and municipal government except in the case of psychiatry. In the latter case the provincial authorities determine the salary in consultation with the universities. This system of decentralised determination of wages has made it very difficult for central government to control inflation and has contributed to the escalation of hospital expenditure discussed above.

Dental care in Italy is poor. The number of dentists is small (about 10,000) because they are trained physicians who have specialised in dental care. This training can take up to ten years and the medical profession is anxious to protect the specialism. Consumers often finance their own dental care. ENPAS for instance, give free dental care only at their clinics. Most funds reimburse the insured and their dependents for the purchase of dentures.

After 180 days in any one year all benefits cease. The person who requires further benefit can have to turn to several sources if he lacks resources to finance further care. He can apply to the Regional Authorities if he is affected by a condition requiring rehabilitation and appliances (this aid is financed by the Ministry of Health). If he has a very low income he can apply for aid from the Municipality. If the Municipality cannot offer help, he can turn to the Public Welfare authorities and once registered as poor can receive free treatment.

INAM, the public sector funds, the seamens' funds and the Trento-Bolzano funds have similar benefit levels. However the self-employed schemes and the schemes covering the liberal professions are different. By and large they tend to cover hospitalisation and outpatient care mainly and expend little money to finance general practitioner services or cover the costs of drugs. If the Health Reform Bill becomes law the picture will be more homogeneous with all groups being entitled in principle at least to all the benefits discussed above. The Bill asserts that these benefits will be free at the point of consumption. It is possible that this may be changed as the Bill goes through Parliament and charges for, e.g. pharmaceutical products, are being discussed.

(b) Cash Benefits

Sickness benefit is paid to all those members of INAM who are insured and incapacitated by illness, and to all those members of INPS's tuberculosis scheme who have TB in an active phase. The daily rate of sickness benefit is equal to half the average daily wage (without ceiling) of the insured person during the first twenty-one days of sickness and two-thirds of the wage from the twenty-first to the one hundred and eightieth day of sickness. No benefit is paid after the 180th day. Workers who register more than eighteen days of sickness, even if spread over two financial years, are not entitled to a second period of compensation unless they can prove they have been in full-time work between the periods of illness. Further regulations can limit benefits paid. No benefit is paid for the first three 'waiting days'. During periods of hospitalisation only forty per cent of the sickness benefit rate is paid to workers with no dependents. An unemployed person whose insu-

177

rance record makes him eligible for benefit can only acquire such benefit at two thirds the normal rate. The limits are not so extensive for tuberculosis patients. The daily post-sanatorium cash sickness benefit is paid for up to twelve months provided the treatment in the sanatorium lasted at least two months. The daily sickness benefit is paid without a duration limit during the period of treatment. However INPS benefits are not earnings related but lump sums and relatively low. These benefits are supplemented by two types of benefit. Normal benefits are provided as of right to assist the recovery of sick insured persons. They consist of a contribution by INAM to the costs of supplying artificial limbs, dental and orthopaedic appliances, spectacles, hearing aids and therapeutic treatments. The contribution does not, as a rule, exceed fifty per cent of the cost of the appliances or treatments. Exceptional benefits are allocated at the discretion of the provincial committee of INAM. The rationale behind these benefits is to provide help in conditions of exceptional hardship. These benefits can include the extension of sickness benefit payments beyond 180 days, the provision of convalescent care, stays at the seaside or in the mountains for insured person's children and sundry other allowances.

The other cash benefits provided by INAM are the death grant and the system of maternity insurance. The death grant is a fixed sum (20,000 lire [£13] in 1970) paid to the deceased's family to defray the costs of the funeral. Maternity insurance is of two types. Maternity care provides benefits in kind and consists of the services of specialised medical dispensaries both before and after confinement. In normal circumstances the birth is supervised by INAM certified midwives (see the medical care section above). In special circumstances a general practitioner may attend the birth. Both the midwife and the general practitioner are paid rates agreed between the professions and INAM. Cash maternity benefits are normally paid by INAM at a rate of eighty per cent of the average daily wage. However women in agriculture receive a single lump sum of between 20,000 and 35,000 lire depending on their work status. Domestic workers and women working at home also get a lump sum benefit but their benefits are paid by INPS. INAM's normal daily maternity allowance is paid for a fixed period whose duration depends on the sector in which the woman works. Women working in industry receive the benefit of three months prior and eight weeks after confinement whilst those working in banking and insurance get the benefit for six weeks prior and eight weeks after confinement. Exceptions to this exist. For instance in the case of certified complications the pregnant woman may leave work earlier and get an extension of maternity benefit allowance.

These benefits are not exactly parallelled by the other funds. For instance ENPAS provides similar maternity and death grants but provides no sickness insurance. This is because the government pays sickness benefit as part of the collective wage bargain. Also some of the white collar workers who are members of INAM receive sick pay from their employers direct, rather than from INAM. All such benefits do not appear to be included in the Health Reform Bill and their fate is unclear.

7. Provision

(a) Medical Personnel

Some details of the methods and levels of remuneration of physicians were given in the previous section. This will be complemented now by an analysis of the stock and flow position of various types of health personnel and of hospitals.

In 1971 there were 107,000 practising physicians in Italy. Some details of the growth in the size of the physician stock are given in Table 9. From this date it can be seen that between 1966 and 1969 the number of physicians increased by 5156, i.e. by 5.4 per cent. Between 1969 and 1971 the increase was 11821, i.e. 12.4 per cent. This large rise is likely to contibue because of university reforms. Since the beginning of the 1970's any high school pupil who matriculates has a right to a university place in the faculty of his choice. This 'open door' policy has led to a very large rise in the size of the student population: between 1961 and 1971 the total number of students rose by 160 per cent to 750,000. The number of medical students taking the six year course rose in the same time period by 288 per cent to 97,000. Although failure rates are relatively high (nearly thirty per cent fail in the first year examinations) this high student population will lead to a large increase in the number of qualified physicians in Italy in the 1970's. It may not lead to an equally large increase in the number of speacialists, however, because post graduate places are limited with the 'open door' policy ending after the completion of the first degree and specialist qualification depends on further full time study.

Table 8 *Remuneration of Hospital Physicians 1971 (per month)* *

Category	Full Time		Part Time	
Assistants	from	428,700 (£285.8)	from	273,700 (£182.4)
	to	955,450 (£636.9)	to	601,200 (£400.8)
First Assistants	from	843,450 (£562.3	from	531.200 (£354.1)
	to	1202,950 (£801.9)	to	756,200 (£504.1)
Consultants	from	1187,200 (£791.4)	from	746,200 (£497.4)
	to	1427,450 (£951.6)	to	896,200 (£597.4)

Source: Vetere (1974).

* The hospital doctor receives 13 monthly payments per year.

Table 9 *Physicians in Italy (selected years)*

Year	Total Number of Physicians
1966	90,020
1967	91,708
1969	95,179
1971	107,000

Sources: *World Health Organisation* (1970 and 1971) and Vetere (1974)

Of the 107,000 doctors practising in Italy 40,000 (thirty-seven per cent) work in hospitals, fifty per cent full time. There are 9000 municipal physicians (9.4 per cent) treating the poor as well as fund members. A further 9000 are involved in public health, administration and the armed forces. There are about 10,000 (9.3. per cent) who are dentists: as yet there is no separate course for dentists and so all Italian dentists have to train as physicians and specialise in dentistry. The remainder, some 39,000 (36.4 per cent) work in private practice. Many private physicians are specialists and of the hospital doctors about forty per cent are specialised.

The progress of the Italian physician is dominated by examinations. The initial six-year course leads to final examinations in five subjects taken from a list of one hundred and fifty. The marks gained in finals are carried forward to subsequent competitions to acquire a hospital post. From 1974 new graduates will undertake one years hospital work at a salary equal to one third of the Assistant (see Table 8). Specialisation requires further study, the duration of which varies between specialisms. Examination is by written papers and theses. Whilst the physician position appears to be one of abundance, that for nursing is one of shortage. The training and deployment of nursing staff was until recently haphazard. The single largest sub-category of nurses, are aids (some 60,000) whose training is completed in one year after at least eight years of school education. The more qualified nurse has to have ten years of school education, of which two years is high school (sixth form) and two years of professional training. At present there are only 35,000 such nurses but a great effort is being made to increase this stock. The number of training schools has risen from 120 in 1968 to 290 in 1973 and the output of nurses has grown from 3000 in 1968 to 8000 in 1973. The 1973 flow was augmented by about 2500 nursing aids being up-graded. Even so there is a shortage of 40,000 trained nurses (Vetere page 20) for hospital care and 20,000 for home care. After the initial two year course the nurse can go on to study to be a ward sister, a health visitor, a midwife or one of several other specialisms. The midwife studies a further two years before

180

completing her training. In 1973 there were 24,000 midwives.

(b) Hospitals

The change in stock of hospital beds in Italy over the period 1961 to
1971 is given in Table 10. The total number of beds increased by 16.2
per cent between 1961 and 1971. The public sector with a growth rate
of twenty-three per cent, grew at a less rapid rate than the private
sector whose growth rate was 35.4 per cent. Private sector psychiatric
beds increased in numner by 36.8 per cent whilst public sector provision in this field fell by 4.8 per cent. By and large the public sector
psychiatric beds are situated in large, old units with a reputation for
poor standards of care. Despite the fall in their bed stock it is likely
that public psychiatric units have increased their through-put because
of the sharp reduction (twenty per cent) in length of stay shown in
Table 11. Both private and public sector tuberculosis provision fell
between 1961 and 1971: by 42.7 per cent in the former sector and
29.2 per cent in the latter. General hospital bed provision increased in
both sectors with the most rapid change taking place in the private
sector: seventy-one per cent as compared with forty-five per cent. The
shares of the public and private sectors in the total general bed
provision changed from 86.2 per cent/13.7 per cent to 84.1 per cent/
15.8 per cent, i.e. a small increase in the importance of the private
sector. The geographical distribution of this bed stock is very unequal.
In some provinces in the South the bed to population ratio is as low as
three per thousand; Other areas — e.g. Veneto — have large bed stocks.

Table 10 *Hospital Bed Provision by Ownership Type 1961, 1967
and 1971*

	General	Type of Hospital Tuberculosis	Psychiatric	Total
Public Hospitals				
1961	236,724	47,245	97,474	381,433
1967	303,451	37,168	91,594	432,213
1971	343,343	33,418	92,708	469,469
Private (for profit)				
1961	37,796	17,903	15,914	71,613
1967	55,892	17,134	23,037	96,063
1971	64,680	10,241	22,099	97,020
TOTAL				
1961	274,520	65,148	113,388	453,056
1967	359,343	54,302	114,631	528,276
1971	408,023	43,659	114,799	526,757
1971 per 1000 pop.	6.87	0.81	2.12	9.77

Sources: *World Health Organisation* (1971) and Vetere (1974) p 12.

Table 11   *Hospital Length of Stay 1961 and 1971*

	1961	1971
Public Sector		
general hospitals	16.0	15.2
TB sanitaria	136.0	114.0
psychiatric	211.0	167.0
Private sector		
general hospitals	11.0	10.0
TB sanitaria	154.0	136.0
psychiatric	138.0	135.0

Source: Vetere (1974) p 12.

The bed population statistics given in the final line of Table 10 are national averages. Ministry of Health propose bed population targets of eight to nine per thousand for general cases and tuberculosis and three per thousand for psychiatric care. These appear to be high and would necessitate considerable expansion of the hospital stock.

As alternative policy which is recognised by the Ministry is that of cutting down the length of stay in hospitals. Table 11 shows that in some hospitals the length of stay in 1961 and 1971 were very similar. Obviously shorter stays plus greater utilisation of specialists hospital beds in particular [16], would obviate the necessity to expand the bed stock. The long-stay patients are often in expensive hospital care because of the lack of community facilities. An expansion of community care would make the three per thousand target for the psychiatric sector redundant. The differences between the private and public sectors in the long-stay hospitals may be due to differences in the case mix. Whether this is the explanation of the general hospital length of stay figures is not known. Of the two sectors have a similar case mix at the general hospital level the public sector may have something to learn from the private sector.

Most private profit making hospitals are operated by physicians and others in partnership. The public hospitals are run by the regions (larger hospitals with specialist departments), by the provinces (mostly psychiatric) and the municipalities (smaller hospitals with fewer specialisms). The 1968 Hospital Law set staff/patient objectives which in some cases have still to be met. These objectives are complex, (e.g. the law set an objective of two hours nursing time per day for each and every patient), and have contributed to the rapid inflation of hospital costs (an annual rate of increase of twenty-three per cent in money terms in the period 1966-70) because they have compelled increased staff employment. In the financial year 1969-70 it is estimated that forty per cent of increased hospital expenditure by INAM was due to the Hospital Law.

Private Hospitals have not been affected by the Hospital Law. There are two broad types of private hospital. The 'high class' private hospital provides luxury facilities and well-known specialists. The 'ordinary' private hospital is usually an adjunct of the public system and its main income is derived from the sickness funds with whom it has has entered agreements. The private sectors fees, particularly in the latter type of hospital, are lower than the public sector because of greater efficiency [17] and the non-applicability of the Hospital Law to the private sector. This position is likely to be changed in the near future as draft legislation has been prepared to extend the Hospital Law. Also legislation has been prepared to prohibit private practice in private hospitals by doctors employed part time in public hospitals. This proposal may reduce the attractions of the private hospitals.

In summarising this section it can be said that the stock and flow position of physicians may lead to 'over-provision' in the near future. The situation for nurses and dentists is one of 'shortage', particularly in the latter category. The provision of hospital beds, by European standards, is quite high although like all the other members of the European Community the geographical distribution of these beds is very unequal.

8. Conclusion

The costs of providing health care in Italy are escalating rapidly. Although administrators and medical opinion favour community care *via* health centres and preventive medicine the trend is one of increased hospitalisation. During the early 1970s substantial reforms have stopped short of the introduction of a National Health Service. The latter continues to be proposed but is not legislated, and could not operate until 1976 at the earliest. It appears likely that costs could be reduced if the present duplication of financial arrangements with about 200 funds could be reformed. Equally the path leading towards greater uniformity in the quality and quantity of medical care could be pursued by a national administrative apparatus. However it is important to realise the reality of the devolution of powers to the Italian Regions. There will be conflict between the central and regional authority which now manifests itself in argument about whether the Hospital Law is a 'fundamental law' (which cannot be overruled by regional governments), which may inhibit progress along the road to greater equality. Many of the problems involved in the more efficient use of health care resources in Italy stand out in stark relief against the background of political machinations. Whether these machinations are capable of producing reform is uncertain.

NOTES

1. The meaning of INAM and ENPAS are given above. ENPDEDP is the National Provident Institution for Employees of Public Law Corporations. *(Ente Nazionale di Providenza per i Dependenti da Enti di Diritto Pubblico)*. INADEL is the National Mutual Benefit Institution for Employees of Local Authorities *(Institute Nazionale di Assistenza ai Dipendenti da Enti Locali)*. The three other funds are:
    Casse mutue provinciali di malltia per gli artigiani e relativa federazione nazionale (Provincial Mutual Sickness Funds for skilled tradesmen (artisans), and the associated National Federation).
    Casse mutue di malttia frazionati, comunali ed interununale e provinciale per id coltivatori diretti e relativa Federazione nazionale (Provincial, communal, intercommunal etc. Sickness Funds of self employed farmers, and the associated National Federation).
    Casse mutue provinciale di malltia per gli esercenti attivata commerciali e relative federazione nazionale (Provincial Mutual Sickness Funds for persons in commercial occupations (traders), and the associated National Federation).
2. *Cassa mutua provinciale de malltie di Trento* (Mutual Sickness Fund for the Province of Trento) and *di Bolzano*. These carry out INAM's functions in these areas as explained below.
3. *Ente nazionale di previdenza o assistenza per i lavoratori dello spettacolo* (the National Provident and Mutual Benefit Institution for the Entertainment Industry – ENPALS).
4. The National Social Insurance Institute *(Instituto Nazionale della Previdenza Sociale* – INPS).
5. Hospital confinements and pharmaceutical costs are met by the municipality in the case of the poor.
6. The Public Health Officer is jointly responsible with the Mayor for local public health matters. However he cannot order any act which implies expenditure.
7. E.g. the national plan for kindergartens, foods and drinks regulations, control of infectious diseases which are the subject of compulsory vaccination, payment of fees for the supply of appliances to crippled persons, drugs registration, etc. See Vetere (1974) p 2.
8. This is especially so if the crucial Ministries are in the hands of coalition members from differing parties.
9. In exceptional circumstances they could be as small as 10,000 people and as large as 100,000 people (Article 7, Health Reform Bill).
10. White collar agricultural employees are compelled to join a special insurance scheme which is run separately by INAM.
11. However entitlement to benefit generally continues for illnesses developing within six months of the termination of the contract of employment for those people in the listed categories. The exception to this is that the entitlement to hospitalisation lapses with the cessation of employment.

12. These categories are entitled to a lump sum payment from INPS (National Social Insurance Institute).
13. I.e. the total (12.61 per cent) minus the employee contribution (0.15 per cent).
14. Part of this expenditure – by local authorities – was to finance the provision of welfare services. The component parts appear to be inseparable.
15. In 1969 the average was 7403 lire per day (£5). So between 1969 and 1871 the average went up by 210 per cent.
16. In some specialisms the utilisation rate is below fifty per cent.
17. Shorter lengths of stay are one indicator of this. See Table 11 and text discussion of this data.

References

Annuario Statistico (1972), 'Relazione Generale sulla Situazione Economica Del Paese – 1971', Rome.
Ente Nazionale Di Previdenza ed Assitenza per I Dependenti Statali – ENPAS (1973), *A Survey of the Institute and Its Activities*, Rome.
European Economic Commission (1973 (a)), *The Cost of Hospitalisation in Social Security*, Department of Social Affairs, Brussels (in French).
European Economic Commission (1973 (b)), *Main Report Covering Three Investigations into the Principal Items of Expenditure in Sickness Insurance by Social Security*, Department of Social Affairs, Bruseels (in French).
European Economic Commission (1973 (c)), *The Cost of Pharmaceutical Consumption in Social Security*, Department of Social Affairs, Brussels (in French).
European Economic Community (1973 (d)), *Report on the Development of the Social Situation in the Community in 1972*, Brussels and Luxembourg.
Instituto Nazionale per L'Assicurazione Contro Le Malattie – INAM (1973), *Il Sistema Assistenziale Dell' INAM*, IX edizione aggiornata Rome, May.
Italian Health Reform Bill, *La Legge di reforma per la sanita* (1973), Rome.
International Social Security Review (1972), 'New Arrangements for the Provision of Medical Benefits to the Insured Persons of the ENPAS and ENPDEDP', No 4.
National Sickness Insurance Institute – INAM (1970), *Health Insurance for Employed Persons*, Rome.
Vetere, C. (1974), *The Organisation of Italian Health Care*. A paper presented to a seminar at the Kings Fund Health Centre, London, March.
World Health Organisation (1970, 1971), *World Health Statistics Annual*, Geneva.

8 UNITED KINGDOM

The Evolution of Health Care in the United Kingdom

Prior to 1911 the degree of government involvement in the finance and provision of health care in the United Kingdom [1] was relatively small. The National Insurance Act 1911 (Part I) altered this situation quite radically. The legislation covered thirteen million workers — all those earning less than £160 per year — and used the existing 'approved societies' as the vehicle for financing two types of benefit. The first type of benefit was sickness benefit. The second type was limited medical care. The medical care was provided by general physicians working in the community. Those physicians who wished to do so could enter the scheme and build up a 'panel' of registered patients. The physicians were paid, in all areas except Manchester and Salford, a capitation fee and the patient received free treatment. However the treatment was limited to what an average general practitioner would provide. The scheme was funded by tripartite contributions, i.e. payments by the employer, the employee and the Government.

During the inter-war years (1919-39) this scheme expanded and was supplemented by changes in other areas of health care. The coverage of the 1911 Act had expanded to fifteen million by 1921 and twenty million by 1938. However its defects were clear and the Lawrence Committee (1926) attempted to rectify some of these by advocating more extensive coverage (e.g. of dependents) and a more comprehensive bundle of benefits (e.g. dental care). Much hospital provision was in the hands of two sets of institutions. The Poor Law hospitals system had grown out of the need to provide hospital care for the poor and destitute. The voluntary (non-profit making) hospitals were largely charitable foundations created by geographically unequal endowments of philanthropy. The latter were much criticised for divergent standards and a lack of coordination in the early part of the century. In 1921 the Voluntary Hospitals Commission was set up to use government grants to encourage these hospitals to collaborate. However change was slow until the local authorities took over the Poor Law hospitals in 1930. After this take-over the local authorities controlled over fifty per cent of hospital establishments (including sanatoria and mental hospitals). This sector became important despite its relative low level of bed provision because the voluntary hospitals found it increasingly difficult to equate income and expenditure. This was so despite the fact that the flow of income to hospitals was augmented by hospital contribution schemes (private insurance) which had five million contributing members and ten million beneficiaries by 1937.

The deficiencies of the situation in 1939 were obvious but as a solution the National Health Service was not necessarily the only logical outcome. The defects were that the 1911 legislation covered only one half of the population. The wives of contributing members received no benefits except when bearing children. No specialist care, no hospital care and no dental care was available: the scheme provided general practitioner care only. The hospital system was criticised as being ill-coordinated and divergent in standards of care and geographical density. Its finances were uncertain. The 'approved societies' (insurance institutions), because they were able to choose their clients, attempted to minimise risks by choosing the healthy. Those societies that succeeded in pursuing this policy and which operated in areas where illness was relatively low were able to offer supplementary benefits to their members. Indeed the health care system in the United Kingdom in 1939 had many of the characteristics which make life difficult for similar systems in Western Europe today.

On the post-war UK the finance and provision problems were tackled by setting up a National Health Service financed by a small amount of ear-marked taxation (the 'Health Stamp') and a large amount of general taxation. Unlike Western Europe where much of the income of the funds is derived from contributions by employers, eighty-five per cent of NHS expenditure is financed out of general taxation. The provision of a 'comprehensive' system of medical care was entrusted to a nationalised system of hospitals and a system of contracted services from medical practitioners (physicians, dentists, pharmacists and opticians). The finance and provision of sickness benefits were separated from medical care and incorporated in a new system of income maintenance governed by the National Insurance Act 1946.

This system is essentially unchanged over twenty-five years later. In 1974 the National Health Service was reorganised to encourage coordination and more efficient management; arguments which were used to rationalise the establishment of the Service prior to 1948. The geographical inequalities in the provision of health care, evident in the inter-war period, have been highlighted in the past decade and, as in other parts of Europe, measures are being taken to ameliorate their impact. The flow of finance to health care is governed by macro-economic factors and the relative politico-economic 'merits' of health care vis-a-vis the other items of public expenditure. With nationalised provision and central government finance the matrix of problems faced by the UK health administrator is different from that of his counterpart in any other part of Europe. However like all other systems of health care analysed in this book the problems of finance and provision are insoluble.

1. Administration

The tripartite provision structure of the National Health Service is shown in Figure 1.

Figure 1 *The Organisation of the National Health Service 1948-74*

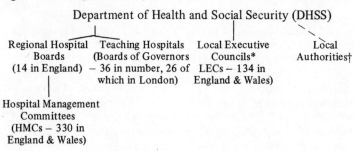

Department of Health and Social Security (DHSS)

| Regional Hospital Boards (14 in England) | Teaching Hospitals (Boards of Governors – 36 in number, 26 of which in London) | Local Executive Councils* LECs – 134 in England & Wales) | Local Authorities† |

Hospital Management
  Committees
(HMCs – 330 in
England & Wales)

Notes:

* These were based on the Local Insurance Committees (created by the 1911 National Insurance Act) which were responsible for the payment of practitioners prior to 1948.

† Prior to 1974 there were 158 local government units with health responsibilities in England, seventeen in Wales and thirty-one in Scotland. Since April 1974 local authority health services have been the responsibility of over seventy new authorities in England, seven in Wales and eight in Scotland. For a discussion of local government reorganisation see Maynard and King (1972).

The first part of the structure was the hospitals. The higher management (e.g. long-range policy) was in the hands of the Regional Hospital Boards (RHB). Day-to-day management and control of the hospital services were in the hands of more numerous Hospital Management Committees (HMC). The Department allocated funds to the Regional Boards largely on the basis of 'last year's budget plus a margin for growth and inflation'. The Boards allocated these funds to the HMCs who spent the money and provided the services. The management of teaching hospitals was separate and directly responsible to the Secretary of State.[2] The Boards of Governors who managed the teaching hospitals and the RHBs were appointed by the Secretary of State. The members of the HMCs were appointed by the RHB.

Medical care outside the hospital was provided by two sets of institutions. The Local Executive Council contracted all physicians, dentists, opticians and pharmacists to provide medical care in each

188

local community. The LECs pay those people who perform contracted services with funds distributed to them by the Department of Health (DHSS). The average size of these bodies varied greatly: ten had populations of over one million whilst twenty-two had populations of less than 75,000.[3] The membership of the councils was appointed by the Secretary of State, the local health authorities and by the profession.

The second body involved in the provision of community medical care was local government. The local health authorities provided general support services such as ante-natal, post-natal and child health clinics, domiciliary midwife services, home nursing and health visiting, vaccination and immunisation, home helps, the ambulance service, family planning and services for the mentally ill and mentally handicapped. During the 1960s the local authorities established Health Centres which by arrangement with the Local Executive Councils and the Hospital Boards provided a range of services. Since the 1974 reorganisation of the NHS all these local authority health services have been handed over to the constituent bodies of the health services. The local authorities were responsible for the provision of welfare[4] services such as residential services for the old, the infirm and the handicapped. Between 1970 and 1974 some of the functions of the local health authorities were transferred to the local social service departments. The local authorities finance all their activities from local taxation (rates[5]) and central government grants. Although there is notional local autonomy this is circumscribed by the DHSS who attempt to pursue their policies by financial inducements (*via* the grants) and mandatory powers.

Since 1st April 1974 this structure has been revised (see Figure 2) to facilitate integration and coordination. The basic unit of the new Health Service is the District which serves of population averaging 250,000 and provides that population with community health services supported by the specialist services of a district general hospital. The key administrative units at the district level are the District Management Teams (DMTs), the District Medical Committees (DMCs), the Community Health Councils (CHCs) and the Health Care Planning Teams (HCPTs). The management, medical and health care teams are concerned with the provision of present and future care. The latter consideration is novel and provides *via* HCPTs a means of local influence in future plans. The CHCs vary in size from eighteen to thirty members. Although Councils are based on the District they are not permitted to question District administrative units and any information they demand about the service is provided by the Area Health Authority. This would not seem to be an efficient way to facilitate the working of a body whose role is to be that of the community's 'watchdog'.

The Area Health Authority (AHA) is the lowest level of statutory authority with planning and operational responsibilities. It has the job of providing comprehensive health services for the Area's population. To do this it has to coordinate its activities closely *via* the Joint Consultative Committees with the new local authorities[6] whose boundaries are commensurate to its own. The AHA's have established Family Practitioner Committees (FMCs) to carry out functions similar to the old Local Executive Councils. However in one respect, health centres, the FMC has lost its power to the Area Health Authority whose job it is to coordinate new units with the local authorities.

The Regional Health Authority (fourteen in England and one in Wales) will be responsible for allocating resources amongst the competing claims of constituent AHAs. In carrying out this allocation they will be compelled to follow national guidance on policy. In addition the RHA will 'review, challenge and approve AHA plans, and subsequently control AHA performance in relation to agreed plans'.[7] All RHAs will be responsible to the Secretary of State for Health and Social Security.

The overall effect of this reorganisation is that the hospital services, the community health services and the former local authority health services[8] are under the direction of one administrative unit and that central control of all the units appears to have been increased. Whether this structure will prove to be a more efficient unit for the delivery of medical care only the future will tell. One area for concern is that many community services remain outside the Health Service being the responsibility of the local authorities' social service, education and housing departments. Unless coordination is close problems could arise which are similar to those existing prior to reogranisation. Another problem is rehabilitation services: the Employment Medical Advisory Service which was reorganised in 1974 on a different basis to the NHS is to remain under the control of the Department of Employment. The continued lack of integration of some groups of personnel, particularly the physicians, into the management of the services is disquieting. Reorganisation has, for instance, left the hospital consultants as a powerful group capable of continuing the over-emphasis on hospitalisation as opposed to community care.

The public provision of medical care is augmented by private non-profit making insurance institutions. These bodies insure about two million subscribers and their dependents against the cost of private medical treatment. This treatment is given in a declining number of places in NHS hospitals, and private hospitals. Subscribers are largely middle grade and senior staff of firms which have 'group' schemes for employees. The major advantages of such treatment are greater

190

Figure 2 *The Organisation of the National Health Services 1974*

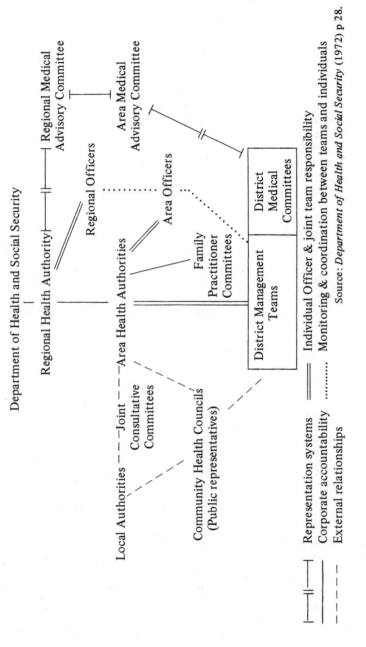

Source: *Department of Health and Social Security* (1972) p 28.

seclusion, the physician of one's choice and 'jumping the queue'[9] for hospital care. Most people in the UK are registered with NHS family physicians and only a small number of people have a family doctor whom they consult privately on a fee paying basis.

2. Coverage

Since 1948 the coverage of the legislation which created the National Health Service — National Health Service Act 1946, National Health Service (Scotland) Act 1947, and the Health Service Act (Northern Ireland) 1948 — has been complete. Sickness benefit is governed by social insurance legislation[10] and covers those who satisfy the contribution requirements of the component parts of legislation — about eighty-two per cent of wage and salary earners in 1970.

3. Qualifying Conditions

Residence in the United Kingdom is the only condition which has to be satisfied for beneficiaries to receive medical care. For sickness benefit the insured must have paid 156 weekly flat rate contributions to be eligible for sick pay. Flat rate benefit is supplemented by graduated payments which are paid according to the insured's contribution record.

4. Finance

A myth popular amongst many people in the 1950s and 1960s was that the NHS was financed by ear-marked taxation. In fact the income derived from ear-marked taxation is very small. A small part of each worker's flat rate National Insurance contribution is a payment to finance the NHS. This payment, when aggregated with an equal payment by the employer, provides less than ten per cent of the income required to finance the NHS. Most of the revenue (over eighty-five per cent) is derived from general taxation.

5. Income and Expenditure

The first difficulty in any analysis of income and expenditure is one of definition. The expenditure in Table 1 follows the format of the Annual Report of the Department of Health and Social Security, but excludes local authority social services and welfare foods expenditure. The income position is simple to describe. Over seventy per cent of NHS income used to finance central government NHS expenditure is derived from the Consolidated Fund i.e. from general taxation. Over fifteen per cent is derived from local taxation (the 'rates') and central government grants financed from general taxation. This portion of the income of the NHS finances local government activity.[11] A further nine per cent of income comes from contributions from those paying National Insurance contributions. About five per cent of income is derived from direct payment by the consumer. Thus in general terms eighty-five per cent of NHS income is derived from general taxation at the central and local level, five per cent is derived from direct payments and ten per cent comes from contributions. These percentages have changed only marginally over the last decades.

Table 1 *NHS Expenditure 1950-1972 (selected years)**

Year	£ million		As a percentage of GNP	
1950	477		4.06	
1955	607		3.56	
1960	902		3.94	
1965	1308		4.14	
1967	1594		4.52	
1969	1886 (	1823)[†]	4.75	(4.59)[†]
1970		2083		4.81
1971		2369		4.86
1972		2832		5.06

Source: *Office of Health Economics* (1974 (b)) Table 1 and Central Statistical Office (1972, 1973) pages 2-3.

*   Includes current and capital expenditure by central and local government and consumer payments.
†   Due to the Social Security Act 1970 the definition of the NHS changes from 1969 onwards. In that year certain local authority health services were transferred from the NHS to local government social service departments.

Table 1 shows that although absolute NHS expenditure has grown throughout the period 1950-72, the expenditure has a percentage of Gross National Product has fluctuated. The nadir of expenditure as a percentage of GNP was reached in 1954 when it was 3.54 per cent. Since then it has steadily grown, so that by 1972 5.06 per cent of GNP was used to finance the NHS.

Table 2 shows expenditure by type as a percentage of total outlay. The series is disturbed in 1969 by the removal of some functions from local authority health departments to local authority social service departments. Whilst the change gives rise to caution in using these

Table 2 *NHS Expenditure by Type 1950-72 (selected years) in percentages**

Year	Hospital Services	Pharmaceutical Services	General Medical Services	General Dental Services	General Opthalmic Services	Local Authority Health Services	Other †	Total
1950	54.9	8.4	11.7	9.9	5.2	7.8	2.0	100
1955	57.3	9.6	10.2	6.3	2.5	8.7	5.4	100
1960	56.4	10.1	9.8	6.3	1.9	9.0	6.5	100
1965	60.5	11.1	7.8	5.1	1.6	10.2	3.7	100
1967	59.9	10.6	7.9	5.0	1.4	10.7	4.5	100
**1969	61.2 (63.1)	10.1 (10.4)	7.8 (8.0)	4.7 (4.8)	1.4 (1.5)	10.4 (7.4)	4.5 (4.8)	100
1970	64.2	10.0	8.3	4.9	1.4	7.0	4.4	100
1971	65.5	9.8	8.1	4.8	1.3	6.9	3.6	100
1972	66.0	9.7	7.9	4.5	1.2	6.8	3.9	100

Source: *Office of Health Economics* (1974 (b)), Table 2.

*   Local and central government expenditure (capital and current) and consumer payments.
†   Includes grants, central administration and such items as research and laboratory costs
     not falling on any one service.
** A new definition of NHS expenditure is used after 1969 due to the creation of local authority
     social service departments.

figures as precise measures their general order of magnitude is good. It can be seen that the hospital services have gained an increased share of expenditure over the period. Pharmaceutical expenditures on the other hand peaked in the mid-1960s and have since fallen away. General medical expenditure after falling in the 1950s levelled off in the 1960s and early 1970s to consume about eight per cent of total expenditure. General dental and general opthalmic expenditures have declined with the latter falling more rapidly. Local health expenditures rose until the 1969 reorganisation of their activities.

The provision of sickness benefit is part of National Insurance.[12] The income of the National Insurance scheme is made up of four components. In 1972 the total income of this scheme was £3696 million, of which forty-two per cent came from contributions by employers, forty per cent came from employees' contributions, 15.5 per cent came from central government and the rest (2.5 per cent) came from sundry small items.[13] Most of the expenditure of this scheme went on non-health items. In 1972 (1962) sickness benefit cost £494 million (£163m), maternity benefit cost £45 million (£26m) and death grants cost £14 million (£6m). These items represented 13.3 per cent (12.5), 1.2 per cent (1.9) and 0.3 (0.4) of total expenditure in 1972. Like all other National Insurance benefits, sickness benefit will be affected by the 1973 Social Security Act which will introduce flat rate benefits financed by graduated contributions and a similar percentage subsidy from central government in 1975.

The importance of health care expenditure as a percentage of Gross National Product is dependent on the definition of 'health'. If the concern is purely medical care such expenditure in 1972 consumed 5.06 per cent of GNP. Alternatively a wider definition which included medical care (£2732 million), sickness and other cash benefits (£553 million), local authority public health activity (£68 million) and local authority social service expenditure [14] (£380 million) implies a total health care expenditure of £3733 million in 1972, i.e. 6.92 per cent of GNP. If cash benefits are removed from the previous totals the result is £3180 million or 5.89 per cent of GNP.

6. Benefits

(a) Medical Care

The family doctor — or general practitioner — plays a primary role in the National Health Service. Everyone over sixteen years old may choose his own physician and the physician is free to accept or reject anyone as a full-time patient. However if he rejects a potential patient from joining his list he has the responsibility to give any necessary treatment if the person applying for such treatment is not on a physician's list or if the physician is absent. A person may change his doctor if he wishes. This may be done if the person changes his address or acquires his physician's consent to transfer. If neither of these things occur the individual can ask his Family Practitioner Committee to sanction a move. Such permission is usually forthcoming although often it is difficult to find a physician who can or will accept a transferee.

The general practitioner is contracted to the NHS to supply medical services free of charge to the consumer. He has complete clinical freedom and his prescribing activities are unregulated. However the individual physician is expected to have due regard to the therapeutic value and the financial cost of individual pharmaceutical products. Malpractice can be investigated by a committee of peers. For any serious condition the patient is referred to a consultant physician who re-diagnoses the patient and, if necessary, refers him for hospital treatment. .

The general practitioner can practise alone or in a group in any area approved by the Medical Practicies Committee.[15] A doctor in a single-handed practice may have up to 3500 patients on his NHS list. If he is a member of a partnership he may have up to 4500 people on his list provided the partnership average list size does not exceed 3500. Any physician who wishes to set up a new practice has to get the approval of the Medical Practices Committee. Their sanction is called for so that the NHS can pursue a policy of 'negative direction' of physicians, i.e. in order get greater geographical equality in the distribution of physicians the Department of Health has adopted policy measures which enable it to make relatively 'over-doctored' areas (e.g. Devon) closed to new entrants. It must be emphasised that the policy does not permit the direction of physicians to relatively 'under-doctored' areas (e g. Wolverhampton).

Over fifty per cent of family doctors are members of partnerships. Group practice has been encouraged by both central and local government. At the local level, local authority medical officers of health have been encouraged by group practice to attach nurses, midwives and health visitors to particular physicians. This has been accompanied by the development of health centres which provide a wide range of community health care provided by physicians, dentists and ancilliary staff. Central government has encouraged local authorities to develop health centres and provided financial inducements for physicians to enter group practice e.g. the General Practice Finance Corporation has, since 1967, provided loans to physicians wishing to convert or improve old premises and erect new premises for group practice.

. This encouragement has manifested itself also in changes in the system of payment for general practitioners. Until the review of 1965-6 the general practitioner was paid by a system of capitation fees. Since then the capitation system has been amended in numerous ways. There is a higher capitation fee for patients aged sixty-five and more. A basic practice allowance is paid to meet necessary expenses. Also additional sums are paid for practising in an area which has been 'under-doctored' for several years,[16] for practising in a group, for seniority, and for vocational training. Specific services such as night-visiting of patients, maternity services, practising in rural areas and the treatment of non-residents are remunerated by further payments. The NHS makes direct payments to meet the cost of premises (rent and rates) and the cost of employing ancilliary staff. ⟨

To acquire dental treatment the consumer merely has to make an appointment; no registration is necessary. The dentist has clinical freedom and may take private and NHS patients if he wishes. General dental practitioners usually provide treatment in their own surgeries and are paid according to a prescribed scale of fees. Unless the patient is exempt, he must pay half the cost of treatment up to a maximum payment of £10 for a course of treatment. There is no charge for examinations. The following categories get free dental care: expectant mothers, or those who have borne a child in the preceding twelve months; children under sixteen; young people under twenty-one who are still in full-time ducation.[17]

Maternity care consists of arrangements for regular pre-natal and post-natal examinations and treatments, and for delivery. The mother can choose usually between pre-natal care provided by her family practitioner or at outpatients facilities at the local hospital. Post-natal care is provided by clinics which are staffed by physicians who examine but do not treat. Treatment is carried out by the family practitioner or hospital to which the child is referred by clinic physician. Confinements usually take place in hospitals and the mother is an inpatient from two to eight days depending on the availability of hospital beds. In 1972 ninety-two per cent of births took place in hospitals. This compares with a statistic of sixty-seven per cent hospital confinements in 1961 and is the result of official policy. This policy is paradoxical in that by and large the emphasis of the NHS is increased community care. Yet in the maternity sector there is an increased use of hospitalisation despite the fact that such treatment is more expensive.

The family doctor can refer any patient to the opthalmic services. Once referred the patient can go to any practitioner. There are three types of personnel working in this area. The opthalmic physician is a doctor who tests sight and prescribes glasses. The opthalmic optician can test sight, prescribe and supply glasses. The optician can only supply glasses to a prescription. The opthalmic optician and physician are paid fees for testing sight. The dispensing opthalmic optician and ordinary optician are paid a dispensing fee together with fees to cover the cost of spectacles with an allowance for breakages. The patient has his sight tested free of charge. However the provision of spectacles and their frames are paid for by the patient. Young people and the poor receive[18] free spectacles whilst older school children are entitled to free lenses but must pay for the frames.

Any pharmaceutical prescriptions made out by the family doctor can be made up at a pharmacy, of which there are 11,000 in England and Wales. The pharmacist is paid by local Family Practitioner Committee. The payment is made up of four parts: the cost of the ingredients, a percentage on cost, a container allowance and a professional fee. The consumer pays a charge of £0.20 for each item on the prescription.[19] Exemptions from this charge are allowed to children under sixteen, retirement pensioners, the poor[20], expectant mothers and those suffering from specific medical conditions.

The cost of pharmaceutical products has been a source of conflict between the suppliers and the NHS. Since the early 1960s various Voluntary Price Regulation Schemes (VPRS) have been in operation. The Coopers (Cooper and Cooper [1972]) have argued that the impact of these agreements between DHSS and the pharmaceutical industry have met with mixed success. Prior to 1964 they argue that their impact was small. However in the period 1964 to 1967 they argue that VPRS 'had a significant downward effect upon (the) prices of prescription medicines in the UK (Cooper and Cooper [1972] page 14). Since 1969 the Sainsbury Report (1967) has led to a new VPRS which emphasises the profitability of the indsutry. This involves the DHSS in great data problems which have not been resolved. The cost of certain pharmaceutical products appears to be lower in the UK than elsewhere in Europe. Whether there is scope for further restriction of the profits of the pharmaceutical industry by such policy instruments as VPRS or even nationalisation is a question which is highly complex and often answered with naive simplicity.

The hospitals and the specialists physicians attached to them, provide inpatient, outpatient, day and night patient care. All the services are provided free of charge. Generally access to such care is by reference of the family doctor. The majority of care takes place in general wards. Amenity beds – beds in single rooms or small wards – are available in some hospitals at a small charge. Pay beds are for private patients who pay fees which meet the full cost of accommodation and treatment. The number of pay beds in NHS hospitals is declining. Since 1966 the hospital bed stock has been modernised by a large hospital building programme, one of whose purposes is to reduce the inequalities in the geographical distribution of beds. Another objective of this programme was to replace old units with modern hospitals of greater efficiency. During the 1960s the hospital bed stock declined but the number of patients treated rose by thirty per cent to 5.5 million due to reductions in the length of stay.

Psychiatric care is provided in hospital units and in the community. Since the early 1960s psychiatric care policy has been to close large, and often geographically remote, mental hospitals and treat patients in the community or in psychiatric wards of general hospitals. This policy was reinforced by the Sir Keith Joseph proposals of 1971 and 1972 which set out provision/population ratios for various types of input. The policy of the 1960s has had some limited success (Maynard and Tingle [1974 (b)]) but the policy of the 1970s which continues previous action by specifying provision objectives will be difficult to prosecute successfully unless the provision of community care facilities by the local authorities is rapidly augmented (Maynard and Tingle [1974 (a)]). The 1974 reorganisation of the NHS left most community care facilities in the hands of the local authorities. Obviously severe problems will arise if the NHS attempts to reduce psychiatric hospital care and turn patients out into a community where mental health facilities are inadequate. The familiar problem of local authority-NHS coordination is particularly acute in this area. Area Health Authorities and local authorities must develop an efficient Joint Consultative Committee system to facilitate coordination in the reorganised service.

(b)   Sickness Benefit ✓

The standard rate of sickness benefit in July 1974 was £8.60 for a single person and £13.90 for a married couple. These payments are supplemented by allowances for each child at an average rate in excess of £3 and, after a means test, Supplementary Benefits[21] which can meet specific expenditures such as rent and rates as well as augment the basic cash payment. Graduated sickness benefit is paid in addition to the standard payment and is related to the graduated contributions made by the individual concerned.

Other cash benefits are death and maternity benefits. The latter is of two types. A lump sum payment of £25 and a weekly payment equal to basic sickness benefit for a single person, paid eleven weeks prior to confinement, the week of confinement and six weeks after the confinement. The death grant is a lump sum payment of £25. Both the death grant and the maternity benefit are paid only if there is an adequate contribution record.

It must be remembered that these cash benefits are separate from the medical care provided by the NHS.

7. Provision

(a) Personnel

The number of physicians in Great Britain increased by 17.5 per cent during the period 1965-72 (see Table 3) to one per thousand population. This was due to a net gain from migration and the beginning of an increased flow of newly qualified physicians. Public policy in the late 1950s was influenced by a Royal Commission who advocated zero expansion of the medical schools because they forecast that there would be an adequate number of physicians in 1970s.[22] By ignoring migration — the so-called 'Brain Drain' of physicians out of the UK — and using poor point estimates of population trends their simplistic forecasts led to an inadequate[23] expansion of the medical schools and a relative increase in the number of 'under-doctored' areas. The reversal of this trend was less than might have been expected by 1972 because the increased employment of physicians was concentrated in the hospitals. The number of family doctors increased by 3.8 per cent in the period covered by Table 3. The number of hospital physicians increased by over thirty-two per cent in the same period and by 1972 nearly fifty-four per cent of physicians were working in hospitals. Current policy emphasises community care but whether such management mechanisms as 'cogwheel', which aims to involve hospital physicians in management, can mitigate consultants' power and facilitate the attainment of current policy objectives is, as yet, unclear. The education of physicians is being slowly changed. Since the late 1960s, when the manpower forecasting errors of the 1950s had been fully recognised, medical schools have been increased in size and number. For the first time university professorships in general practice have been established and slowly the curricula of the medical student is being altered, so that more emphasis is being placed on subjects directly relevant to the physician entering general practice. The criticism is still made that medical schools aim to train hospital specialists and ignore the needs of the community physician. This argument is less pertinent than it was ten years ago but it continues to contain an element of truth. It is argued by some that the six-year course plus one year in hospital training should place more emphasis on mental illness, management skills, the use of cooperant factors of production and an intensive study of subjects such as psychology, sociology and statistics. Like most areas of education the problems of medical education are insoluble but a more scientific approach could increase efficiency and facilitate the attainment of policy objectives.

The geographical distribution of physicians is unequal. This problem has been analysed at length by various authors (Cooper and Culyer

Table 3 *Medical Personnel in Great Britain 1965-72 (percentages)*

Category	1965		1967		1969		1971		1972	
(a) Physicians										
hospital medical staff	22123	(47.6)	23791	(29.7)	25674	(51.4)	27867	(53.0)	29360	(53.8)
general practitioners	24260	(52.3)	24005	(51.3)	24239	(48.6)	24668	(47.0)	25184	(46.2)
Total	46383		47796		49913		52535		54544	
(b) Dentists										
hospital dental staff	663	(5.4)	761	(6.1)	840	(6.6)	904	(6.9)	938	(7.0)
general practitioners	11572	(95.6)	11570	(93.9)	11761	(93.4)	12054	(93.1)	12332	(93.0)
Total	12235		12331		12601		12958		13270	
(c) Nurses										
hospital nursing staff	264683	(93.7)	288438	(93.9)	300598	(93.7)	331190	(93.7)	350330	(93.6)
local authority nurses	17933	(6.3)	19001	(6.1)	20042	(6.3)	22226	(6.3)	23950	(6.4)
Total	282616		307429		320640		353416		374280	
(d) Midwives										
hospital midwives	17333	(74.5)	18368	(76.3)	19438	(79.0)	19934	(80.5)	20680	(81.6)
local authority midwives	5921	(5.5)	5685	(21.0)	5159	(21.0)	4852	(19.5)	4654	(18.4)
Total	23254		24053		24597		24768		25334	
(e) Other Executive Council Medical Staff										
Opthalmic Opticians	887		939		950		986		988	
Opticians	7317		6956		6729		6694		6639	
(f) Other hospital staff										
Professional & technical	31659		34941		37930		42092		44328	
Auxiliary staff	241037		255307		257351		270154		274189	

Source: *Central Statistical Office* (1973 (B)) Table 56 pages 68-9.

[1971] and Lavers and Rees [1972]). Until the 1965-6 review the general practitioner was paid on a capitation basis. Although 'negative direction' was used to prevent physicians working in 'over-doctored' areas no positive attempts were made to attract doctors to specific areas. Since 1966 the attractions of the relatively deprived areas have been increased by means of financial inducements, the nature of which are shown in Table 4.

Table 4 *The Remuneration of General Practitioners 1974*

	Physician A	Physician B
Basic practice allowance	1815	1815
2050 patients under 65	3075	3075
450 patients over 65	945	945
Supplementary capitation fee*	420	420
Out-of-hours- duties	350	350
50 night visits†	150	150
100 vaccinations††	50	50
Group practice allowance	270	270
Designated area allowance	NA	750***
Payment for receptionist's income**	700	700
Rent payments†††	150	150
Seniority payment	910	910
Total Income	8835	9585

*   Payment of £0.28 for each patient on the list in excess of 1000.
†   Night visits take place between 11 pm and 7 am and are paid at the rate of £3 each.
†† Payment rates of £0.50 each.
** Only part of the receptionist's income (£1000) is reimbursed.
*** Only part of the rent of premises (£500) is reimbursed.
††† There are two types of Designated Area payment. Type 1 is where the area is designated as 'under-doctored' and the payment (£490 pa) is paid for three-year periods. Type 2 payment (£750) are made for one year to areas with more than 3000 patients per doctor.

Table 4 shows the components of two physicians' incomes – one in an 'under-doctored' (or designated) area and the other outside. The characteristics of the two physicians are identical. They each have been practising for thirty years and are members of a partnership. They have 2500 patients each, 2050 under sixty-five years old and 450 over sixty-five. They carry out night visits, vaccinations and out of hours duties. Physician A has an income of £8,835 p.a. whose major components are the capitation fees, the basic practice allowance and the seniority payment. Physician B working in a desiganted area receives an income of £9,585. The designated area allowance and the items given for physician A are the major compenents of his income. Table 4 gives the gross income level of UK physicians. Receptionist income, practice expenses and other items can be set off against tax liability. The individual physicians income can vary from one area to another and from one physician to another depending on their circumstances. In 1973-4 the target average income[24] was £8110, of which £2360 was to cover expenses, i.e. the net average income target was £5750. During the years since the large pay increase of twenty per cent in 1970 average incomes have risen by five per cent per annum. This income from general practice can be augmented by payments for services carried out for local authorities and other bodies. The 1971 Review Body Report estimated that on average these payments equalled about ten per cent of NHS income. If this percentage was static in the early 1970s the average general practitioner earned about £6300 in 1974. Financial inducements may mitigate the unequal geographical distribution of general practitioners. The more efficient solution may be to increase the stock of general practitioners but if this is done very rapidly it may have an adverse effect on salaries because of the capitation and other elements in the payment system.

The successful hospital physician proceeds through the grades of house officer, senior house officer, registrar and senior registrar and consultant. The house officer salary range begins at £1914 and the consultant range goes from £5085 to £7599 in nine steps. The latter range is for a full-time consultant. Part-time consultants are paid proportionally lower rates although they can supplement their incomes from private sources. Both full- and part-time consultants are eligible for 'distinction awards'. These payments are awarded on four categories categories[25] and can double a consultant's salary. About thirty per cent of consultants receive an award of some kind. Recently the basis on which awards are given, medical excellence, has been blurred as an attempt has been made to distribute the awards in more geographically 'equitable' manner. The teaching hospitals, traditional centres of medical excellence, are concentrated in London and as a result a large proportion of awards went to consultants working in the south-east. In an attempt to offset this concentration pressure has been exerted by the medical profession and others to increase the number of awards and allocate them to the other regions. This blending of the medically excellent and the geographically equitable objectives is not without its difficulties. Two primary difficulties are apparent. Firstly one of semantics: what is medical excellence? What is geographical equality? Secondly, any definition of these terms must, if it is to be useful for policy purposes, indicate the trade-off between the two objectives, i.e. how much equity? What is the cost of greater equity in terms of rewarding excellence? These problems have not been widely debated and are inherently difficult to answer.

There was also a large increase in the number of hospital dentists during the period 1965-72. However this high percentage increase — forty-two — was on a small base, and the majority of dentists continued to work as general practitioners. The total stock of dentists grew by eight per cent, or 1035, during the period to reach 0.24 per 1000 population in 1972. The stock of general dental practitioners grew six and a half per cent during the seven year period but was very unevenly distributed geographically. In 1971 the average number of patients per dentist in Great Britain was 4460. In the North of England and the East Midlands of England the numbers (6128 and 6152) were well above this average whilst near London and South-West England there were fewer patients per dentist (3280 and 4007 respectively). During the period 1965-72 this relatively static, unevenly distributed stock of dentists increased the number of courses of treatment given to patients by over thirty-one per cent. The remuneration of dentists is fixed by the same body as that for physicians. In 1974 the target average income for a dentist was about £5300. Individual incomes depend on treatment given as the majority of the remuneration of dentists is based on fee per item of service.

° The stock of nurses and midwives grew rapidly during the late 1960s. The number of nurses in Great Britain during the period 1965-72 grew by thirty-two per cent to 374,280 in 1972, i.e. 6.89 per 1000 population. The majority of these nurses worked for the hospital system. The number of nurses working for local authorities rose by 4000 in the period 1965 to 1972. Due to reorganisation many of these nurses are employed by the NHS. There are two categories of nurse: the State Registered Nurse (SRN) — thirty per cent of the total number of nurses in England and Wales in 1972; and State Enrolled Nurse (SEN) — fifteen per cent of all nurses in England and Wales in 1972. The minimum entrance age is eighteen for both categories and the SRN entrance requirements include at least two Ordinary Level passes in the General Certificate of Education. The SRN's course takes three years and includes a higher proportion of theory than the SEN's course which lasts two years. There are about seven hundred training schools for nurses in Great Britain and usually they are attached to the hospitals in which the nurses acquire their practical training. Trainee nurses amounted to twenty-five per cent of the total number of nurses in England and Wales in 1972. Auxilary and assistant nurses have little formal training although their numbers are significant — twenty-nine per cent of the total.

A similar change in employer has been experienced by midwives. The number of midwives grew by nine per cent over the period 1965 to 1972 to 25,334 i.e. 0.46 per 1000 population. The midwife is usually a qualified SRN who has undergone further specialised training.

Three categories of staff in Table 3 remain to be discussed. Opthalmic Local Executive Council staff declined over the period due to the reduction in the number of opticians being uncompensated by the increase in the number of opthalmic physicians. In 1972 there were 7627 opthalmic staff — a fall of 577 compared with 1965. The number of hospital professional and technical staff increased by forty per cent to 44,328 in the period 1965-72. This increase was greater than that experienced by ancillary hospital staff whose numbers grew by thirteen per cent to 274,189 in 1972.

(b) Hospitals

The total hospital bed stock in Great Britain increased by 21,000 to 508,000 in the period 1963-71. The behaviour of the components of this aggregate can be seen in Table 5. The non-psychiatric bed stock declined marginally to 294,000 (5.44 per 1000 population) during the period with the largest change taking place in the surgical category: an 8.69 per cent increase. The psychiatric bed stock declined by 19,000 to 215,000. This figure is the product of two contrary forces. These are the decline in the number of mental illness beds by 21,000 to 146,000 in 1972, and the increase of 2,000 to 68,000 in the number of beds for the mentally handicapped. The overall bed-patient ratio was 9.40 in 1971, of which 3.97 were psychiatric.

Table 5 *Hospital Beds in Great Britain 1963-71* (alternate years and in thousands)*

Category	1963	1965	1967	1969	1971	1971 beds per 1000 population
Medical	80	79	76	73	72	1.33
Surgical	92	93	94	94	100	1.85
Obstetrics and Maternity	23	24	25	26	27	0.49
Geriatrics and Chronic sick	64	65	66	68	70	1.29
Other	36	34	34	34	25	0.46
Sub-Total: Non-Psychiatric	295	295	295	295	294	5.44

Table 5 *(Cont)*

	1963	1965	1967	1969	1971	Beds per 1000
Psychiatric	234	233	229	223	215	3.97
Total	529	528	524	518	508	9.40

Source: *Department of Health and Social Security* (1973) Table 4.2 pages 58-9.

* Average number of beds available each day.

The geographical distribution of the hospital bed stock is very unequal. This inequality has been the object of much attention from academics and policy makers alike during the 1960s and 1970s. Feldstein (1965, 1967) used 1960 data to indicate the paradoxes of the UK hospital system. He noted substantial regional inequalities in bed stocks and demonstrated that the Regional Hospital Boards' response to these differences were strange. For instance the Sheffield Region had less beds per 1000 population than the Liverpool Region. Despite this difference the average length of stay in the Sheffield Region exceeded that of the Liverpool Region, whereas it might have been expected that the Region with the low bed stock (Sheffield) might have responded to relative scarcity by cutting the length of stay. The relative deprivation of the Sheffield Region was driven home by Cooper and Culyer (1970, 1971) who showed that on thirty-one provision indices the Sheffield Region was worse off than the Oxford Region. The disparities remain in the 1970s.[26] For instance the South-West Metropolitan Hospital Region had thirteen beds per 1000 population in 1970. The Sheffield Region in the same year had 7.7 beds i.e. sixty-nine per cent less than the SW Metropolitan Region.

Policy makers have not been blind to these regional disparities and have reacted in a number of ways. It was noted above that a policy of 'negative direction' was adopted in 1966-7 to acquire greater equality in the distribution of general practitioners. The policy makers response to the inequalities in the distribution of hospital beds and expenditure have been twofold: the regional allocation formula and the hospital building programme. The regional allocation formula was circulated by the Department in 1970. The main element in the formula is the adjusted[27] population of the regions. Two other elements, bed stocks and case flow, are incorporated into the formula. These elements are highly correlated and reflect the effects of history rather than the relative 'needs' of the regions. The formula is used to determine regional hospital allocations and whilst it may tend to equalise revenue between the regions, it ignores the level of co-operant resources in the regions (e.g. the level of general practitioner care) and does little to equalise the stock of hospital beds.

The principal instrument used to equalise the stocks of hospital beds is the hospital building programme. Whilst the allocation formula services the stocks of beds that exist, the building programme attempts to reduce the inequalities produced by wide variations in the distribution of resources and philanthropy prior to nationalisation in 1948. The history of the NHS between 1948 and the early 1960s was one in which the prime concern was to constrain the rate of growth of expenditure. As far as the capital expenditure programme was concerned this policy was very successful. The result was that the Administration found itself with an antiquated and geographically unequal stock of hospital beds at the beginning of the 1960s. In 1962 the Government published long-term plans for modernising the hospital service. These plans were revised in 1966 when a ten-year hospital building programme was announced. This programme cost £500 million in the five years which followed and, at 1971 prices, a further £800 million was ear-marked for hospital building in the period up to 1976. The product of this programme will be a national network of general hospitals each equipped with a wide range of diagnostic and care facilities, and a mitigation of geographical inequalities in the hospital bed stock.

The building programme has been accompanied by a sustained effort to increase the efficiency with which existing facilities are used. Although the total bed stock has declined, through-put in terms of patients increased by thirty per cent in the 1960s. This outcome was achieved by the shortening of the average length of stay. Table 6 shows average length of stay data for selected years during the period 1961-72. The overall average length of stay fell by nearly thirty per cent to 34.5 days. If long-stay patients are excluded the average length of stay statistic fell by thirty per cent to 10.2 days. The attractions in terms of cost savings of further reductions in the length of stay are substantial. However, during the early 1970s the hospital system was being relatively unresponsive to further efforts in this direction. The onset of diminishing returns may be reversed in the psychiatric sector if the current attempts to care for patients in the community are successful.

Table 6   *Average length of stay in Hospital*

	1961	1966	1970	1971	1972
All patients	34.5	29.4	25.7	24.7	24.2
Excluding long-stay patients*	14.5	12.4	10.8	10.4	10.2

Source: *Central Statistical Office* (1973 (c)) Table 78 page 130.

*   i.e. psychiatric, geriatric and the chronic ill.

However, such attempts, when successful, reduce hospital expenditures but require increased expenditure elsewhere. The problems of these efforts are discussed elsewhere (Maynard and Tingle 1974 (a) and Maynard and Tingle 1974 (b)).

8. Conclusion

The objective of the reorganisation of the National Health Service in 1974 was to increase the efficiency with which medical care is provided in the United Kingdom. To attain this objective an increased emphasis has been placed on improvements in the management of the service, in particular the integration of various groups of personnel, such as physicians, into the management structure. A more careful approach to the allocation of funds to the regional hospital authorities has been adopted although its efficacy in furthering the efficient allocation of resources can be questioned (West 1973). The basic overall allocational formula is still what we had last year plus x per cent. The priorities of the Service are usually those elements which pressure groups and scandals have demonstrated to be 'inadequate' in some stark manner. The Service component in the lime light during the last ten years has been the psychiatric service with its legacy of antiquated equipment and a hospital population some of whom were confined as a result of illegitimate pregnancies in less liberal times.

The problems posed by the provision of medical care in the UK are enormous. No adequate measure of output exists although elementary efforts to develop social indicators have been undertaken (Culyer, Lavers and Williams [1971]). The scope for the application of more rigorous techniques is realised by all concerned with the administration of the Service. Certain economic techniques may be of use. Cost effectiveness studies which take the policy objective as given and then attempt to estimate the full costs of the various methods of attaining the objective, can provide the policy maker with fuller information about the costs of present procedures and the cost of alternative methods of attaining the same end.[28] Output budgeting, which selects intermediate measures such as bed population ratios and attempts to rank them by priority, is at worst an excellent technique for concentrating attention on what the Service is trying to do, and is at best an aid to those seeking to measure whether the Service is doing what it is alleged to be doing. The Department of Health and Social Security are preparing an output budget for the NHS, elementary elements of which are already published (see Maynard and Tingle 1974 (a)). The use of these and other techniques, and the development of social indicators should lead to a more efficient use of resources.

Whilst such techniques may lead to a more efficient use of resources within the NHS there are no comparable techniques to enable the politicians and the administrators to decide which is the most efficient way of allocating resources between different types of expenditure. It is impossible to compare the outputs and hence the relative virtues of investing in defence or health. Decisions to allocate resources to particular services are the outcome of a complex system of filtering departmental resource demands. In any particular year 98.5 per cent of total public expenditure is pledged by policy decisions made in previous years. The political fights are concerned with about 1.5 per cent of the total resources available to finance expenditure. As Heclo and Wildavsky (1974) have argued the winners of this fight are those with charisma and political strength in their Departments and in the Cabinet.

It might be argued by some that Health Ministers in the UK have been relatively unsuccessful in these competitions for resources. An indicator of their relative failure could be the low percentage of GNP spent on medical care in the UK. This would be a dangerous argument. GNP league tables are dubious measures of anything, let alone the political weight of Health Ministers. An equally plausible explanation of the GNP figure, if we assume it is meaningful to some degree, is that it is the product of the monopsonist influence of the Department of Health and Social Security. Unlike many other European health ministries the DHSS is the sole buyer (monopsonist) of many medical care goods and services. This market power may have constrained the powers of monopolies such as the medical profession and the pharmaceutical industry: a plausible indicator of this in the pharmaceutical industry is the lower level of prices charged for many drugs in the UK compared with Western Europe (see Cooper and Cooper [1972]). If the monopsony has constrained the monopolies costs and hence expenditure may have been cut to produce a lower GNP percentage for the UK. The exercise of this power is not costless however, and if taken too far it may precipitate migration of physicians and lower research expenditures by the pharmaceutical industry.[29]

The British National Health Service is financed by general taxation and provided by an administration which is increasingly constrained by the decisions of the DHSS. By placing medical care outside the market place and inside the public sector the British have removed one set of problems and replaced them with another set. Whilst students of foreign health usually have to study the interaction of financers and providers of medical care, the student of the NHS has to study the interation of politicians, administrators and pressure groups. The institutions differ and the respective problems set differ accordingly. However, behind each set of problems lies the basic question of what

209

medical care, how much medical care, how should it be produced and to whom should it go. The nationalisation of medical care facilities and their finance out of general taxation does not solve these problems. Indeed given that society changes, the answers must change and with all the time-lags due to the inflexibility of individuals and institutions, and the basic problem of the scarcity of resources, the problems of medical care systems may never be solved.

NOTES

1. The United Kingdom consists of England, Wales, Scotland and Northern Ireland. Later the term Great Britain is used; this consists of England, Wales and Scotland alone, and its use is necessitated by a lack, in certain areas, of UK statistics.
2. The Minister in charge of the NHS is the Secretary of State for Health and Social Security.
3. Ministry of Health (1968) p 8, n 1.
4. National Assistance Act 1948, Social Security Act 1970. This function remains with the local authorities after the 1974 reorganisation.
5. The rate is a property tax levied as a proportion of every £ of notional rental value.
6. Local Government was reformed as from 1st April 1974. The social services responsibilities of these new authorities lie with the Districts and Metropolitan Areas of England and with the Counties outside Metropolitan Areas. In all areas except London the AHA covers one local authority unit to facilitate coordination. There are ninety AHAs in England and fifteen in Scotland. The AHAs in Scotland are responsible to the Scottish Home and Health Department.
7. Department of Health and Social Security (1972) pp 24-5.
8. These include the ambulance services, home nursing and midwifery, maternity and child care, vaccination and immunisation, health visiting, health centres, family planning and epidemiological surveys. An excellent discussion of reorganisation can be found in Office of Health Economics (1974 (a)).
9. I.e. avoiding the NHS waiting list. For e.g. hernias, the waiting time can be six weeks in some areas.
10. National Insurance Act 1946 (flat rate benefits), supplemented in 1966 (graduated benefits), and to be replaced in 1975 (Social Security Act 1973). For a survey of this legislation see Maynard (1973) reprinted in Cooper (1974).
11. Due to the NHS reorganisation discussed in the previous section, this percentage will fall as some local functions will be transferred to the NHS proper.
12. National Insurance covers benefits to the old, the sick, the unemployed, widows, guardians, expectant mothers and various other groups. All benefits are in cash.
13. E.g. £72 million was interest on the National Insurance Fund – the latter is a residue of the insurance myth.

14. Many of the activities of local authorities Social Service Departments are complementary to the medical care of the NHS.
15. This Committee is appointed by the Secretary of State for Health.
16. One effect of this may be that practitioners, once established in an 'under-doctored' area, attempt to prevent any further inflow of physicians. New entrants can depress established physicians' levels of remuneration if they remove the area from the 'under-doctored' category.
17. Other young people under twenty-one are exempt from all charges except charges for the supply and modification of dentures and bridges.
18. The 'poor' are defined as those in receipt of Supplementary Benefits.
19. Except for elastic hosiery, which is charged at a rate of £0.25 or £0.50.
20. See note 18 above.
21. One extraordinary characteristic of UK social security is that basic National Insurance rates are less than Supplementary Benefit (SB) rates. The latter benefit is paid to the uninsured and those whose insurance benefit has expired and is means-tested. Many people on National Insurance can supplement their benefits by SB if they know their 'welfare rights' and are prepared to undergo the means test. See Maynard (1973) reprinted in Cooper (1974).
22. The Willink Committee (1957) was a classic exercise in bad manpower forecasting. See Peacock and Shannon (1968).
23. Adequacy here is related to a policy objective of one physician per 2500 people.
24. There is a permanent Review Body which reports annually on the remuneration of doctors and dentists. The present body was set up in 1970 and has reported three times prior to 1974 (1971 [Command Paper 4825]; 1972 [Command Paper 5010]; 1973 [Command Paper 5353]).
25. In 1974 there were 115-119 A plus awards (£7350), 420-434 A awards (£5577), 1215-1256 B awards (£3273), and 2605-2743 C awards (£1392). The awards are allocated by a committee of physicians.
26. See Maynard (1972) and Maynard and Tingle (1974 (b)) for a discussion of this with reference to psychiatric care.
27. The adjustments take account of the migration of patients across regional boundaries and the existence of teaching hospitals (which are funded separately).
28. For an example of this see Culyer and Maynard (1970).
29. H.G. Johnson, has argued that the use of monopsonist powers by the British Government in the 1960s contributed to the 'Brain Drain'. For a full account of this debate see Blaug (1968).

References

M. Blaug (1968) editor *The Economics of Education: Selected Readings.* Vol II Penguin Books, London.
Central Office of Information (1973) *Health Services in Britain*, Reference Pamphlet 20 HMSO, London.

References *(Cont)*

Central Statistical Office (1972, 1973 (a)), *National Income and Expenditure 1972, 1973*, HMSO, London.

Central Statistical Office (1973 (b)), *Annual Abstract of Statistics*, HMSO, London.

Central Statistical Office (1973 (c)), *Social Trends*, No 4 HMSO, London.

M. Cooper and A.J. Culyer (1970), 'An Economic Assessment of Some Aspects of the Operation of the National Health Service' in the British Medical Association's publication *Health Services Financing*, Appendix A.

M. Cooper and A.J. Culyer (1971), 'An Economic Survey of Nature and Intent of the British National Health Service' *Social Science and Medicine*, Vol 5 pp 1-13.

M.H. Cooper and A.J. Cooper (1972), *International Price Comparison: a study of the prices of pharmaceuticals in the UK and eight other countries in 1970*, National Economic Development Office, August, London.

A.J. Culyer and A.K. Maynard (1970), 'The Costs of Dangerous Drugs Legislation in England and Wales' *Medical Care*, Vol 8, No 6, November-December.

A.J. Culyer, R. Lavers and A. Williams (1971), 'Social Indicators: Health' *Social Trends*, No 2 HMSO London.

Department of Health and Social Security (1972), *Management Arrangements for the Reorganised National Health Service*, HMSO, London.

Department of Health and Social Security (1973), *Health and Personal Social Services Statistics for England and Wales 1972*, HMSO, London.

M.S. Feldstein (1965) 'Hospital Bed Scarcity: An Analysis of the Effects of Inter-regional Differences', *Economica*.

M.S. Feldstein (1967) *An Economic Analysis of Health Service Efficiency: econometric studies of the British National Health Service*, North Holland.

M. Heclo and A. Wildavsky (1974) *The Private Government of Public Money*, Macmillan, London.

R. Lavers and M. Rees (1972) 'The Distinction Award System in England and Wales' in Nuffield Provincial Hospitals Trust *Problems of and Progress in Medical Care*, Seventh Series, Oxford University Press.

A. Maynard (1972) 'Inequalities in Psychiatric Care in England and Wales', *Social Science and Medicare*, Vol 6, pp 221-7.

A. Maynard (1973) 'A Survey of Social Security in the UK', pp 39-57. *Social and Economic Administration*, Vol 7, No 1, January. Reprinted in M.H. Cooper (1974) editor *Social Policy*, Blackwells, Oxford.

Alan K. Maynard and David N. King (1972) *Rates or Prices?*, Institute of Economic Affairs Hobart Paper, London.

A. Maynard and R. Tingle (1974 (a)) 'The Mental Health Services: A Review of the Statistical Sources and a Critical Assessment of their Usefulness', *British Journal of Psychiatry*, April.

A. Maynard and R. Tingle (1974 (b)) 'The Objectives and Performance of the Mental Health Service in England and Wales in the 1960's', *Journal of Social Policy*, forthcoming.

Ministry of Health (1968) *The National Health Service* , HMSO, London.

National Health Service Reorganisation: England (1972), Command Paper 5055, August, HMSO, London.

Office of Health Economics (1974 (B)), *The Cost of the NHS*, Information Sheet No 24, March, London.

Office of Health Economics (1974 (c)) *The NHS Reorganisation*, London.

212

References *(Cont)*

Alan T. Peacock and J.R. Shannon (1968) 'The New Doctor's Dilemma', *Lloyds Bank Review*, January.

Review Body Reports (1971, 1972 and 1973) *Report of the Review Body on Doctors and Dentists Remuneration Number 1, 2 and 3*, Command Papers 4825 (December 1971), 5010 (June 1972) and 5353 (July 1973) HMSO, London.

The Sainsbury Report (1967) *Report of the Committee of Enquiry into the relationship of the pharmaceutical industry with the National Health Service*, HMSO, London.

P. West (1973) 'Allocation and Equity in the Public Sector: the Hospital Revenue Allocation Formula', *Applied Economica*, Vol 5, No 3, pp 153-66, September.

The Willink Committee (1957) *Report of the Committee to Consider the Future Number of Medical Practitioners and the Appropriate Intake of Medical Students*, HMSO, London.

9 IRELAND

The Evolution of Health Care in Ireland

Prior to Independence the evolution of medical care in Ireland
paralleled developments in the United Kingdom. The Irish Poor Law
Commissioners, appointed in 1847, lost some of their health powers in
1872 to the Irish Local Government Board. This body administered,
by a system of local government, health care (in particular public
health) in Ireland until after Independence. The local authorities
financed their own activities and subsidised the provision of medical
care by the Poor Law Workhouses. The Poor Law administration
provided hospitals and compelled each local Poor Law Union to be
divided into dispensary districts. These dispensary districts, which
remained the basic health administration areas until 1970, were provided with a physician whose duty it was to attend, without charge, the
sick poor in his area. The physician was permitted to supplement his
Poor Law income with fees received from treating the non-poor sick of
his area. Voluntary hospitals were few in number but relatively large in
importance, and were concentrated geographically in the Dublin area.

Independence was followed by some reorganisation. The Local
Government Board was replaced by a Minister who could initiate
change rather than only administer the medical care system. The finance of medical care was derived primarily from local taxation
although this was augmented by such measures as the 1933 Public
Hospitals Act which set up a horse-racing sweepstake whose profit went
to finance hospital capital expenditure. Although plans for comprehensive health insurance were not put forward until after 1945, reform
prior to 1960 was not as substantive as some wished. Legislation in
1947 and 1953 transformed the county council into the local health
authority in charge of all medical care except mental health, which
remained the responsibility of special joint boards, in most parts of the
country. In Dublin, Cork, Limerick and Wexford medical care was
delivered by a complex system of boards until 1960 when legislation
unified provision under comprehensive health authorities. This change
reduced to twenty-seven the number of local health care units.

These changes in administration were accompanies by an increase in
the magnitude of the financial role of central government and an
increase in social insurance coverage. By 1947 State grants met sixteen
per cent[1] of the total costs of providing health services. New legislation

214

in 1947 resulted in the State making grants which met all increases in expenditure after 31st March 1948 until central payments equalled local payments. Thereafter the State agreed to meet fifty per cent of any further increase in expenditure on medical care. The coverage of the medical care system was increased by the Health Act 1953.[2] The eligibility criterion of this legislation was that each socio-economic class should be eligible for services 'which persons in it could not afford'. This rather vague criterion was spelt out in detail in the legislation. The general practitioner service was provided free of charge to a limited number of people and was means-tested. Institutional care, being more expensive, was open to a wider section of society whose characteristics were specified by group rather than by individual means test.[3]

Since 1961 central administration has changed little[4] although significant changes may occur as a result of work taking place at present. Local administration was radically reformed in 1971 when health care was taken out of the hands of the local government authorities and handed over to regional bodies who are made up of local and central government representatives and health profession organisations. The finance of the service changed in 1966 when the local financial contribution was frozen. By 1970 fifty-six per cent of the total cost was met by central government which reacted to this increased burden by introducing contributions by eligible persons in October 1971. These radical changes are discussed in more detail below.

State activity in the medical care field has been supplemented by voluntary insurance. In 1957 a State sponsored Voluntary Health Insurance Board (VHIB) was set up to aid and encourage the more affluent groups of Irish society to cover themselves against the risk of medical care expenses. By the beginning of 1973, 506,162 people were covered by the Board's scheme. Private health insurance bodies can operate if they hold a Ministerial Licence to do so. This is issued only if the company does not compete with the VHIB. Contributions to both private and VHIB insurance schemes are tax deductible.

The system of cash sickness benefit is the responsibility of the Department of Social Welfare and has evolved from a partial system introduced in 1911 to full coverage in 1974. Prior to 1974 benefits were given only to those groups who came within the scope of legislation which related coverage to the income and wealth characteristics of the population. These characteristics were the same as those used in deciding limited and full coverage for medical care until 1974.

1. Administration

Since 1971 Irish medical care administration has had the structure which is shown in Figure 1.

215

Figure 1 *The Organisation of Medical Care in Ireland since 1971*

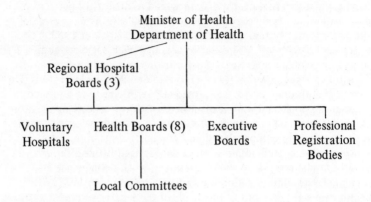

Source: *Hensey* (1972) p 42.

The task of administering the day to day running of the Irish health service lies in the hands of the eight Health Boards.[5] These bodies are comprised of local government officials who are in the majority, and representatives of the medical professions. The latter will be elected by the professions when the first appointments made by the Minister, on grounds of short-term expediency, retire. The Boards coordinate their activities with the local authorities and the voluntary health bodies. The management structure of the Boards has been largely determined by the work of the consultants, McKinsey. The Chief Executive of each Board administers an organisation with a tripartite structure. Each component of this structure covers a broad health area: community care, general hospital services and 'special'hospital services (services for the mentally handicapped and the mentally ill). The larger Boards have a 'programme manager' for each component of their structure, and a group of 'functional officers' in charge of finance, personnel and planning. These managers and officers form the Board's 'management team'. The smaller areas[6] have two managers, one of whom is responsible for the general and the special hospitals.

The community care component for the Area Board's work covers preventive health activities, general practitioner services, social workers and dental and public health nursing services. These services are not administered at the Area level but at the local government level and

216

overseen by a director of community services who is responsible to the Area's programme director in this field.

This disaggregation of the Area Board's activities is supported by local committees. The function of these bodies is advisory and they are based on the local government structure. These bodies will enable the Board to keep in contact with local opinion as the chief executive officer or another senior officer of the Board is required to attend the meetings of the local committee.

The hospital programme director is responsible for the general hospitals and special hospitals in public ownership. The latter group is sub-divided into mental illness, mental handicap and geriatric facilities, and each has a director. The problem of coordinating public and voluntary hospital activities is to be resolved, it is hoped, by the Regional Hospital Boards. The three Regional Hospital Boards[7] are concerned with 'the general organisation and development of hospital services' rather than the day-to-day provision of services. Their activities are related closely to those of the Department of Health and the communication of views about 'needs' and 'priorities' between the two organisations is important. It is possible that the organisation of these bodies may be changed in the light of problems observed during the first year of their operation.

The 'Executive Bodies' shown in Figure 1 are the result of 1961 legislation which empowered the Minister of Health to set up corporate bodies. Hensey[8] gives a list of such bodies which include the Blood Transfusion Service Board, the National Rehabilitation Board, the Medico-Social Research Board and the National Drugs Advisory Board. The functions of these bodies are usually apparent from their names.

The function of the Registration Bodies is apparent to those interested in the provision of medical care. Each of the medical professions have registers of their members' names. The registration of physicians is controlled by the Medical Registration Council. The main costs to those physicians who choose to practise but are not registered, is that they can be fined if they claim they are registered, they are ineligible for any public appointment, and they are not entitled to sue for non-payment of fees. The dentists, the pharmacists, the nurses and the opticians have similar registration bodies: the Dental Board, the Pharmaceutical Society of Ireland, An Bord Altrannis and the Bord na Radharemhastoire.

It is not yet clear whether this organisation is effective because of its recent implementation. The radical changes of 1971, which withdrew health functions from local government agencies, have created a structure whose weak points are clearly apparent. The most obvious of these is the dual ownership of the hospital system and the problem of coordinating their activities to provide the comprehensive hospital

217

system envisaged by the Fitzgerald report[9], and the problem of coordinating the activities of the Health Boards and the local authorities which provide social services.

Cash sickness benefits are administered by the Department of Social Welfare which has a network of local offices.

2. Coverage

The recent reform of medical care institutions has been accompanied by changes in the coverage of the services provided. The extent of coverage depends on the type of benefit which the consumer demands. It was hoped that from 1st April 1974 every Irish citizen would be entitled to limited eligibility, i.e. free hospital inpatient and outpatient care, free maternity services and free infant welfare services. Furthermore no family was to have been required to pay more than £4 per month for pharmaceutical products. Prior to the legislation outlining these plans only manual workers and persons earning less than £1600 per year, farmers whose farms were valued at less than £60, and those in receipt of social welfare payments were entitled to these services. However the extension of coverage has had to be limited because of the opposition of the physicians. The intention is to extend coverage as planned when the physicians agree. in the meantime limited eligibility has been extended so that all those employees earning less than £2250 are covered. By 1975 it is hoped that limited eligibility will cover all Irish residents.

The limited eligibility which is to apply to all groups is augmented by full eligibility for some groups. The groups who get all medical care free of charge are those who, in the opinion of the Chief Executive Officer of the Health Board, are unable to afford general practitioner services for themselves and their dependents. All persons so designated received exemption cards which when produced prove eligibility for free general medical practitioner service with free choice of physician, free pharmaceuticals and appliances, a supply of milk for expectant and nursing mothers and for children under five years of age, dental and opthalmic services, travel facilities for parents of children who are long-stay patients in hospitals, and for all the benefits received by those with limited eligibility. Prior to 1974 the means test used to determine full eligibility differed from one area to another. Since 1st April 1974 a standard means test has been applied and as a result about one-third (1,034,083 at 31st March 1974) of the Irish population gets free medical care. Details of this means test are given in Table 1. From this it can be seen that any married couple with two children and an income below £23.50 per week would be designated as fully eligible.

218

Table 1 *Standards Adopted as Guidelines by all Health Boards with effect from 1st January 1974*

Single person living alone	£14.00
Single person living with family	£12.00
Married couple	£20.00
Allowance per child	£ 1.75
Allowance for other dependents	£ 2.75
Allowance per outgoing on house excess over	£ 2.00 pw
Other allowance	Reasonable expenses necessarily incurred in travelling to work.

1. Persons in receipt of the following pensions and allowances under the Social Welfare and Health Acts are regarded as eligible for medical cards without any further assessment of means: Old Age (Non-Contributory) Pension; Widows: (Non-Contributory) Pension; Orphans' (Non-Contributory) Pension; Deserted Wife's Allowance; Blind Pension. In addition to the above the following in certain areas are also regarded as eligible for medical cards without any further assessment of means:- Persons in receipt of Infectious Diseases (Maintenance) Allowances, Disabled Persons (Maintenance) Allowance, (South-Eastern, Southern and North-Western) and Home Assistance (as a basic income) in the South-Eastern Health Board area.

2. *Farmers*: Valuation as such is not the sole determining factor in assessing applications from farmers. Individual cases are assessed on all relevant factors including income, in accordance with the above standards.

Both those with limited and full eligibility receive free treatment of tuberculosis and other infectious diseases. Also children with long-term diseases and disabilities and adults who are mentally ill or handicapped receive free care.

Social insurance coverage is augmented by private insurance which covers over half a million people and is principally the concern of the Voluntary Health Insurance Board. The principal benefit given by this insurance is aid to 'top-up' public coverage for hospitalisation. This enables the privately insured patient to have a private room and treatment. Private insurance generally covers pharmaceutical expenditures only if they exceed a certain annual level e.g. £25. Most of the cost of

219

general practitioner care is financed out of private funds as relatively few people have private insurance to cover this type of care.

The overall coverage of the medical care service in Ireland is nearly complete. The poor receive free care. The relatively affluent will have limited eligibility and finance other types of care (e.g. private hospitalisation services) by insuring with the Voluntary Health Insurance Board, private insurers or by financing such care out of their current income.

Since 1974 sickness insurance has covered all Irish citizens. Prior to 1974 only those employees earning less than £1600 per year were covered. This change has been accompanies by the introduction of a second sickness and maternity benefit scheme which gives graduated or wage-related benefits to the insured.

3. Qualifying Conditions

The qualifying conditions for medical care benefits depend on the person's eligibility category. The qualifying condition for limited eligibility is residence in Ireland. For full eligibility the qualifying conditions are residence, citizenship and the Health Boards' means test, details of which are given in the previous Section.

Sickness benefit is paid for an unlimited duration provided 156 weekly contributions have been made by the insured person. The duration of benefits is limited to fifty-two weeks if forty-eight weekly contributions have been paid or credited in the last year and the 156 contribution record is absent. Reduced benefits are paid for fifty-two weeks if the contribution record in the last year shows only twenty-seven to forty-seven weekly payments. Maternity benefits are paid if twenty-six xontributions were made in the last year. Any person with less than twenty-six payments in the last year appears to have to have recourse to the public assistance system. Graduated benefits depend on the graduated contribution record of the insured person.

4. Finance

Until recently medical care was financed out of local taxation (the rates) and central taxation. Since late 1971 there has been a system of health contributions for those citizens in the limited eligibility category only. All contributors pay £0.15 per week or £7.00 per year. Those who contribute to social insurance schemes pay their health contribution with their social insurance contribution. Farmers pay £7 per year directly to the Health Boards and the self-employed contributions are collected by the Revenue Commissioners. These contributions meet only a small part of the cost of medical care in Ireland. Ninety-three per cent of income in 1972-3 was derived from the general taxation revenues of local and central government.

The finance of sickness benefits varies between the flat rate and the wage related scheme. The former is financed by flat rate employer and employee contributions which finances retirement pensions as well as sickness benefits. The contribution of a male employee in 1974 was £1.21; his employer paid £1.72. The wage related scheme is financed by a proportional contribution paid by the employer and the employee on incomes up to £2500 per annum. These contributions are collected by the income tax system.

5. Income and Expenditure

The finance and expenditure characteristics of the Irish health service are changing rapidly at present. By 1977 they should have reached a state of rest. In the financial year 1972-3 the total expenditure of the State provided Irish medical care system was just over £103 million. Nearly ninety per cent of this money was spent by the Health Boards as can be seen from Table 2. The remaining ten per cent financed the operating deficits of the voluntary (non-profit making) hospitals. In 1972-3 this latter item was the second part of a process of supplementation of the voluntary hospital systems income. The other part was a payment of capitation fees by the Health Boards. Since April 1974 this two-part system has been replaced by an annual grant made by the State to those hospitals which fulfill the necessary regulations and submit annual budgets in advance of expenditure. These budgets are used to determine the level of State grant.

The expenditure was financed by income from various sources. Health contributions by the population make up a very small part of the total income — less than five per cent. Apart from this income and a small payment which results from the horse sweepstake, the system is financed by various forms of taxation. The central government finances, *via* the health vote and the Exchequer vote, over sixty per cent of expenditure. This finance is raised by general taxation. In 1972-73 local government met just over thirty-three per cent of the total cost of State provided medical care. Since April 1973 the financial picture has been altered radically. The share of the Exchequer (central government), which has been increasing since the last war, has increased still further as a result of the implementation of a policy to transfer from local to central taxation that part of the cost of the medical care services which is met out of local rates. This policy is to be executed over a four-year period ending in 1977. The effect of the decision in 1973-4 was that the Exchequer bore all increase in medical care expenditure plus an amount equivalent to a reduction in 1972-3 local

221

government rates of twenty-five per cent. A further twenty-five per cent will be taken over by the Exchequer each year so that by 1977 all medical expenditures will be financed by central government. As a result of this policy the Irish public medical care system will be financed from central sources only.

Table 2 *State Health Care in Ireland, Income and Current Expenditure 1972-3*

	£m	Percentage
1. Income		
Local Government taxation (the rates)	35.00	33.83
Exchequer vote	53.03	51.27
Health contributions	4.75	4.59
Health vote	9.40	9.08
Sweepstake income	1.25	1.20
Total	103.43	100.00
2. Expenditure by spending authority		
Health Boards	92.78	89.70
Voluntary Hospital Deficit	10.65	10.29
Total	103.43	100.00
3. Expenditure by Type		
General hospital care	48.835	47.21
Psychiatric and mental handicap hospital care	21.760	21.03
Other hospitals and homes	5.776	5.58
General medicine and general practitioner service	12.567	12.15
Other	14.492	14.01
Total	103.430	100.00

Source: Personal correspondence with the Department of Health, Dublin, May 1974.

Details of how the income was expended in 1972-3 are shown in the final section of Table 2. General hospital care was the largest consumer of resources taking up over forty-seven per cent of the total. Psychiatric and mental handicap hospital care took up a further twenty-one per cent and general medicine and the general practitioner service for those with full eligibility consumed over twelve per cent of total expenditure.

The capital expenditure programme of the public medical care programme is financed partly out of the proceeds of the Hospitals Trust Fund which administers a sweepstake on horse-racing events in Ireland and the United Kingdom. The administration of this Fund is in the hands of a Board which finances only those capital programmes approved by the Minister of Health. During the period 1933 to 1971-2 £57.5 million was spent on capital projects for the public medical care services in Ireland. Of this total, £32 million (55.6 per cent) was derived from the Hospitals Trust Fund, £12.6 million (21.9 per cent) from State supplements to the Fund, and £12.9 million (22.4 per cent) from the local government and other sources. The sector which benefitted most from this expenditure was general hospitals – 37.7 per cent. Mental illness and mental handicap units received 17.7 per cent and tuberculosis units 18.4 per cent of total expenditure. The remaining twenty-six per cent of capital expenditure in this period was spent on maternity and childrens' hospitals (7.8 per cent), clinics and dispensaries (2.9 per cent), country homes (8.3 per cent), and miscellaneous items (6.9 per cent).[10]

There are two further expenditure sources in the Irish medical care system. The first is insurance. The Voluntary Health Insurance Board paid out £4.095 million in the financial year 1971-2. This money was paid as a result of the claims of the insured and financed hospital care in the large majority of cases. The expenses of pharmaceutical products and general practitioner care is usually met out of current income by those citizens with limited eligibility status.

It is difficult to calculate the exact size of private expenditure on health care in Ireland. The Dublin Ministry of Health has no estimate available. The total expenditure of the State and Voluntary Health Insurance Board was £107.25 million in the financial year 1972-3.

6. Benefits

(a)   Medical Care

The general practitioner service has changed in the last five years. Until the early 1970s those people with full eligibility received free general practitioner care from the physician who practised in each local authority dispensary area. The new arrangements, which have covered all Ireland since late 1972, attempt to offer free care to the one third of the population who have full eligibility. In practically all areas the arrangement is governed by an agreement between the physicians and the local Health Board. The physicians are paid per item of service. The agreed fee since 1972 for a consultation in normal working hours has been £0.80. Consultations outside normal hours other than those between 12 midnight and 8 am are paid at a rate of £1.15. Those between 12 midnight and 8 am earn the physician £2.25. The fees paid for visits to patients by the physician vary according to the distance which the physician has to travel, e.g. if it is less than three miles it is £1.15. Only those physicians who sign the standard agreement with the Boards are able to care for fully eligible patients. The number of physicians involved with this service will be determined by the Boards in relation to 'need'. The physician is forbidden to discriminate between private and public patients. The majority of the population (sixty-six per cent) who do not have full eligibility to medical care services are private patients when demanding general medical care. The fees charged by physicians are not regulated by the State.

The cost of pharmaceutical products differs from one group of society to another. All those who suffer from certain diseases or disabilities of a long-term or permanent nature receive free drugs regardless of their income. The benefit categories are specified[11] and the pharmacist is refunded by the local Health Board. Those people who are not in these groups and have full eligibility status get free pharmaceutical products whilst those families with limited eligibility have to pay no more than £4 per month for drugs: the State pays fifty per cent of expenditures between £3 and £5 and a hundred per cent of those those expenditures over £5 in any month.

Some dispensing is done by physicians and both they and the pharmacists are paid by a central bureau.

Dental care may extend to both limited and full eligibility categories in the late 1970s. At present this type of care is restricted to children of families with full eligibility. Care is provided by the Health Boards who employ full-time dentists (141 in 1971) supplemented in some areas by part-time employment of private practitioners. The geographical distribution of these facilities is unequal and in some areas there is no such care for the fully eligible patients.

Both limited and fully eligible groups get free maternity care and free infant welfare services. Maternity care consists of care by the physician during pregnancy, and of infants for the first six weeks of their life. Normal care consists of four visits prior to confinement and two after. Most babies are born in hospitals and so the need to finance midwife services for home confinements − now only four per cent of the total − has been removed to a considerable extent. Where domiciliary care continues the Health Board finances care. The infant welfare services cover children up to the age of six years and the intention is to inspect children regularly: in urban areas clinics are to be set up for this purpose.

The provision of home helps and financial assistance for the aged and others is the responsibility of the local authority. These services are wholly financed by local government and, as in the United Kingdom there is the problem of coordinating provision in this area with the demands of the medical care programme which encourages short hospital stays to economise. General hospital care will be provided free of charge for all when limited eligibility is extended. There are three types of institution. The public hospitals are operated by the Health Boards and largely financed out of central government taxation. The voluntary (non-profit making) public hospitals vary in size and characteristics. They are located in urban areas, principally Dublin, Cork and Limerick, and are financed largely from public funds. The third part of the hospital sector is private (for profit) hospitals. These are relatively few in number (see Section 7 below).

Special hospital care is provided free of charge and caters for the mentally ill, the mentally handicapped and the old. The emphasis of public policy is to return as many of the groups to the community as soon as possible. Between 1958 and 1970 the number of mentally ill inpatients fell by twenty-seven per cent to 15,392. The number of mentally handicapped hospital places has been supplemented by a programme involving an increase in residential places and day centres for the handicapped. The mentally handicapped adult (over the age of sixteen) is provided with care only after a means test. However this test is related to the individual's income and usually means that he gets free aid.

(b)   Cash Benefits
Flat rate sickness benefits are paid after a three-day waiting period for an unlimited duration provided the insured person has paid 156 contributions. If such a contribution record is absent, benefits last for fifty-two weeks and if less than forty-seven but more than twenty-six weekly contributions are shown for the preceding year, the benefit rate is reduced. The weekly benefit for a married man whose spouse is a housewife and a single adult is £11.90 and £6.55. This benefit is paid if less than twenty-six contributions have been made in the last year. The maternity benefit is paid for six weeks prior, and six weeks after the confinement at a weekly rate of £6.55.

The graduated benefit system was introduced in April 1974 and benefits are determined by the graduated contribution record. The benefits are not paid for the first two weeks of illness and their amount is limited to forty per cent of average weekly earnings during the previous tax year between £14 and an upper limit.

7. Provision

(a)   Medical Personnel

The data concerning medical personnel in Ireland is rather imprecise. This lack of precision is partly the result of registration procedures practised by various professions. Table 3 shows the number of people practising in six medical professions in 1971. The physicians' data is an estimate because the Irish Medical Register shows those physicians who are fully registered in Ireland as medical practitioners. In 1971 the register had 9412 such physicians but many of these people were not resident in Ireland. In 1966 there were 3011 resident medical practitioners and the statistic shown for 1971 is an estimate derived from EEC sources.[12] The statistics for the other professions are not complicated by such problems.

Table 3 *Health Personnel 1971*

	Total	Number per 1000 population
Physicians	3100	1.03
Dentists	785	0.26
Midwives	16140	5.38
General nurses	30814	10.27
Pharmacists	2033	0.67
Opthalmic opticians) Opticians)	558*	0.18

Source: *Hensey* (1972) Chapter 6.
*   246 opthalmic opticians and 312 opticians.

The medical personnel/population ratios are given in the second column of Table 3. The number of physicians per thousand population in 1971 — 1.03 — was one of the lowest in the European Economic Community and has been relatively stable since the middle of the 1960s. The level of provision of dentists was low by European standards. However the number of nurses and midwives was high. The number of pharmacists was near the arithmetic mean of the Western European distribution.

The labour markets for medical personnel in the United Kingdom and Ireland are very interdependent. The Irish trained physician, for instance, is free to migrate to England and set up in practice within the National Health Service. Some Western areas of the UK in particular (e.g. Liverpool) have a high proportion of Irish born nurses. The factors affecting the migration of personnel are complex and vary from time to time. It is usually assumed that relative wage levels are of importance.

(b) Hospitals

There are three types of principal general hospitals in Ireland. The public (government owned) hospitals, formerly run by the local authorities and now administered and financed by the Health Boards, contain fifty-three per cent of all Irish general hospital beds, and their average size (185 beds) is larger than that of the other categories. The voluntary hospitals contain thirty-five per cent of all general hospital beds and their average size is only slightly smaller than that of the public hospitals. These hospitals are centred on the cities — Dublin in particular — and although run by autonomous boards they are dependent on the Department of Health for most of their finance. The channels for this finance — ninety-one per cent of an expenditure total of £22 million in 1970-71 — were, until 1974, capitation grants paid by the Health Boards for patients from their areas and payments by the Minister which met deficits. Since 1974 each voluntary hospital administration has been obliged to submit in advance to the Department of Health their planned budget for the year. The Department then finances those items — usually all items are approved — which it deems are necessary. The third hospital sector — private, profit making units — contains twelve per cent of all general hospital beds and are relatively small in size (see Table 4), The income of these units comes from patients paying for private care with their own resources and/or private insurance.

Table 4 *Hospitals 1969*

	Number of units	Number of beds	Average size
Principal General Hospitals			
Public	33	6102	185
Voluntary (non-profit)	22	4031	183
Private (profit making)	19	1353	71
Total	74	11486	155
Local Hospitals			
Public	52	1982	38
Voluntary (non-profit)	6	164	27
Total	58	2146	37
Maternity Hospitals and centres			
Public	2	132	66
Voluntary (non-profit)	5	787	157
Private (profit making)	48	705	14
Total	55	1624	29

227

Table 4 *(Cont)*

Paediatric hospitals (all voluntary)	5	754	150
Orthopaedic hospitals: Total*	10	1363	136
Infectious diseases hospitals (all State owned)	9	636	
Tuberculosis hospitals†	7	917	
Cancer hospitals (all voluntary)	3	299	
Opthalmic hospitals (all voluntary)	2	233	
Total (all hospital beds)	233	19448	

Source: *World Health Organisation* (1973) 'World Health Statistics Annual' 1969 Vol 3 Geneva.

* Of these 5 (651 beds) are owned by public bodies and 5 (712 beds) are owned by voluntary bodies.

† Of these 6 (721 beds) are owned by public bodies and 1 (196 beds) is owned by voluntary bodies.

The principal general hospital system is augmented by a local hospital system which contains a further 2146 beds. Of these additional beds, ninety-five per cent are in public institutions. Also there are units specialising in particular types of care. Fifty-five publicly and privately owned maternity centres and hospitals provide 1624 beds for confinements. Orthpaedic hospitals, paediatric hospitals, infectious diseases hospitals, tuberculosis hospitals, cancer hospitals, and opthalmic units provide specialised treatment in institutions owned by a variety of public and private bodies. When all these units are aggregated Ireland has over 19,000 non-psychiatric hospital beds in 1969. The average hospital size was eighty-seven beds and there are 6.5 non-psychiatric beds per 1000 population.

Table 5 supplements the data provided in Table 4 by showing the distribution of all hospital beds by Health Board Area in 1972. All the data is shown as beds per 1000 population. In 1972 there were 5.86 acute beds per population in Ireland. The best provided area — the Eastern — included Dublin and this area had fifty-nine per cent more beds than the North-Western Health Board area which had fewest beds per 1000 population of this type. The distribution of mental illness and mental handicap beds is also very unequal as can be seen from Table 5. If the final category of beds (homes for the aged, etc.) is omitted it can be seen that there were 8.35 beds per 1000 population in Ireland in 1972.

The coordination of this system of hospitals is not easy because of the diversion of ownership. Table 4 shows that the majority of beds

Table 5 *Distribution of hospital beds by Health Board Area (1972) – beds per 1000 population*

Speciality	HEALTH BOARD								
	Eastern	Midland	Mid-Western	North-East	North-West	South-East	Southern	Western	Total
General Medical	1.85	0.64	0.98	1.18	0.58	0.83	1.04	1.23	1.26
General Surgical	1.28	1.03	0.99	1.32	0.68	0.89	1.04	1.20	1.12
Obstetrics	0.62	0.49	0.53	0.69	0.56	0.63	0.54	0.58	0.59
Gynaecology	0.24	0.06	0.13	0.08	0.05	0.01	0.06	0.19	0.14
Paediatrics	0.90	0.22	0.55	0.41	0.22	0.34	0.37	0.37	0.54
Other (Regional) specialities	2.07	0.67	0.78	0.39	-	0.69	0.98	1.14	1.19
Private (non-participating) hospitals*	0.55	-	0.26	-	-	-	0.77	0.45	0.37
Medical and minor surgical†	0.08	1.02	0.64	0.29	1.02	0.93	1.66	0.53	0.65
Total Acute Beds	7.61	4.14	4.87	4.38	3.12	4.32	6.46	5.70	5.86
Mental Illness	3.74	8.09	5.27	3.83	7.19	7.39	3.78	8.32	5.25
Mental Handicap	2.17	1.12	1.13	1.50	1.40	1.06	1.78	0.94	1.60
Other non-acute care (Homes for the aged, nursing homes, etc.)††	na	na	na	na	na	na	na	na	4.36
Total beds (excluding last speciality)	13.52	13.35	11.27	9.71	11.71	12.77	12.02	14.96	12.71

Source: Department of Health, Dublin, Personal correspondence, 1974.

*   These hospitals are outside the ambit of
   (i) state hospitals
   (ii) voluntary hospitals whose deficits are met by the state.
   Details of beds by speciality are not available.
†   These are the general practitioner staffed District and Cottage Hospitals.
††   Estimated.

are in hospitals owned by the government or the voluntary bodies. Since 1974 the latter have been directly financed by central government and this will enable the government to be much more rigorous in analysing the management of these bodies in future years. With the central government paying the piper the next step is that they will try to call the tune even more rigorously than at present. The continuing drive to increase the efficiency of the Irish medical care system which is being promoted by the employment of the consultants McKinsey, will necessitate a much higher degree of coordination between the sectors of the hospital system than has existed prior to 1974.

8. Conclusion

Since the middle of the 1960s the Irish health system has been going through a period of radical change. This process has altered the modes of delivering and financing medical care. The execution of medical care provision policy has been placed in the hands of eight area Health Boards. Many of the functions previously reserved for the central government have been devolved down to these Boards. The role of central government has changed into one of financing, supervising and monitoring. It is impossible to see how well this system will perform. No doubt some problems will arise. The obvious candidates for this role are the hospital system and the provision of complementary local authority welfare service. The Irish are aware of difficulties in these areas and substantial efforts will be made to mitigate their impact.

Ireland is a small country which had a poorly structured health service until recently. One result of recent changes has been that the health care structure has been simplified with the roles of participants clearly specified. The basic problems of resource allocation remain but\within the newly evolved programme budgeting framework it may be easier to discuss objectives and assess the performance of the health care system in relation to these objectives.

NOTES

1. See Hensey (1972) p 22.
2. Hensey (1972) p 26.
3. The groups were as follows: persons insured for social welfare; persons with family incomes less than £600 per year; farmers with farms valued at or under £50; and those not in these groups who could deminstare need.
4. See Hensey (1972) pp 29-30.

5. The eight Health Boards are the Eastern, Midland, North-Eastern, South-Western, Mid-Western, Southern, North-Western and Western. They vary in size from 987,000 population (Eastern Board) to 179,000 (Midland Board).
6. The Midland, Mid-Western, North-Eastern and North Western Boards.
7. The three Regional Hospital Boards are the Dublin RHB (covering the Eastern, Midland, Morth-Eastern and South-Eastern Health Board Areas), the Cork RHB (covering the Mid-Western and the Southern Health Boards) and the Galway RHB (covering the North-Western and the Western Health Boards).
8. Hensey (1972) Appendix C and pp 61-2.
9. The Report of the Consultative Council on the General Hospital Services (The Fitzgerald Report) 1968.
10. See Hensey (1972) p 91.
11. The categories are mental handicap, mentally ill, children under the age of sixteen (after sixteen a means test is carried out on the handicapped person's income. This means that most get free drugs after sixteen), phenylketonuria, cystic fibrosis, spina bifida, hydrocephalus, haemophilia, cerebral palsy, diabetes mellitus, diabetes insipidus and epilepsy. See Hensey (1972) page 119-20.
12. EEC (1974), pp 228-9.

References

Department of Health (1973), Press Releases.
European Economic Community (1973, 1974), *Report on the Development of the Social Situation in the Community in 1972 (in 1973)*, Brussels and Luxembourg, February.
B. Hensey (1972) *The Health Services of Ireland*, Institute of Public Administration, Dublin.
US Department of Health, Education and Welfare (1972), *Social Security Programs throughout the World, 1971*, Washington.
World Health Organisation (1973) *World Health Statistics Annual 1969*, Vol 3, Geneva.

The Evolution of Health Care in Denmark

The Danish health care system provides medical care and sickness benefit for its five million residents and has evolved in a manner similar to many other European countries. A specialised hospital service was established in Copenhagen in 1757 when the Royal Frederiks Hospital was established. Ever since that date any Dane suffering from a disease which could not be diagnosed or treated in local hospitals has had the right to free treatment in this hospital. In 1818 a State employed district physician service was established which as well as looking after public health matters also had the task of treating the poor free of charge. The State has regulated the fees charged by Danish physicians since 1619 and it was this group of medical personnel who initiated the creation of sickness funds in the middle of the nineteenth century. State regulation extended to the rules of these funds by the 1890s and from 1933 until the recent reforms membership of a fund was compulsory. The health laws were revised in 1960 to provide greater national control and more uniformity among the basic benefits provided by the 1100 sickness funds. During the 1960s the number of sickness funds declined due to amalgamation and by the beginning of 1971 there were 275 approved funds in operation.

These funds had geographical limits corresponding to the municpalities except for the Danish State Railways fund which covered the whole country. In 1971 forty per cent of these funds had less than 5000 members. All residents could voluntarily become active members of their local fund and by 1971 ninety-five per cent of those Danes aged over sixteen were members. There were various membership categories. Fully active members were divided into two groups, A and B, according to income. A-type members received benefits which fully covered the costs of medical care. Group B members were those above the income limits and their memberships entitled them to partial reimbursement from the funds of the costs of medical care. Danish residents who were not active members were compelled to be passive members of their local fund. They paid 48 kroner per year in the early 1970s as a 'contribution' but received no benefits. Passive members could become active members after contribution to the fund at the active rate for three months. These complex arrangements did not provide sufficient income for the funds to be solvent without substantial State subsidisation: in 1970 nearly twenty-five per cent of the total sickness funds' income of 1,460,451,000 kroner (£104m) was derived from State grants. In addition to this most of the 4,300 million kroner (£306m) spent on hospital care of all types was financed by the State.

Since 1st April 1973 the sickness funds have been abolished and their role as a provider of medical care and sickness benefits has been transferred to the municipalities and the county councils. Individual contributions as a source of income have been replaced by a financial system which is dependent on general taxation revenues. Thus, in Denmark the system of the State working through sickness funds has been ended and replaced by a system which is financed and provided by the organs of central and local government.

1. Administration

The responsibility for providing health care in Denmark is divided up amongst three levels of government: the central government, the counties (*amtskommuner*) and the municipalities (*kommuner*). The country is divided up into fourteen counties with a population of 250,000 to 500,000 each. Each county is divided up into a number of municipalities of which there are 217 in Denmark as a whole.[1] Each of the local government organisations is governed by a council whose members are elected every four years and has the power to levy land taxes and a proportional income tax. Also they receive certain block grants from central government which finances its activities by progressive income taxation and various additional forms of taxation.

The discretion of the local authority is circumscribed by central government legislation. The central government determines which services will be provided by the local government units and also often determines the standards or norms of provision. For example, the 1969 Hospital Act obliged each county to establish and operate a sufficient number of hospitals and convalescent homes for its population and compelled them to offer hospital services free of charge to the population. Also the Act required each county administration to prepare a detailed plan of the operation and future development of its hospital system. This plan has to be submitted to the central government for approval and until such plans are drawn up and approved all new developments must have prior clearance from Copenhagen. Other legislation compelled municipalities to provide a sufficient number of health visitors and to provide adequate dental facilities to furnish preventive and curative dental care for all children.

233

These functions can be carried out with greater efficiency because the recently reformed local authority units have an adequate tax base to provide finance and an adequate population to give some scope to the administrations which wish to exploit potential economies of large scale provision. The exploitation of potential scale economies is an idea which attracted the attention of the committee whose proposals were translated into local government reformation. Their hope was that the present county areas would be sufficient for the full exploitation of large specialised medical units to be possible. Within the new local authority units the hospital system is governed by one committee of the county council. This is an improvement compared with the period prior to 1973 because during that period each hospital had its own governing body and coordination was difficult.

Although medical care functions have been delegated to local authorities in most cases, some activities remain the preserve of the central government. Central government provides care and rehabilitation services for the mentally ill, the mentally handicapped, alcoholics, epileptics, the blind and the deaf. Some of these activities will be transferred to the counties in the future — e.g. psychiatric care will be transferred in 1976 — so that they can fully integrate with the various types of hospital care. It is planned to devolve all central government activities to the local authorities with the exception of Copenhagen University Hospital, the most specialised unit in Denmark, and the national clinical microbiological services (State Seruminstitute).

The role of the private sector is small. In the hospital field the national policy has been to provide an adequate system.[2] The consumer cost of utilising the hospital service has been kept low by central government subsidisation. This policy of keeping hospital fee levels low has caused the private hospital system to contract. Those private hospitals which continue to operate have been forced to become heavily dependent on central and local government and are, as a consequence, under detailed State control. Private health insurance continues in Denmark. This is because the A and B membership types have been maintained and the relatively affluent B members get reimbursement which does not fully cover the cost of care. Consequently they insure privately in order to 'top-up' their public benefits. There is discussion about the abolition of the A- and B-type distinction. If there was only one membership type and full reimbursement the private insurance sector's future would be bleak.

The relationship between the government and the medical profession is governed by several bodies. Each county appoints a committee of four to six members whose object is to facilitate cooperation and coordination between physicians, hospitals and the other health and welfare services. In addition there is a Central Negotiation Committee

234

of seven councillors. This committee is responsible for the conclusion
of agreements with the professional organisations of the physicians, the
dentists, and other medical professions. These agreements have to be
confirmed by the Ministry of Social Affairs. Three members of the
Central Negotiation Committee and three representatives of the Danish
Medical Association form a committee to supervise the interpretation
of these agreements. Similar machinery has been created for some of
the other medical professions. In all cases where there is failure to reach
agreement, arbitration machinery takes over and its decision is binding
on both parties. It is to be noted that hospital physicians are government employees whilst general practitioners are in private practice.

Figure 1 *The Organisation of Danish Health Care*

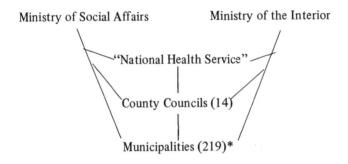

* The number of municipalities is 217 plus Copenhagen and
   Fredericksberg (see Note 1 to the text).

These administrative arrangements are summarised in Figure 1. As can
be seen from this figure there are two central government ministries
involved in health care. The Ministry of the Interior is primarily concerned with supervision of local government. As one of the main
functions of local government is health care, the Ministry of the
Interior has most health care responsibilities. The Ministry of Social
Affairs is involved in the regulation of professional fees and the
provision of care for the mentally handicapped and all those other
groups where care has not, as yet, been devolved to the local authorities.
Neither of the Ministries employs a member of the medical professions.
All professional advice is provided by what Koch[3] calls the National

235

Health Service. This institution is directed by a physician who is appointed by the Ministry of the Interior and is responsible for providing professional advice to the Ministries and any other public agencies who request such advice. The National Health Service is involved in advising local government in matters relating to the planning, organisation and management of their local health service.

The finance and provision of health care[4] has been delegated to two sets of local authority be the central government. The nature of this delegation has been carefully detailed and the degree of central supervision is substantial. It is claimed that the virtue of this structure is that the delivery of health care is the responsibility of democratically elected councils who are responsible to consumer/elector pressures. This virtue is constrained by the desire for efficiency so that in some cases the popular local demands for, for example, a specialised hospital unit, may be rejected on the grounds that it would not be fully utilised. The performance of this system of local demands constrained by central planning cannot be judged as yet because it has been in operation for such a short time.

2. Coverage

Since April 1973 the coverage of the Danish Health Service has been complete. The twenty per cent of the population who, prior to 1973, elected to be non-participating members who paid a fixed contribution and received no benefit have been drawn into the social insurance system. The distinction between A- and B-type membership has been maintained. At the end of 1973, A-type membership covered all those breadwinners whose income was below 68,700 kroner (£4983) in Copenhagen and 60,100 kroner (£4280) elsewhere. For single persons the dividing line between A- and B-type membership is 51,500 kroner (£3668) in Copenhagen and 45,100 kroner (£3212) elsewhere. For each child under sixteen the limits are raised by 8,900 kroner (£634). These rates are revised every January and at present eighty per cent of the population are in the A group. It is possible that the present A- and B-type membership categories may be abolished. There are two plans being considered by the Danish government. The first plan proposes to give all citizens, regardless of income, the same A-type benefits. The second proposal is that B-type members should be entitled to opt for A-type membership even if their income is above the income ceiling of A members. The latter proposal is favoured by the Danish Medical Association.

3. Qualifying Conditions

Before April 1973 all residents of Denmark were covered by the social insurance legislation. Membership and complete contribution records entitled A- and B-type members to the prescribed benefits. Since April 1973 all residents of Denmark are entitled to medical care and sickness benefits. Benefits are no longer dependent on membership of a fund or a contribution.

4. Finance

The system of medical care and sickness benefit contributions which existed prior to 1973 has been altered radically. In 1971 the annual contribution rate payable by A-type members varied from fund to fund. Fifty funds had rates which varied between 264 and 312 kroner (£18.8 and £22.2). Two hundred and nine funds had annual contribution rates which varied between 324 and 396 kroner (£23.0 and £28.2). A further sixteen funds had rates which varied between 408 and 480 kroner (£29.0 and £34.2). B-type members had to pay a contribution which exceeded those of A-type members by an amount corresponding to the average difference per member between the public contributions received by the funds. In 1970 the average A-type contribution was 325 kroner (£23) per year and the relevant difference was 72 kroner (£5). Thus the average B-type member paid a contribution of 397 kroner (£28.2). Contributory members (those who received no benefit) paid a contribution of 48 kroner (£3.4) in 1970.

Since April 1973 social health insurance has been completely financed by the taxation revenues of local and central government. The county is free to levy a proportional income tax at whatever rate it thinks necessary. The use of the other local taxation instrument, the land tax, is limited by agricultural pressure groups and the maximum tax rate that can be levied is two per cent of the value of the estate. The central government uses a system of grants to equalise and supplement local resources. Prior to the reform of local government this grant was expressed as a percentage of the cost of a particular service e.g. in the early 1970s a grant of sixty-five per cent of the cost of hospital care was made to local authorities. Since reform the grant system's base has been changed to one of 'demands and needs'. A formula which incorporates population, age structure, and load variables is used to provide blanket grants to the local authorities. No ear-marked contributions are made to finance medical care.

The administration of sickness benefit was transferred from the funds to the local authorities at the same time as medical care. Prior to April 1973 sickness benefit expenditure was financed by contributions paid by employers and employees, and by government grants. Since April 1973 any sickness benefit payable during the first five weeks of illness are financed normally by the employer who pays the benefit out of his own income. If any person is sick for a period in excess of five weeks the sickness benefit is paid by the local authority. Each employee pays a contribution equal to nine per cent of taxable income. This revenue goes into the Daily Cash Benefit Fund which refunds seventy-five per cent of the outlay of local authorities on sickness benefits. The central government guarantees the liquidity of this Fund by meeting any deficits. The local authorities finance their twenty-five per cent share of the cost of benefits our of their own tax resources.

5. Income and Expenditure

The latest available expenditure statistics for the Danish medical care system are reproduced in Table 1. The data in this Table are for the financial year ending 31st March 1972, i.e. it predates the reform of the Danish health service. Total medical care expenditure in 1971-2 was about 7000 million kroner (£498m). Expenditure by the funds and local and central government was 6930 million kroner (£493m). The difference between these two figures is accounted for by an esti-mate of B-type members' expenditure on fees which were only partly reimbursed by the funds. Koch estimates that this type of expenditure was about 60 million kroner (£4.3m). In 1973 the first three categories of benefit under primary care were taken over by the local authorities. Since this take-over all medical care has been financed by the local authority taxation supplemented by grants from the central govern-ment.

The most expensive single item in the medical care budget of Denmark is the hospital system. Capital and current expenditure on hospitals of all types in 1971-2 amounted to 5290 million kroner (£376m) or slightly more than seventy-five per cent of total expendi-ture. Current psychiatric hospital outlays (520 million kroner [£37m]) was a relatively small part of this expenditure. Seventy-two per cent of current hospital expenditure goes towards meeting the costs of employing labour. The next largest expenditure items were physicians' fees, dentists' fees and pharmaceutical products. These items were relatively small in absolute and relative terms: 790 million kroner (£56m)[5], 250 million kroner (£18m) and 340 million kroner (£24m), or 11.2 per cent, 3.5 per cent, and 4.8 per cent respectively. Expendi-ture on sickness benefits and other cash benefits such as maternity and funeral benefits provided by the funds was just over 72 million kroner (£5m) in 1970.[6]

The rate of growth of expenditure on all medical care was seventeen

238

Table 1 *Danish Medical Care Expenditure 1971-2*

Current Expenditure	Absolute level of expenditure in millions of kroner	Percentage rate of growth 1966-71
Primary Care		
Physicians fees * †	730	15
Dentists fees*	250	16
Pharmaceutical products*	340	17
Preventive services	100)	
School health	110)	12
Domiciliary nursing services	110)	
Total	1.640	15
Hospital Care		
General Hospitals	3.600	16
Psychiatric Hospitals	520	13
Somatic specialised hospitals	180	12
Total	4.300	16
Total (Primary and Hospital Care)	5,940	
Capital Expenditure		
Construction of hospitals	870	26
Hospital equipment	120	21
Total	990	25
Overall Total (current and capital expenditure)	6.930 (£493m)	17

Source: *J.H. Koch* (1974) p 19.

* These expenditures were financed by the sickness funds prior to 1973, since then they have been financed by local government.
† B-type members paid an estimated additiona fee total of 60 million kroner: see Koch p 20 1974.

per cent per annum during the period 1966-71. The rate of growth of capital expenditure on hospital construction (twenty-six per cent) and hospital equipment (twenty-one per cent) were the fastest growing individual rates. Pharmaceutical expenditures, (seventeen per cent), general hospital expenditure (sixteen per cent), dentists' fees expenditures (sixteen per cent) and the expenditure on the remuneration of physicians (fifteen per cent) were further areas where, although the rates were below the average, considerable increases in outlay can be seen to have occurred.

Like so many other European countries Danish medical care expenditure is escalating at a very rapid rate. A simple extrapolation of present trends would result in a hundred per cent of Danish GNP being spent on medical care before the end of the century. In 1971 5.46 per cent of the Danish GNP was spent on medical care. The 1973 reorganisation of the system may improve efficiency and enable central government to constrain the rate of growth of expenditure. Without such constraint of demand the financial situation will be dire if we accept that the already high taxation levels cannot be raised.[7]

6. Benefits

(a) Medical Care

The distinction between A- and B-type membership must be borne in mind throughout the following discussion of medical care benefits.[8] Those citizens who are A-type members of the public health care system are entitled to free medical care from general practice physicians and specialists. Each citizen has a free choice of doctor and is permitted to change his registration once every twelve months if he so wishes. If specialist care is given to an A-type member by a physician with no approved agreement with the public health system grants meeting only part of the fees are made. B-type citizens (those above the income limit) receive refunds equal to the benefits received by A-type citizens. Thus if the public health authorities agree a fee of 100 kroner with the physicians' profession for the treatment of a category of illness, the local authority (the county) pays the physician 100 kroner. If the patient is a B-type member the physician will be free to charge in excess of 100 kroner and the member is paid 100 kroner by the local authority, meeting the deficit out of private insurance or his income and savings.

If the family physician prescribes hospitalisation both A- and B-type members receive free treatment at public hospitals and free treatment at special hospitals and institutions which have been publicly recognised. These hospital services are almost wholly provided by the county hospital service which is obliged by law to provide an adequate service for its residents at zero cost. This stipulation is supplemented by a law which obliges each county to provide facilities for the delivery of babies in obstetric hospitals or special clinics. Furthermore since 1973 midwifery services have been 'socialised' in that each county is now obliged to employ sufficient midwives to provide the local population with examinations, before and after birth, free of charge. For the most part these services are provided at centres which house four to six midwives who serve populations of about 75,000 people.

For other types of care the discrimination between A- and B-type members is not always continued. The county pays to all A- and B-type members seventy-five per cent of the cost of pharmaceutical products prescribed by physicians. The State controls the price of pharmaceutical products and controls their distribution through a State-owned system of pharmacies.[9] Physiotherapy treatment is given on the usual A- and B-type arrangement, i.e. the A-type member gets free treatment provided it is approved by the family physician. The financial burden of dental care and the provision of appliances such as spectacles differs between A- and B-type members as does the provision of transport to and from medical care facilities. A domiciliary nursing service has been provided free of charge since 1957.

(b) Cash Benefits

For the first five weeks of sickness the employer is responsible for paying sick pay to the individual worker, usually at a rate equal to ninety per cent of his normal wage. After the fifth week the local authority pays benefits equal to ninety per cent of the average income of the sick worker in the previous year up to a ceiling of 698 kroner (£49.7) per week. Similar benefits are paid to eligible mothers for fourteen weeks. The self-employed can insure on a voluntary basis so that they get coverage both during the first five weeks of illness and subsequently. Those persons who are not 'economically active' (e.g. housewives) can join the scheme and obtain the same benefits if they wish. Both the self-employed and the economically inactive can pay contributions at varying rates which make them eligible for varying benefit levels. This system which came into force in April 1973 is a radical departure from previous practice which gave only flat rate benefits and did not cover the self-employed. The long-term sick become eligible for invalidity pensions.

7. Provision

(a) Medical Personnel

The familiar conclusion that there is a shortage of physicians in Denmark can be seen from some of the early 1970s literature on the subject.[10] As is so often the case with such conclusions the arguments upon which they were based were notable only for their arbitariness.

The Danes have adopted an arbitary GP/patient ratio objective of one to 1500. During the 1960s the ratio was static but by 1972 it was declining and equal to about one to 1925. The reason for this change is the opening up of the medical schools to which students now have free access. There are three medical schools in Denmark, one at each of the universities of Copenhagen (founded 1479), Aarhus (1928) and Odense (1966). These universities are open to all those students who graduated from a gymnasium (about fifteen per cent of each age cohort). The medical schools have thus no power to limit or select the students. Each year about ten per cent of the intake decide to study medicine (1100 to 1200 students) and about sixty per cent of these graduate. This policy has lead to a sharp rise in the output of medical schools: between 1969 and 1971 graduate output doubled to 600. Each trainee physician has a basic seven-year course followed by a two-year period of hospital training during which the physician rotates

Table 2 *Danish Physicians 1966 and 1971-2*

		1966	1971-2
General Practitioners		2579	2600
Specialists			
of which:	internists	393	419
	obstetricians†	256	167
	surgeons	376	407
	paediatrists	91	95
	geriatrics	*	101
	psychiatrists	243	304
	Others	1382	1553
	Total specialists	2741	3046
Physicians in post graduate training		*	1500
(Other)**		(2374)	(968)
Total number of Physicians		7694	8114

Source: *Koch* (1974) Appendix, p 3.

* No data available.
† Includes gynaecologists.
** This is calculated by summing the specialist and GP statistics with/without those in post-graduate training in 1966/1971-2. These physicians are employed in administration and the public health service.

round the hospital's departments and his training is augmented by theory courses. The average Danish physician spends five or six years in a hospital after graduation. The overall physician patient ratio is low — one physician to every 616 people. Given present trends the GP/population ratio will be achieved by 1980 when it is estimated that there will be over 11,300 physicians.[11] Then public policy will have to concern itself with a reduction in the rate of expansion of the physician stock.

Table 2 shows that the largest group of Danish physicians are specialists' 3046 in 1971/2 or over thirty-seven per cent. This group increased in size by 305 during the period 1966 to 1971/2. The number of general practitioners in 1971/2 was 2600, a net increase of twenty-one during the same period. Many of the physicians undertaking postgraduate training in 1971-2 will augment the supply of hospital physicians in the short run. However it is anticipated that the stock of general practitioners will expand rapidly during the period 1972-80.

The physicians are remunerated by a system which varies geographically. Those physicians who practise in Copenhagen where there are only a limited number of positions are paid on a capitation fee basis. All other general practitioners are paid by a system which goes on a basic capitation fee payment and supplements this by a system of fees per item of service (each component of this fee arrangement makes up about fifty per cent of the physician's income). A B-type patient is charged a fee in the region of 150 kroner for each consultation with a GP. Of this fee the B-type member gets only 60 kroner reimbursement. The B-type patient is obviously attractive to the general practitioner and the larger the proportion of such patients in his care the higher his salary. An average GP salary estimate for 1972 by Toftemark was 100,000 kroner per year (£7122). Hospital physicians are government employees and their salary depends on their grade. A head of department receives an annual remuneration of 180,000 (£12820): this is a gross figure of which about sixty per cent goes to the State in income tax.

Table 3 gives some indication of the number of qualified nurses and other paramedical personnel employed by the Danish health service. Unfortunately there are some data gaps which have proved difficult to fill. The number of qualified nurses working in acute and psychiatric hospitals rose by 1400 (10.6 per cent) and 100 (six per cent) during the period 1966 to 1971-2. The number of nurses completing training in 1971 was 1400. The number of other paramedical personnel in acute and psychiatric hospitals rose by 8200 (forty-six per cent) and 2150 (eighty-one per cent) in the same period. These significant increases in the quantity of labour employed by the health service have contributed to the escalation of expenditure. In 1971 the costs of personnel

Table 3 *Other Danish Health Personnel 1966 and 1971-2*

	1966	1971/2
1) Nurses		
in general acute hospitals	13200	14600
in psychiatric hospitals	1630	1750
in geriatric hospitals	*	*
in homes for the aged	*	2750
in institutions for the handicapped	*	*
2. Other Paramedical Personnel†		
in general acute hospitals	17700	25900
in psychiatric hospitals	2625	4775
in geriatric hospitals	*	*
in homes for the aged	*	5834
in institutions for the handicapped	*	*

Source: *Koch* (1974) Appendix p 4.

* No information available.

† Includes nursing assistants and other unqualified nurses, and
physiotherapists.

represented seventy-two per cent of total running costs of hospitals.

The retail pharmaceutical trade is a nationalised concern. Central
government controls the number and location of pharmacies. The
pharmacists are appointed by the government and in many ways they
are treated like any other civil servants, e.g. they get a state pension on
retirement. It is illegal to sell pharmaceutical products outside the 360
unit State pharmacy system and the prices of its products are carefully
regulated. This price control enables the State to control the income
levels of the pharmacies and further powers enable it to equalise
incomes between pharmacies by levying special fees on the high earning
units. These fees are paid into a central fund which is used to subsidise
the less prosperous pharmacies and to loan funds to those who wish to
redevelop their premises.

(b) Hospitals

During the development of this Chapter a considerable amount of
information has been produced about the hospital system in Denmark.
The most important institution in the provision of hospital care is the

county council. Each county is obliged to provide sufficient facilities for the population at zero cost to the patient. The general practitioner usually refers his patients to one of the local county hospitals. If the patient requires highly specialised care (e.g. transplants, neurosurgery, etc.) he may be transferred out of his home county, if the facilities are inadequate, to specialised units in Copenhagen, Odense, Aarhus and a few other locations. When such transfers are necessary the patient's home county meets the cost of care. The exception to this rule is the Copenhagen University Hospital which is financed by the central government and provides free care to those patients referred to it. This exception may be removed by the central government charging the counties for the services the hospital renders. The logic of such a charge is that it is alleged that the counties are acting rationally and in cases of need for specialised care they are transferring patients to zero cost Copenhagen rather than positive cost Odense and Aarhus which are operated by the counties. If the patient wishes to have treatment outside his county of residence and his county does not agree to transfer him, the patient may elect to go to the hospital of his choice but in doing so he has to pay an all-inclusive fee of 100 kroner (£7.1) a day.[12]

Table 4 *Hospital Bed Provision in Denmark 1966 and 1971-2*

	Total number of beds 1971-2*	Beds per 1000 population 1966	Beds per 1000 population 1971-2
General acute hospitals	30870	6.0	6.3
Medicine and obstetrics	12250	-	2.5
Surgery	13720	-	2.8
Paediatrics	1470	-	0.3
Geriatrics	2450	-	0.5
Psychiatric	1470	-	0.3
Psychiatric hospitals	9800	2.0	2.0
Homes for the aged and nursing homes	40180	6.6	8.2†
Institutions for the handicapped	30870	6.0	6.3

* These figures have been calculated by multiplying the bed population rate by 4.9 (the population in 1971 in millions). As a result the individual items sum to a figure larger than the total.

† This datum is for 1972.

Since the reform of local government the county administration has been responsible for all the public hospitals within its boundaries. Instead of one governing board for each hospital there is one hospital committee for each county area. Each county has appointed a county hospital manager who is responsible to the hospital committee for the smooth running of the local hospital system. This system is financed by local taxation and State subsidies.[13]

Table 4 gives an indication of the number of hospital beds by type which are available in Denmark. The acute hospital bed ratio per 1000 population is 6.3 and the psychiatric statistic is 2.0. As can be seen from the Table there are 0.3 per 1000 psychiatric beds in general hospitals, so the overall psychiatric bed statistic is 2.3 per 1000. The number of beds in homes for the aged and nursing homes has been increased sharply of late — twenty-four per cent increase during the period 1966 to 1971-2. The expansion of homes for the aged is a cost effective way of providing care for the aged outside the expensive general hospital system.

Table 5 *Hospital Efficiency Indicators*

	1966	1971-2
1. Average length of stay (in days)		
General acute hospitals of which	14.2	12.3
medicine	n.a.	16.0
obstetrics	n.a.	8.0
surgery	n.a.	11.0
paediatrics	n.a.	15.0
geriatric care	n.a.	53.0
psychiatric care	n.a.	23.0
Psychiatric hospitals	200.0	147.0
2. Average occupancy (in per cent)		
General acute hospitals	87	87
Psychiatric hospitals	99	100
3. Costs (in kroner)	per patient	per day
General acute hospitals	3800	310
General psychiatric hospitals	2000	133

Source: *Koch* (1974) Appendix p 2.

The data in Table 5 gives some indication of the level of efficiency at which the Danish hospital system works. The average length of stay in acute hospitals was reduced by thirteen per cent to 12.3 days between 1966 and 1971-2. The reduction in the corresponding psychiatric statistic was twenty-six per cent to 147 days. The average length of stay in psychiatric units of general hospitals was twenty-three days in 1971-2. These levels are relatively low by European standards. The scope for improving occupancy rates was limited as can be seen from the Table. The one hundred per cent occupancy rate for psychiatric hospitals is very high. The 1971-2 costs of care in general acute hospitals was 3800 kroner (£270.6) per patient or 310 kroner (£22.0) per day. In psychiatric hospitals the corresponding statistics were 2000 kroner (£142.4) and 133 kroner (£9.4).

8. Conclusion

The result of the recent reforms of the Danish medical system has been that the local authority (the county) has been endowed with responsibility of providing sufficient coordinated medical care (inside and outside the hospital) for its resident population. Whilst the counties own and can control the activities of the hospitals there is a large part of the primary medical care system which is outside its control. The general practitioner is a relatively free agent who pursues an independent policy and who attempts *via* his professional organisation to extract 'reasonable' fees for the services he provides. At present there is no problem with regard to the geographical distribution of physicians and related medical professions such as the midwives continue to cooperate with the local authorities, the latter will be able to fulfill their objectives.

The cost of the Danish medical care system grew at an annual rate of seventeen per cent during the period 1966 to 1971-2. This rate of expansion cannot continue, and the problem of constraining the expenditure growth is the major problem facing the Danes. The labour component of costs is high and if the medical professions are not to have relative wage reductions their employers will have to pay large salary increases. The problem of containing the expenditure growth in the health sector is a familiar one. The answers to this problem are not readily apparent.

NOTES

1. Local government was reorganised in 1970. Prior to this reorganisation there were 1200 rural municipalities, ninety city municipalities and twenty-three counties. Now there are 217 municipalities and fourteen counties. This reform leaves Copenhagen and the neighbouring municipality of Fredericksberg unaffected. These two areas have had s special status for over a hundred years.
2. The concepts of 'adequacy' and 'sufficiency' used in this section are being defined by a national hospital plan as was explained above.
3. See J.H. Koch (1974), pp 17-18.
4. Both medical care *and* sickness insurance.
5. This includes additional B-type members' expenditure.
6. Beretning fra Direktoren for Sygekassevaesenet for 1970 (1971).
7. In May 1974 the Danish government raised income tax levels and their action precipitated widespread strikes. The popularist sections of the political spectrum have made significant gains in recent elections on a programme which includes radical reductions in the levels of taxation.
8. See Section (2) Coverage, above.
9. See Section (7) Provision, below, for more details of this arrangement.
10. For instance see the periodical 'Junior Hospital Physicians' (1971).
11. See Junior Hospital Physicians (1971), p 14.
12. This represents only about ten per cent of the cost of care.
13. See Section (4) Finance, above, for further details.

References

Beretning fra Direktoren for Sygelkassevaesenet for 1970 (1971), Copenhagen.
Daily Cash Benefit (Sickness or Maternity) Act 1972.
Danish Medical Bulletin (1972) *Educating Tomorrow's Doctors*, September.
European Economic Community (1973, 1974), *Report on the Development of the Social Situation in the Community in 1972, 1973*, Brussels and Luxembourg.
Junior Hospital Physicians (1971), *The Expected Number of Physicians in Denmark 1971-85*, August 20th, Copenhagen.
J.H. Koch (1974), *Health Services in Denmark*, Paper presented to a seminar at the Kings Fund Centre, London, April.
Public Health Security Act 1971.
C. Toftemark (1974) *The Organisation, Planning and Problem of the Danish Health Services*. Paper presented to a seminar at the Kings Fund Centre, London, April.
US Department of Health, Education and Welfare (1972) *Social Security Programs Throughout the World 1971*, Washington.
J. Worm-Paterson (1972), *National Health Services; their Impact on Medical Education and their Role in Prevention*, International Macy Conference, June 19th-22nd, Copenhagen.

11   SOME INTERNATIONAL COMPARISONS

The object of this chapter is to bring together and compare some of the characteristics of the nine health care systems analysed in the previous chapters. The analyses follow the same sectional divisions as was employed in the previous chapters and concentrates on the finance and provision of medical care.

1. Administration

In West Germany the primary financial institutions are the 1800 sickness funds of seven broad types and the various levels of government. The funds set the contribution rates within limits determined by the central government. These rates and the earnings' ceiling, which are determined by central government also, determine the flow of finance to the funds. Because of various factors, some argue the most important of which is the monopolist power of the medical profession, the funds usually spend most of their income on the purchase of primary medical care. Their finance of hospitalisation has been inadequate and the consequent deficits are met by the *Länder* and central governments, who are seeking to rationalise the hospital system. The physicians involved in the provision of primary medical care are members of professional *Länder* organisations which negotiate fees with the seven types of fund.

As in West Germany, the Dutch central government is not directly involved in the provision of medical care. The ninety-one Dutch sickness funds receive their income from a General Fund administered by the national Sickness Funds Council, and provide insurance cover for those compelled to be members of the system and those who opt in. Expensive medical care protection, which is covered by the AWBZ legislation, covers all the population and is operated by private insurers in the case of those people who are not members of sickness funds. The majority of hospitals are operated by private non-profit making bodies which are often of a religious nature.

Although a multitude of Ministries are involved in the compulsory medical care system in Belgium, financial involvement is delegated. All social security contributions are paid to an independent organ (ONSS) of the Ministry of Social Affairs which redistributes part of the funds to another autonomous institution – INAMI. The latter distributes the funds to six health care organisations, five groups of sickness funds and an auxiliary fund set up by the government. Each group of funds distributes this income to its members. The funds negotiate fees with the providers of medical care — the physicians, the hospitals, etc. There are special arrangements for railwaymen and civil servants.

The pattern is similar in France. The general scheme which covers seventy per cent of the population is financed by contributions paid to a central fund (National Sickness Insurance Fund) at a uniform rate. Sixteen regional sickness funds carry out functions such as monitoring physicians fee scales.One hundred and twenty-one sickness funds register the insured, dispense benefits and ensure the provision of benefits. There are special schemes for civil servants, servicemen, miners, seamen, railwaymen, and the employees of the gas and electricity industries.

In Luxembourg the eleven sickness funds are responsible for organising the provision and meeting the cost of some medical care. The roles of government are two in number: it provides hospitals and is responsible for the general supervision of the system.

Italy is in a state of flux as far as medical care is concerned. At present six large and two hundred small funds provide insurance coverage which varies from fund to fund. INAM, the largest of the big six funds, covers over fifty-three per cent of the Italian population, and like the other funds agrees fees with the providers of medical care. It is proposed that a National Health Service be introduced in Italy. This will be financed by one central institution drawing its money from a proportional ear-marked income tax. The provision of medical care will be devolved to the recently introduced system of regional government.

In the United Kingdom medical care is largely financed out of general taxation and is provided by a structure which is directly controlled by the Department of Health and Social Security. The Area Health Authority is responsible for providing a comprehensive health service for its population. These authorities have, since April 1974, controlled all medical care activity in their areas and are responsible to the Regional Health Authorities who have the power to 'review, challenge and approve' all Area Health Authority activity in their area. In turn the Regional Health Authorities are directly responsible to the Secretary of State for Health and Social Security.

A body similar to the Area Health Authority is of primary importance in the Irish medical care system. There are eight Health Boards in Ireland and it is their job to provide medical care for the inhabitants of their areas. Their activities are financed largely by central government funds and they are responsible to the Department of Health in Dublin for the efficient execution of their responsibilities.

In Denmark the organisation of the provision of medical care has been devolved by central government legislation to the counties and the municipalities. The providers of medical care finance their activities by local taxation and central government subsidies. The Danish sickness funds which operated as financiers prior to 1973 have been abolished.

2. Coverage

Table 1 *Medical Care Compulsory Social Insurance Coverage*

Percentage of the population covered*

Western Germany	88 †
The Netherlands	69.8†† (100.00)
Belgium	99.3
France	99.0
Luxembourg	98.9
Italy	92.0
United Kingdom	100.0
Ireland	34.46 (100.00)**
Denmark	100.00 ***

* Some of those covered by compulsory social insurance have opted in although above the earnings' ceiling (e.g. Germany and the Netherlands). Those not covered by compulsory legislation either have private insurance (if rich) or are eligible for public assistance/social aid programmes (if poor).

† An additional ten per cent had private insurance cover.

†† Most of those not covered by compulsory insurance (i.e. the more affluent) had private insurance cover. AWBZ (expensive medical care) legislation covers 100.00 per cent of the Dutch population.

** Thirty-four per cent of the population had full eligibility. By 1975 all the Irish should have limited eligibility. (See text for a discussion of the different types of eligibility.)

*** There are type groups of beneficiary: A- and B-type members. Their benefits vary (see text).

In any international comparison the statistics have to be treated with caution. The data in Table 1 is no exception. Each of the statistics cited in the Table relates to a particular system of compulsory medical care insurance, and each system gives rise to a different array of contribution costs and benefits.

251

In West Germany those workers who are below the earnings ceiling — DM 1875 per month (£313) in 1974 — are obliged to join a sickness fund. In the early 1970s this meant that eighty-eight per cent of the German population were covered by compulsory sickness insurance. In the late 1960s and early 1970s the rapid escalation of the ceiling, which is now related to an index, increased the coverage of the scheme. Those above the ceiling (the relatively rich) can opt into the scheme if they so wish or take out private insurance cover to meet the cost of medical care. Those exhausting their hospitalisation benefits which are limited to seventy-eight weeks for any one period of illness, have recourse ro public assistance or self-finance.

In the Netherlands fewer people are covered by the general scheme. This scheme usually covers those earning less than 20,000 florins (£3200) per year (1973), i.e. about seventy per cent of the population. However it is to be remembered that the AWBZ legislation which covers the costs of particularly expensive types of medical care, is comprehensive i.e. its coverage is one hundred per cent. Those not covered by the general scheme are usually privately insured.

The coverage of compulsory medical care legislation in Belgium was almost complete by 1970. However it is important to note that although the self-employed are covered, their benefits are for certain types of care only: heavy risks. Also there is only partial reimbursement of the costs of many types of medical care, e.g. only seventy-five per cent of the agreed tariff is reimbursed in the case of general medical care. As a result of these qualifications there is considerable scope for private insurance, sometimes this takes the form of the funds compelling their members to supplement their benefits, and supplementation of benefits by employers.

A similar system operates in France. Although the coverage of the various schemes is almost complete, benefits usually take the form of partial reimbursement of the costs of medical care. A law of 1967 made it illegal for any insurer or fund to cover the complete residual cost of medical care. However this legislation appears to be ignored by many French citizens who 'top-up' their insurance by taking our private cover.

In Luxembourg a similar state of affairs exists. Although coverage is almost complete the costs of medical care benefits are not met in full and the duration of hospital benefits is limited to twenty-six weeks. These benefits are supplemented by private insurance for the rich and by public assistance for the poor.

The Italian coverage statistic of ninety-two per cent of the total population hides a considerable distirbution of benefit levels. Under the direct assistance scheme INAM meets the full costs of medical care except for certain benefits such as false teeth and hearing aids. However

252

hospitalisation benefits are limited to twenty-six weeks in any one year and if a member opts for indirect assistance whereby he is treated as a private patient at a private patient rate, he acquires a refund equal to an agreed fee and has to meet the residue either by private insurance or out of his income.

In the United Kingdom the coverage of the scheme is complete. Only in a few cases – e.g. prescription charges of £0.20 per item – does the British consumer not have complete immunity from meeting the direct costs of care. Those who wish to purchase private insurance can do so and they use their benefits to purchase private treatment in public and private hospitals. The advantages of this insurance are that the patient can 'jump the queue' and avoid a wait for surgery, and purchase a different, more secluded, type of care.

In Ireland full eligibility gives the right to free medical care inside and outside the hospital. At present thirty-four per cent of Irish residents are in the full eligibility category. By 1975 all Irish residents will be members of the limited eligibility category. This designation will make them eligible for free hospital care and the provision of subsidised pahrmaceutical care. Primary medical care will not be covered by this change and the relatively affluent Irish citizens will have to meet the cost of general practitioner care out of their own incomes. Private insurance exists in Ireland but it is largely used to purchase private hospitalisation benefits rather than meet the costs of primary medical care.

In Denmark medical care insurance covers all residents but benefits are related to the membership category of the individual citizen. Eighty per cent of the Danes are A-type members and the costs of their care is met in full by the local county authorities. The B-type member receives benefits equal to the benefits of the A-type member but the physician is free to charge the B-type member a fee in excess of that met by the county on the A-type member's behalf. Both type of members receive free hospital care and both have to meet twenty-five per cent of the cost of pharmaceutical products.

It is hoped that this discussion of the bald statistics of Table 1 will have established the fact that any discussion of medical care coverage in terms of mere percentages is mischievous.

3. Qualifying Conditions

The conditions which qualify the member and his dependents for benefits vary from country to country. In West Germany the membership of a fund is sufficient to generate benefits for the member. A similar rule is the requirement in the Netherlands, and in neither case is there a need to fulfill a contribution minima. In Belgium the rules are more onerous: membership has to supplemented with a contribution record showing 120 days of work in the previous six months and contribution vouchers have to have been submitted to the fund. These rules are relaxed for widows, pensioners, orphans and the handicapped. In France the individual has to have completed at least 200 hours of work in the three months or 120 hours in the month prior to claiming benefits before he is a registered member eligible for benefits. In Luxembourg membership alone is sufficient for benefits to be paid and this is the case in Italy as well. In the United Kingdom any resident can acquire medical care. The Irish situation is more complex: full eligibility status is available to any resident who meets the means' test; limited eligibility status will be available to all without a means' test. In Denmark the dividing line between A- and B-type members affects benefit levels but there is no qualifying condition or period.

There are several groups with regard to qualifying conditions. In West Germany, the Netherlands, Luxembourg and Italy the general rule is membership of a sickness fund. In Belgium and France this rule is supplemented by a contribution requirement. In the United Kingdom, Ireland and Denmark the sickness funds have been replaced by government activity. In Ireland a means' test determines eligibility. In Denmark and the United Kingdom medical care is available to all residents.

4. Finance

Table 2 is another illustration of the difficulties of international comparisons. The footnotes to the Table qualify the data considerably due to the fact that contribution rates vary between schemes in many of the countries with which we are interested. Several groupings suggest themselves. The Dutch and the Belgians have a two-tier system of contributions. Their general scheme contributions, 8.9 per cent and 5.75 per cent respectively of earnings up to the individual ceilings, are divided between the employee and employer in equal parts in the case of the Netherlands and in unequal parts (35:65) in the case of Belgium. Heavy risks, such as long-term hospitalisation, are financed by separate contributions. In the Netherlands these are financed wholly by the employer at a rate of 2.8 per cent of earnings. Employee participation in Belgium, which may be emulated in the Netherlands in the near future, is limited to two-fifths of the three per cent total contribution rate.

Another group is France, West Germany and Luxembourg. These three countries have only one tier of contribution. The proportional share of the employer in the total varies from fifty per cent in West

254

Table 2 *Contribution rates*[1]

		Employee[4]	Employer	Total Contribution	Ceiling[10]
West Germany		4.00	4.00	8.00	DM 22500 (£3762)
The Netherlands					
	(a)[2]	4.45	4.45	8.9	17680f (£2707)
	(b)[3]	0.00	2.60	2.60	24300f (£3721)
Belgium					
	(a)[5]	2.00	3.75	5.75	345300 (£3761)
	(b)[6]	1.20	2.80	3.00	345300 (£3761)
France		3.50[7]	12.45[8]	15.95	27840 (£2646)
Luxembourg[9]		2.25	4.50	6.75	292000 (£3173)
Italy[11]		0.15	12.61	12.76	No ceiling
United Kingdom		16 pence	8 pence	24 pence	(Flat rate)
Ireland			15 pence	15 pence	(Flat rate)
Denmark		None	None	None	

Notes

1. In percentage of earnings up to the ceiling unless otherwise stated.
2. General Scheme.
3. AWBZ – heavy risks only. Employee participation may be introduced in the near future.
4. Average. Each fund has limited discretion to fix its rates.
5. General scheme only.
6. Heavy risks.
7. General scheme. Of the 3.5 per cent, 1.00 per cent is levied on all income above and below the ceiling.
8. Of the 12.45, 2.00 per cent is levied on all income above and below the ceiling.
9. Blue collar workers only, white collar contributions are 3.9%-2.6% by the employer and 1.3% by the employee.
10. All ceiling data is 1973 except for Germany and France whose data are for 1974.
11. This includes pension contributions and is not purely for health care.

Germany, to sixty-six per cent in Luxembourg, and to seventy-eight per cent in France. France is a slight exception to this group in that one per cent of the employee contribution and two per cent of the employer contribution is levied on total income. All other contributions in this group are levied on earnings up to the ceiling.

Italy is a category on its own. The share of the employer is very high (over ninety-eight per cent) and the contributions finance health care, one type of retirement pension and subsidies to the agricultural sickness insurance scheme. If a National Health Service is introduced in Italy this contribution is to be replaced by an ear-marked proportional income tax.

Ireland and the United Kingdom form a fourth grouping. In both countries there is a token contribution by the individual. In the United Kingdom this is paid as part of the National Insurance contribution by the employer and the employee. In Ireland those people in the limited eligibility category have, since 1971, paid £0.15 per month (£7 per year). In both countries most of the cost of providing medical care is financed out of general taxation.

Denmark finances its medical care system without contributions by the potential beneficiary. The cost of the care provided by the local government is met out of local taxation (a proportional income tax and a land tax) and central government subsidies.

It can be seen that the nine countries of the European Community rely on widely differing system of contribution finance. The United Kingdom, Ireland, Denmark and Italy are moving or already use a system involving general taxation with varying degrees of reliance on ear-marked regressive[1] or proportional[2] income taxation. The other five countries of the community use contribution rates which are proportional to income but whose revenues go to the funds rather than the government. This difference is little more than academic in some ways as the governments' control of the use of these funds is substantial and, perhaps, increasing. Perhaps the major difference between the two groups is the extent of reliance on contributions by the employers. In the latter group it is relatively large. This may be seen as an unfair advantage to the employer in the former group because their costs may be lower. Such arguments have been important in tax harmonisation reforms in the Community and if the objective of equal treatment is pursued in relation to health care contributions, radical changes in the financial arrangements of some countries will be inevitable.

5. Income and Expenditure

One of the areas into which much research effort has been allocated is

Table 3 *Expenditure: Absolute figures and as a percentage of GNP*

	Absolute expenditure in £m (and in millions of national currency units)		Expenditure as a percentage of GNP
West Germany (1972)*	£5670	(33908m)	5.84
The Netherlands (1972)†	£1154	(7610m)	6.71
Belgium (1971)††	(£ 457)	(42030m)	(3.90)
France (1971)**	£4752	(50000m)	5.50
Italy (1971)	£3130	(4095500m)	6.00
United Kingdom (1972)	£2832		5.06
Ireland	£ 107		4.96
Denmark (1971)	£ 498	(7000m)	5.46

*   Estimated data (see Chapter on West Germany and this Chapter for discussion).

†   Incomplete data. The expenditure figure includes AWBZ and general scheme expenditure. It ignores private outlays from income and own savings. (See Chapter on the Netherlands.)

††   Incomplete data. The expenditure figure includes the outlay of the general scheme and the self-employed scheme only (see Chapter on Belgium and discussion in this Chapter).

**   See *Revue Française des Affaires Sociales* 1973 'L'Hospitalisation publique en France', p 119.

health care expenditure in relation to Gross National Product. These efforts have usually produced estimates hedged round with assumptions and caveats which their authors have been at pains to point out. However the statistics have often been adopted by callow observers and used in 'league table' exercises to show the 'inadequacies' of medical care expenditure in a particular country. Such an approach is mischievous because it tends to gloss over the fact that individual medical care expenditures are the result of particular medical care structures. Each of these structures differs in the scope of benefits it offers, e.g. 'cures' are still popular in continental Europe but do not enter the schemes in Ireland and the United Kingdom. As can be seen in the Chapter on West Germany (the Szemeitat estimate, Table 11) if health care is defined broadly to include research, public health activities and current and capital expenditure, the size of total health care outlays can be very large in absolute and relative terms. Another complicating factor is that individual countries differ in the degree to which legislation demands consumer participation in the cost of using medical care facilities. Thus in England the degree of participation in the cost of care at the point of consumption is small. In France for a particular type of care it can amount to twenty-five per cent of the cost of care. These differences compel the analyst to acquire estimates of medical care expenditure financed by private insurers and out of the income and wealth of private individuals. Such exercises are fraught with difficulties and although they are discussed in Chapters on individual countries they are not always included in Table 3. This is because the author suspects their accuracy and does not wish to be a party to the perpetration of new myths about relative medical care expenditures.

Table 3 representes an attempt to determine the levels of current expenditure in the member countries of the EEC in the early 1960s. Luxembourg is omitted because of its relatively small size and the difficulties in acquiring data referred to in the Chapter on that country. The first column shows absolute expenditure in £ million and, in brackets, in millions of units of the national currency. The recent fluctuations in exchange rates make the sterling figures look somewhat unreal. The second column shows the level of current expenditure on medical care as a percentage of GNP for 1971 or 1972.

Each of the statistics needs to be considered carefully. The 1972 level of sickness fund expenditure on medical care in Germany was DM 27003 million. This figure relates to expenditure on goods and services consumed by those covered by compulsory medical insurance. A further ten to eleven per cent of the population lie outside the scope of this insurance. If we were to assume, as a plausible estimate[3], that this ten per cent consumed at an equal rate to those covered by compulsory insurance the total expenditure figure would rise by DM 3000 million. In fact this group is likely to have spent more because of its affluence. However, let us maintain this assumption and add DM 900m as an estimate of hospital deficits financed by the government and DM 3000m as an estimate of private insurance benefits.[4] Then a conservative expenditure outcome is a figure equal to 5.84 per cent of GNP.

In the Netherlands the general scheme (ZFW) covers seventy per cent of the population and cost 4321 million florins in 1972. The AWBZ heavy risk scheme covered all Dutch residents and cost 1993 million florins. If it is assumed that the thirty per cent not covered by ZFW spent a proportionally equal amount on medical care as those in the scheme, an estimate of their expenditure is 1296 million florins. As a result the total expenditure estimate for 1972 is 7610 million florins, or 6.71 per cent of GNP. This estimate seems rather high.

The use of the strong assumtpions to derive expenditure figures for West Germany and the Netherlands cannot be extended to Belgium. In the Belgian case coverage is nearly complete and the expenditure of the general and self-employed funds is the result of this coverage.

However, because Belgian citizens augment their compulsory insurance with voluntary and coluntary-compulsory cover[5] the expenditure of the funds is only part of expenditure on medical care. Furthermore the self-employed are insured for heavy risks only. These two factors make the Belgian statistic a serious underestimate of actual medical care expenditure. Due to the paucity of Begian data no satisfactory statistic can be provided.

The estimate for France is an official estimate whose source is cited in the Table. The French statistics are, by and large, very good because of the activities of CREDOC — Centre de Recherches et de Documentation sur la Consommation — a government agency which analyses consumption patterns in France. The 1971 expenditure figure of 50,000 million francs represented 5.50 per cent of GNP.

The remaining three statistics are discussed in the Chapters covering the countries concerned. Denmark spent 5.46 per cent of its GNP on medical care in 1971. Ireland spent 4.96 per cent of its GNP on medical care in 1972. In the same year the United Kingdom spent 5.06 per cent of its GNP on medical care.

Although these statistics are hedged round by bold assumptions and estimates the interesting implication of all nine statistics is that the relative share of medical care expenditure as a percentage of GNP appears to be rising. This is the inevitable result of medical care expenditure rising at a rate far in excess of the rate of growth of GNP. The growth rate of expenditure is discussed in each chapter. A good example of the general problem is Denmark where during the period 1966-71 expenditure was rising at an annual average rate of seventeen per cent. Simple linear extrapolation of such trends implies that a hundred per cent of GNP will be consumed by medical care by the end of the twentieth century!

The causes of this expenditure escalation are complex. One important factor is that by their very nature medical care services are highly labour intensive, e.g. fifty to sixty per cent of the cost of hospital services in the Nine are due to the payment of labour. As a result wage inflation can affect the cost of medical care quickly and directly. Another important factor is that the suppliers of certain goods and services are in a monopoly position. This position gives certain groups the power to extract monopoly profits in some market conditions. The groups with such potential powers are physicians, the producers of pharmaceutical products, the suppliers of some types of medical equipment (especially that supplied to hospitals) and perhaps some other sections of the medical personnel group. The necessary condition for the use of monopoly power is that there be no close substitute for the goods or services which are being supplied. The only countervailing actions available to governments in such situations are that they attempt to reduce the monopoly power by, for instance, anti-trust legislation[6] or the formation of a monopsony or sole buying agency which means that the monoplist can sell its services to only one agency and thus there is no potential to play one buyer off against another, and raise prices all the while. This does not necessarily imply State provision and finance of medical care. Although the role of the State is increasing in the Nine as a result of financial pressures and the desire to 'rationalise by planning' the State could counter monopolies by regulations affecting fee determination and by implementing anti-trust legislation.

6. Benefits

Table 4 *Social Insurance Benefits – How Much does the Patient Pay?* *

	Hospital Care	General Practitioner Care	Prescribed Pharmaceutical Products
West Germany	Free 78 weeks max.	Free	20% of the cost up to a maximum of DM 2050
Netherlands	ZFW – free for 365 days: AWBZ from 365th day	ZFW free	ZFW free
Belgium†	Free	25% of agreed tariffs	BF 25-50
France†	20% of cost	25% of agreed tariffs	30% in general – 10% for expensive 'special' products
Luxembourg	Free for 180 days	Free for 180 days	Free for 180 days
Italy (INAM)	Free for 26 weeks	20% of agreed tariffs	25% of cost
United Kingdom	Free to all	Free	£0.20 per item unless 'poor'**
Ireland	Free to all***	Full eligibility free. Limited eligibility – full cost.	Full eligibility – Limited eligibility††
Denmark	Free to all	Free to A-type members. B-type pay excess.	25% of cost

Table 4 *(Cont)*

Table 4 attempts to show the level of costs facing individuals in various countries when they consume medical care. Three types of benefit are shown: hospitalisation; the primary medical care provided by the general practitioner; and prescribed pharmaceutical products.

Hospital care is provided free of charge in every country except France. The duration of hospital benefits are limited in West Germany (seventy-eight weeks), Luxembourg (180 days), and Italy (twenty-six weeks). In the Netherlands and Belgium two types of scheme are responsible for insuring short term and long term hospital risks. These together give full cover. In France where the consumer can be obliged to pay twenty per cent of hospital care, certain groups (e.g. old age pensioners) are exempted.

Primary medical care is provided free of charge without duration in the United Kingdom and West Germany only. In the Netherlands the seventy per cent of the population covered by ZFW (the general scheme) get free care whilst the rest meet the costs out of private insurance or income. In Luxembourg care is free but limited to 180 days. In Belgium and Italy and France the patient pays twenty-five per cent, twenty-five per cent and twenty per cent respectively of the agreed tariff. In these countries if the patient pays in excess of agreed tariff rates he meets all excesses out of his own pocket. In Ireland primary medical care is free to the poor: those who are fully eligible. Those with limited eligibility status get no State assistance to meet the cost of care. In Denmark A-type members have their agreed fees paid by the county authorities. B-type members get benefits equal to the fees agreed between the physicians and the counties but are charged fees in excess of the county rate. This excess they meet out of their own pockets.

In the Netherlands (ZFW members only) and Luxembourg prescribed pharmaceutical products are free. In the United Kingdom and Ireland those designated as 'poor' by virute of a means test and the chronic sick get free benefits. In the case of all other countries similar tests give free benefits sometimes as a result of the public assistance system. In

Belgium and the United Kingdom the insured pays a lump sum of BF 25 to 50 and £0.20 respectively. Italy and Denmark charge the consumer twenty-five per cent of the cost of the products, and in West Germany the consumer pays twenty-five per cent of the cost up to a maximum of DM 2.50. In France the participation percentage is thirty per cent for normal products and ten per cent for expensive 'special' items.

These three types of care consume upwards of seventy-five per cent of the cost of medical care in the Nine. It can be seen that the degree of consumer participation in terms of meeting the cost of care is, in general, quite limited. Details concerning other benefits can be found in the Chapters for each country.

7. Provision

(a) Medical Personnel

The medical personnel statistics contain some ambiguities. An attempt is made to overcome these problems by various measures, the products of which are shown in Table 5. The first two columns of the Table show physicians per 1000 population data for the nine members of the Community. The first column is derived from a single source: the European Community's Social Report for 1973. The second column is derived from the statistics used in the Chapters covering individual countries in this book. The two sources act as checks on accuracy. The Social Report series varies from 1.03 per 1000 in Ireland to 1.80 per 1000 in Italy (1970). The other series varies from 1.00 in Britain to 1.97 in Italy (1971). The growth of the Italian statistic is rapid and, in part at least, this is accounted for by the rapid expansion of the input and output of Italian medical schools. A similar expansion has taken place in Belgium and this will maintain Belgium's position as a country, together with West Germany, Italy and Denmark, with a physician/population ratio above the average for the Nine.

The Table gives data for three other types of medical personnel. Dentists in Italy are specialist physicians and consequently there is no Italian dental statistic. Of the remainder, only Denmark, France and West Germany have above average endowment of dentists. The picture for nursing is confused. The variations in this series are so substantial that it would seem that statistics stated as being derived on similar definitions may, in fact, be based on dissimilar bases. If this is not so we can only marvel at the high levels of nursing staff available in Ireland and the United Kingdom in particular. The variation in the pharmacist series is substantial. This data is derived from the Nine's Social Report. Denmark, the United Kingdom, West Germany and the Netherlands

Table 5 *Medical Personnel per 1000 population*

	Physicians (a)		Physicians (b)		Dentist		Nurses **		Pharmacists	
West Germany	1.78	(1971)	1.79	(1970)	0.51	(1970)	2.26	(1969)	0.37	(1971)
Netherlands	1.19	(1970)	1.36	(1972)	0.27	(1972)	4.46	(1969)	0.08	(1970)
Belgium	1.61	(1971)	1.55	(1970)	0.19	(1970)	1.45	(1970)	0.71	(1971)
Luxembourg	1.09	(1972)	1.15	(1972)	0.34	(1972)	2.32	(1972)	1.50	(1972)
Italy	1.80	(1970)	1.97	(1971)	†		1.88	(1968)	1.65	(1970)
United Kingdom	1.26	(1972)	1.00	(1972)*	1.24	(1972)*	6.89	(1972)	0.28	(1972)
Ireland	1.03	(1971)	1.03	(1971)	0.26	(1971)	10.20	(1971)	0.55	(1971)
Denmark	1.45	(1971)	1.62	(1971-2)	0.67	(1971-2)	3.82	(1971-2)	0.40	(1971)
Average	1.39		1.42		0.36		3.02		0.46	

Source: *European Economic Community* (1974) 'Report on the Development of the Social
Situation in the Community in 1973' Luxembourg and Brussels. Page 215; *World
Health Organisation* (1972, 1973) 'World Health Statistics Annual 1968, 1969' Geneva;
data cited in the individual Chapters of the book.

* This data is for Great Britain, i.e. Northern Ireland is excluded.

† All dentists in Italy are physicians who have specialised in dental surgery. The number of
such specialists is relatively small.

** This includes nurses in psychiatric and general hospitals, and homes for the aged.

have below average provision levels. The Netherlands statistic is, perhaps, in a category on its own being a mere seventeen per cent of the average endowment.

The significance of deficiencies amd surpluses are difficult to ascertain. National commentators discuss the adequacy, or lack of it, of provision in various sectors as if there was some scientific way of determining the optimum. In fact the targets used in policy discussions are arbitary and differ from one country to another.[7]

(b)   Hospitals

Table 6 *Hospital Beds and Length of Stay**

	Beds (a)	Beds (b)	Average length of stay
West Germany	11.20 (1971)	11.03 (1969)	18.6 (1969)***
Netherlands	5.26 (1970)	10.52 (1971)	20.7 (1969)***
Belgium	8.35 (1971)	7.70 (1971)	17.9 (1969)***
France	8.85 (1969)	10.39 (1972)	15.7 (1971)**
Luxembourg	11.46 (1972)	12.21 (1972)	14.5 (1969)***
Italy	10.55 (1970)	9.77 (1972)	15.2 / 10.0 (1971)††
United Kingdom	9.61 (1971)	9.40 (1971)	10.2 (1972)
Ireland	13.33 (1971)	12.71 (1972)	13.1 (1971)
Denmark	8.81 (1970)	8.30 (1971-2)†	12.3 (1971-2)
Average	9.71	10.22	15.32

Source: *op. cit.* and *European Economic Community* (1973 (a)) 'The Cost of Hospitalisation in Social Security' in French and unpublished, Brussels.

*   Hospital beds (acute, psychiatric and other types) per 1000 population, and average length of stay in acute (general) hospitals.
†   Includes general and psychiatric hospital beds only. A further 14.3 beds are available in institutions for the handicapped, homes for the aged and nursing homes.
***   The source for this data is European Economic Community (1973 (a)) p 28.
**This statistic is for public hospitals.
†† 15.2 is for public hospitals statistic, 10.00 is the private hospital statistic. The former is used in the calculation of the average.

Table six gives hospital bed and average length of stay data for each of the nine member states of the EEC. These statistics return us to speculation about the accuracy of sources. The first two columns of the Table give two separate series of bed per 1000 population ratios. The first column (a) is derived from the Community's 1973 Social Report and in some cases gives statistics wildly at variance with the data in column (b) which is derived from the Chapters on individual countries in this book. Perhaps the most glaring discrepancy is that for the Netherlands. This seems to be accounted for by the fact that although the Community's statistics are meant to include 'clinics, psychiatric hospitals, sanatoriums, nursing homes and old person's homes' this statistic excludes them. A further discrepancy whose magnitude is large concerns Denmark. The data in column (b) is for general and psychiatric hospitals only. This is similar to the EEC statistic which includes homes for the aged and nursing homes. As is pointed out in the footnote to this Table Danish sources cite considerably larger statistics for the EEC definition. In 1971-2 there were 8.2 beds per 1000 population in homes for the aged and nursing homes and 6.3 beds per 1000 population in homes for the handicapped. The former statistic boosts the Danish endowment to 16.5 beds per 1000 population[8], and such a definition excludes provision for the handicapped. These differences are similar to those given in World Health Organisation statistics and put their accuracy in serious doubt. If the data difficulties are put to one side the series in Table 6 indicate that Belgium and the United Kingdom have the lowest bed endowment.[9] Luxembourg, Italy, West Germany, Ireland and perhaps Denmark, if the statistic is adjusted as outlined above, appear to have the largest provision of hospital beds in the Community.

Whether these beds are efficiently used is another matter. Obviously those countries with low hospital bed endowments may utilise their beds more efficiently by minimising the length of stay in hospital. This would appear to be the case in the United Kingdom where the average length of stay in acute (general) hospitals appears to be the lowest in the Community. However, in Belgium it does not appear to be the case as her low provision level is accompanied by an above average length of stay. Average lengths of stay were lowest in the United Kingdom, Denmark and Ireland. They are particularly high in Belgium, the Netherlands and West Germany.

8. Conclusion

Regardless of the aspect of medical care which is compared the diversity in the nine member countries of the European Economic Community is substantial. Throughout this Chapter it has been emphasised that international comparisons are exercises which must be treated with extreme caution. In each part of the foregoing coverage great pains have been taken to highlight defects in the data and to question the accuracy of many sources of data. A substantial part of the data differences is due to the simple problem of semantics. Words mean different things to different people. This results in different definitions of hospital beds, for instance, being used in some comparative studies. It also brings into high relief the inherent difficulties of international comparisons of medical care expenditure. It is believed that the data used in the final analysis were of reasonable accuracy and it is hoped their interpretation casts more light than dark.

NOTES

1. Flat rate contributions are used by Ireland and the United kingdom. These are regressive, i.e. proportionally they are a relatively greater burden to the low income earner.
2. Italy will, if it adopts a National Health Service, be wholly dependent on an ear-marked proportional income tax. Denmark does not ear-mark but uses local proportional income tax revenues.
3. The rich may consume more medical care because of their affluence compared with the relatively poor covered by Social Insurance. However this tendency is countered, in part at least, by the lower incidence of illness amongst more affluent groups. The relative weighting of these and other influences is not known.
4. These estimates are derived from the text of the Chapter on West Germany.
5. See Chapter on Belgium for an explanation of this statement.
6. Thus the British and West German governments are attempting to counter the alleged monopoly power of pharmaceutical products by investigating companies (e.g. La Roche) believed to be in breach of the relevant legislation.
7. Further analysis of the process of determining and attaining input provision targets in West Germany, France and the United Kingdom will take place in 1974-5.
8. I.e. 8.30 in column (b) Table 6 plus 8.20 beds per 1000 population in homes for the aged and nursing homes.
9. Denmark and the Netherlands are not in this category for the reasons cited in the previous paragraph. Also the French EEC statistic is low in comparison to the source used in this book.

The preceding eleven Chapters of this book have been concerned with the functioning of medical care systems. This brief Chapter develops some arguments mentioned in the text to highlight the problems common to each system and concludes with the advocacy of increased research effort.

1. The Insurance Myth

A considerable portion of the social welfare programme of Western Europe continues to be administered as 'insurance'. The insurance is not funded[1] and is administered on an annual 'pay-as-you-go' basis. The contributions levied by the sickness funds are equivalent to tax payments in that they are compulsory. The contributions are paid directly to the funds, which are creatures of the State in that their activities are monitored and often subsidised by government, or to 'autonomous' agencies whose function it is to distribute contribution income and, in some cases, State subsidies to the local funds. The best way of describing this process is by saying that it is a process of ear-marked taxation paid to the approved, and regulated, agencies of the State. The constraints placed upon the activities of the funds vary from one country to another. Such ear-marked taxation is the primary source of finance in the former Six of the EEC[2], and is a relatively unimportant source of finance in Ireland and the United Kingdom.[3] In Denmark there are no longer individual ear-marked taxation payments to finance the provision of medical care.

The economic case for the continued operation of the sickness fund system has to be based on evidence that the funds are the least costly way of meeting the objectives of the State. Some writers[4] argue that the funds are an inefficient means of minimising the resource costs of financing a medical care system. This argument usually rests on the observation that with a multitude of funds administration costs are a high proportion of the total cost of medical care insurance. It is possible that this argument is incorrect or correct. If the objective of the State is to minimise costs the argument may be correct and would imply the abolition of funds and their replacement by more centralised institutions. On the other hand the argument may be incorrect because the objective function of the State may have more than one variable in it. Thus the State may wish to minimise costs but it may also wish to avoid the centralisation of power. For instance the Danes have recently abolished their sickness funds and replaced them with a system of local government provision and local and central government finance. One of the arguments used to advance this change was that by placing provision in the hands of the locally elected representatives the desires of the community could be heard, and met, more effectively. It is unfortunate that analyses of the relative costs and benefits of alternative market and non-market institution is thin at both the theoretical and empirical levels. Without more evidence about the relative virtues of alternative ways of funding and providing medical care it will remain impossible to be definitive about such matters. This ignorance will not facilitate harmonisation of financial structures if and when it comes.

2. Monopsony

One factor which may influence institutional reform is the recognition of the market power of particular groups. The physicians and the pharmaceutical industry are usually used as examples in relation to this argument. The belief is that these two groups have monopoly power, i.e. they are the sole sellers of particular services or goods which have no close substitutes. As a result of this power it is argued that they can offer their services on an all-or-nothing basis at a high price. The consumer must pay the price or else he will not get the goods or service. Obviously this is a caricature of the market situation where market power may be constrained by the Hypocratic oath and the fear of government intervention. However it is a matter of degree. Friedman and Kusnets[5] have argued that the physicians in the United States have used their monopoly power to restrict the supply of physicians and force up their relative wages. Although these results have been disputed they retain some validity and there is no reason to believe that the American physician's counterparts in Europe do not exploit their market power.

The German situation could be regarded as a valid example of this argument. The financers — the sickness funds — pay the *Länder* association of physicians, which all practitioners have to join, money which it redistributes to its members. The sickness funds are legally obliged to provide medical care and as a result they have to reach an agreement with the physicians. The physicians operating at the Federal and regional level manage to conclude agreements which ensure that their 'first bite' of the funds' financial 'cake' is large. Indeed their market power has been such that the residue of the 'cake' has been insufficient to finance the hospital system which, as a result, has gone into deficit and is subsidised by the *Länder* and Federal Governments. Most physicians are paid on a basis of a fee for each item of service and this system, like any piece-rate arrangement, invites a tendency for physicians to execute unnecessary medical acts in an effort to maximise their income.

The validation of the monopoly hypothesis is far from simple. However, even if the policy makers were convinced of its accuracy the solution which is often proposed is not without its difficulties. The usual solution is that the monopoly power of the seller should be countered by the construction of a monopsony, i.e. a sole buyer. The market is then one in which there is one buyer and one seller. The outcome of the price determination process is indeterminate and rests on the relative power of the two sides. It is often the case that the argument infers that a State monopsony will effectively counteract any market monopoly such as that possessed by the physicians. The problem lies in the determination of the meaning of the term 'counteract'. If the State exercises its market power 'too effectively' it will generate a new array of problems.

Some argue that this array of problems can be seen to exist in the United Kingdom. The argument at its simplest is that the UK Department of Health and Social Security has used agencies which have driven down the relative wages of United Kingdom physicians to a level which encourages them to migrate to countries which offer them a higher wage.[6] This explanation of the 'brain drain' is plausible and, as yet, has not been bettered by an alternative hypothesis. The policy implications are simple: if the State uses its powers 'too effectively' it will negate the monopoly profits of the physicians and encourage them to migrate. Another example of this propensity is the remuneration of nurses. In 1974 the payment of nurses was such that it created a crisis involving strike action by the profession. The problem was that the relative remuneration of nurses had become so depressed that, in London in particular, it was difficult to staff the hospitals and wards were threatened with closure. Here the problems appeared to be monopsonistic tendencies complicated by the inability of the NHS bureaucracy to react swiftly to correct the decline of nurses' real wages in the face of rapid inflation. It is simplistic to believe that State intervention removes the disadvantages of market imperfections. In many cases it replaces one type of market imperfection by another and it is difficult to see which is the lesser of the two evils.

A similar type of argument can be followed in relation to the products of the pharmaceutical industry. The firms in this industry whose products have no close substitutes in many cases and are protected by patents, are subject to monopoly (anti-trust) legislation, but this is executed with minimal activity in many of the countries. In the United Kingdom the monopoly power of the industry has been countered by the monopsony power of the National Health Service. The price of pharmaceutical products is informally regulated by the Voluntary Price Regulation Scheme (VPRS) and as Cooper and Cooper (1972) have shown one effect of this appears to be that the UK pharmaceutical prices are lower than their counterparts in the rest of Europe. It has been estimated, on the basis of certain assumptions, that the costs of prescription medicines to the NHS during 1970 were reduced by £18 million as a result of the price cutting effects of the VPRS scheme.[7]

To argue that this reduction was an unambiguous gain to the British community, let alone to its European counterpart, is naive. In the first place the international pharmaceutical industry may be selling at lower prices in the UK and recouping their losses by charging high prices elsewhere. If they are doing this, or if they are merely accepting lower worldwide profits as a result of VPRS, the effects on the industry could be significant. If pharmaceutical producers are maintaining their profits by charging higher prices elsewhere their total profit levels may be relatively unaffected. However, if their profit levels decline it is possible that their investment on research will be reduced. At the present level of knowledge it is impossible to know the relationship between profit and research in the pharmaceutical industry. It is apparent that massive sums are invested by private firms every year but the effects of reducing profits by State intervention cannot be foreseen. Once again there is a conundrum: it is a popular idea to cut the 'excessive' profits of the industry, but will this kill the golden goose which has 'laid' the significant therapeutic advances of the last two decades?

3. Restrictive Practices

Entry into professional medical groups is usually the result of satisfying examination and training goals which are determined by the group. It is an observable fact that each group strives after State registration: the medical profession achived this objective in 1858 in the United Kingdom. Such registration makes the group's products different from that of its rivals, and superior. This superiority gives rise to greater status and earnings. In most cases the group is not a monopoly on the legal sense[8] but by differentiating its product it acquires monopoly powers. To maintain these powers the groups restrict competition within the profession by limiting activities such as advertising. Physicians in Switzerland and dentists in the United States are exceptions in that they are permitted to advertise their services. Elsewhere such behaviour is viewed as unprofessional and the group's rules often make it illegal. This attitude protects the older established members of the profession from the potential price cutting activities of new entrants who are seeking to acquire a share of the market.

Competition from other groups is restricted also. A good example of this is described by Lees.[9] In the UK physicians may not work with, or even mention, the name of an osteopath. The osteopath profession in the United Kingdom is governed by two associations which regulate training, maintain a register of qualified osteopaths and 'guide' ethics, e.g. prohibit advertising. The associations have made several attempts to acquire registration but have, so far, failed. Indeed it is difficult to see why registration is necessary because the present voluntary agreements give adequate guidance and protection to the consumer.

The grounds for defending professional monopolies, whether they are registered or not, are weak if not non-existent. The first argument in favour of monopoly is that the consumer is unable to distinguish the unqualified from the qualified. If this is the case the implication is an increase in the supply of information about the groups concerned so that the consumer is more fully informed. The second argument implies that even though the consumer may be informed about alternatives he should not be permitted to purchase services from unqualified personnel. This is an argument about values and, at present, it is unfortunate that society is prepared to condone such paternalism.

The maintenance of restrictive practices perpetuates inefficient practices especially with respect to training. The prestige of the physician, in particular, has been transformed in the last one hundred years. In the early twentieth century some physicians remained as exponents of the art of leeching and the status of the profession was not high. In the course of seventy years, the pharmaceutical revolution in particular has resulted in the transformation of the profession's image. This position has resulted in an all too uncritical appraisal of training methods within the profession. It is hardly unfair to argue that in many countries the physician's training consists of the implantation of skills appropriate to a hospital physician. Yet in most countries at least half of the profession is involved in general practice. The appropriate skills for the two roles are significantly different. It would be sensible to train personnel in separate programmes for the two types of job. In the future the extension of community care will result in specialist physicians practising in health centres: where there is no need for specialised skills there is a need to replace skilled physicians with personnel whose training is more relevant. It is argued by many that much of the general practitioner's work-load is of the nature of social work. The patients are in need of the skills of a social worker rather than a person trained to rectify physical ailments. At present the trend is towards diluting the skills of the physician in order to turn him into a quasi-social worker. Whether it is sensible to dilute skills and create Jacks-of-all-trades who are masters of none is a matter which is debatable.

The restrictive practices of the medical profession should not be condoned. The activities of physicians are very similar to those of shop floor workers and there is no reason why society should not treat both groups in a similar, critical manner. Restrictive practices have sheltered uneconomic training activities for many years. The logic of the expansion of the medical care market should be that there should be more specialisation. This implies that there should be substitution of some physicians' services by the services of other professions. Efficient treatment of the patient demands that personnel should be fully utilised practising the skills in which they have been trained.

4. The Need for more Research

This final section has indicated some areas in which policy changes have been put forward. The argument has indicated that these 'solutions' are not unambiguously better and their side effects may be significant and deleterious. At present there is a need to be cautious because the present state of knowledge is such that agnosticism is, perhaps, the best policy. The current trend is to argue that the market has failed and that there is a need to supplement or supplant it by increased State finance and provision of medical care. There are, without doubt, serious imperfections in the medical care market. However to cast the market aside will solve few problems. It will merely change their nature. As time goes by our knowledge of the operation of the market is increasing. If the State involvement in the provision and finance of medical care is to be effective there is a need to devise ways of analysing the behaviour of the State and the non-profit maximising bodies which it creates to administer medical care. If institutions do not maximise profits, what do they maximise?[10]

The need to understand the behaviour of non-profit institutions is parallelled by the need to devise a thorough-going theory of the State. This book has been concerned with State and private activity in nine medical care markets. There is a need to understand why the State has increased its involvement in the finance and provision of medical care during the course of the twentieth century. The economist's view of government activity is based on the theory of externalities and public goods.[11] These ideas are in their infancy. However they need to be developed with rapidity if we are to understand more fully why the State has become increasingly involved in the provision and finance of goods and services. Whilst it is both useful and interesting to analyse the medical care system of various countries, the limitations of the theories at present used by social scientists make it difficult to examine the systems with the rigour that is necessary. There is a need to devise new theories, to improve old theories and to generate information with which these theories can be tested. Only then can we move towards a greater understanding of why medical care systems are what they are.

NOTES

1. Funded means that income is invested to produce resources flows which finance activity in the future.
2. West Germany, France, Luxembourg, The Netherlands, Belgium and Italy.
3. In the United Kingdom and Ireland approximately five per cent of total income is derived from contributions.
4. For instance Alhbourn in British Medical Association (1971), pp 431-8.
5. Friedman and Kusnets (1945).
6. For instance the United States, Canada and Australia.
7. See the Association of British Pharmaceutical Industries Annual Report 1970-1.
8. For instance the British Medical profession is not a legal monopoly in that anyone is free to practise medicine for gain provided he does not claim to be a qualified practitioner. See D. Lees (1966), p 10.
9. Lees (1966), p 29.
10. A quiet life or the satisfaction of the managers are but two possible answers. Economists are involved in interesting developments in this area, e.g. Newhouse (1970) and Niskanen (1971).
11. See Cooper and Culyer (1973), pt 1.

References

M.H. Cooper and A.J. Culyer (1973) editors, *Health Economics*, Penguin, London.
A.J. Cooper and M.H. Cooper (1972) *An International Price Comparison of Pharmaceuticals*, National Economic Development Council, London.
W. Niskanen (1971) *Bureaucracy and Representative Government*, Aldine-Atherton.
British Medical Association (1971) *Health Services Financing*, London.
J.P. Newhouse (1970) 'An Economic Model of a Hospital', *American Economic Review*, vol 60, pp 64-74. (Reprinted in M.H. Cooper and A.J. Culyer [1973]).
M. Friedman and S. Kusnets (1945) *Income from Independent Professional Practice*, National Bureau of Economic Research, New York.
D. Lees (1966) *The Economic Consequences of the Professions*, Institute of Economic Affairs Research, Monograph 2.

APPENDIX 1

Exchange Rates

In each of the Chapters the financial values are translated into £ sterling to give an approximate indication of the orders of magnitude involved. The indication is approximate due to the significant variations which the international monetary system has experienced during the last few years. The values used are listed below and pertain to September 1973. The foreign currency equivalents of £1 sterling were:-

West Germany	5.98 DM
The Netherlands	6.53 florins
Belgium	91.80 BF
France	10.52 NF
Luxembourg	91.80 F*
Italy	1500.00 lire
Denmark	14.04 kroner
United States	2.44 US dollars

* The Luxembourg exchange rate is related to that of Belgium.

APPENDIX 2

Population and other Statistics of the EEC

(i) Population

	Population 1972 in millions	Average annual rate of growth 1958-72 as a %	Percentage of the aged 0-14	65 and over
West Germany	61.7	0.9	21.3	10.4
The Netherlands	13.3	1.3	30.1	8.8
Belgium	9.7	0.5	23.2	11.8
France	51.7	1.0	25.9	11.6
Luxembourg	0.35	0.7	-	-
Italy	54.3	0.7	24.6	9.0
United Kingdom	55.8	0.5	23.2	11.5
Ireland	3.0	0.4	30.4	10.8
Denmark	5.0	0.7	26.1	10.3
Average/Total	254.6	0.8	24.4	10.5

Source: *European Economic Community* (1974) 'Report on the Development of the Social Situation in the Community in 1973' pp 214-5, Luxembourg and Brussels.

(ii)   Population Trends 1958 and 1972.

	Live births per 1000 population		Deaths per 1000 population		Infant mortality per 1000 live births	
	1958	1972	1958	1972	1958	1972
West Germany	16.7	11.3	11.0	11.8	36.2	22.8
Netherlands	21.2	16.1	7.6	8.5	17.2	11.7
Belgium	17.1	13.8	11.7	12.0	31.3	18.2
France	18.1	16.9	11.2	10.6	31.5	13.3
Luxembourg	16.0	11.8	11.3	11.8	34.7	16.7
Italy	17.7	16.3	9.3	9.6	48.2	22.1
United Kingdom	16.8	14.9	11.6	12.1	23.4	17.6
Ireland	20.9	22.6	12.0	11.3	35.4	18.0*
Denmark	16.5	15.1	9.2	10.1	22.4†	14.2†
Average	17.5	14.9	10.6	10.9	33.5†	20.7†

Source: *op. cit.* and *World Health Organisation* (various) 'World Health Statistics Report' Geneva.

*   1971 data.
†   1970 data.

(iii) Gross National Product per capita *in US Dollars*

	1958	1972	Annual Rate of Change as a percentage
West Germany	1096	3840	17.88
Netherlands	845	3193	19.84
Belgium	1154	3351	13.59
France	1196	3489	13.69
Luxembourg	1402	3255	9.44
Italy	612	2008	16.29
United Kingdom	1252	2641	7.92
Ireland	578	1760	14.60
Denmark	1101	3889	18.08
Average	1029	3039	13.95

Source: *op. cit.* pp 222-3.

INDEX

Administration, *see* by country
Agricultural workers, France, 107,
109, 117-8, 122-3, 126;
Italy, 164, 167-8, 178, 184n;
Lux., 148
Algemene Kas, 48, 249
*Algemene Wet Bizondere Ziektc-
kosten*, 1967 (AHBZ), 46, 49,
53, 55, 59, 66, 67, 249, 251, 257
Ambulance Service, Neth., 60; UK,
189, 210n
Area Health Authority (UK), 190,
199, 210n, 250
Artificial limbs, Italy, 178; Lux., 152;
W. Germ., 28
Auxiliary fund (Belg.), 79, 81, 83,
105n

Belgium, birth, death, infant mortality rates, 276; GNP, 277;
pop., 275; medical care: admin.,
79-81, 249-50; benefits, 93-8,
260-2; coverage, 82-4, 252;
expend., 86-93, 257-9; finance,
84-6, 254; hist., 78; hospitals,
94, 101-3, 264-5; personnel,
98-101, 262-3
Benefits, *see* by country
Betreibskrankenkassen (BKK), 7-8,
11, 18-9, 31, 43n
Birth rates, 276

*Caisse Auxiliare de l'Assurance
Maladie-invalidité*, 81, 83, 105n
*Caisse Nationale d'Assurance
Maladie* (CANAM), 108, 109,
110-2, 115-22, 126, 127-34,
144-5n, 250
Cancer treatment, Belg., 87, 91, 97;
France, 138; Ireland, 228;
Neth., 71; W. Germ., 28
Certificates, W. Germ., 26, 29, 42
Chemists, *see* Pharmacists
Chiropodists, France, 137
Chronic sick, Belg., 95, 103;

Denmark, 241; France, 114, 119,
132, 133; Ireland, 261;
Neth., 49, 66, 71, 74; UK, 205,
261; W. Germ., 27, 43
Civil Servants, Belg., 79, 81, 250;
France, 107, 109, 110-1, 117, 122,
125, 250; Italy, 157, 169;
Lux., 147, 152; Neth., 49, 76n;
W. Germ., 14
Community Health Councils (UK),
189
Company sickness funds, Neth., 48;
W. Germ., 7-8, 11, 18-9, 31, 43n
Consultants (UK), 196, 200, 203-4
Copenhagen University Hospital,
234, 245
Cross Associations, Belg., 81;
Neth., 49-50, 66-7

Daily Cash Benefit Fund (Denmark),
238
Danish Health Service, *see* Denmark
Danish Medical Association, 235,
236
Death benefits, Belg., 87-8, 92, 98;
France, 115, 117-8, 122-3, 124;
Italy, 178; Neth., 68; UK, 199;
W. Germ., 20-1, 22, 29
Death rates, 276
Denmark, birth, death, infant
mortality rates, 276; GNP, 277;
pop., 275; medical care: admin.,
233-6, 250-1; benefits, 237-8,
240-1, 260-2; coverage, 236, 253;
expend., 238-40, 257, 259;
finance, 237-8, 256; hist., 232-3;
hospitals, 244-7, 254-5;
personnel, 241-4, 262-3
Dental care, Belg., 89, 94, 96;
Denmark, 233, 241; France, 119,
127; Ireland, 224; Italy, 164, 177;
Lux., 152; Neth., 65; UK, 187,
194-5, 197; W. Germ., 21-3,
26-28
Dentists, Belg., 86, 94, 96;

279

Gross National Products, 3, 4, 277;
& health expend., Denmark, 240;
France, 127; Italy, 172; UK, 193,
195, 209
Guaranteed wage (W. Germ.), 17-8,
20-1, 29, 42, 44n
Guild sickness funds (W. Germ.),
7-8, 11, 18, 31

Handicapped, Belg., 79, 84, 87,
91, 92, 97-8; Denmark, 234, 235;
France, 115, 134; Ireland, 219,
225; Neth., 49, 51, 67, 72;
UK, 189; W. Germ., 10-1
Health Act, 1953 (Ireland), 215
Health Boards (Ireland), 216, 218,
220, 222-5, 229, 230, 231n,
250
Health Care Planning Teams (UK),
189
Health Insurance, complementary,
Belg., 81; France, 132; Neth., 48,
66, 68
Health insurance, compulsory, 1, 2,
3, 251, 267-8; Belg., 79-98,
251, 252; Denmark, 233-47,
251; France, 107, 108, 110-3,
115, 119-22, 130-4, 145n,
251; Ireland, 214-30, 251;
Italy, 159, 163-79; Lux., 147-56,
251; Neth., 47-69, 73, 75;
UK, 187-213, 251; W. Germ.,
9-30, 251
Health insurance, private, 251;
Belg., 93, 252; Denmark, 234,
240; France, 126; Ireland, 215,
219, 252; Italy, 253; Lux., 252;
Neth., 46, 63, 66; UK, 186-7,
190-2; W. Germ., 9, 11, 12, 15,
16, 25
Health insurance, voluntary, Belg.,
81, 83, 93; France, 122; Lux.,
147; Neth., 48-9, 50, 52, 54-5,
56, 57; W. Germ., 9, 11
Health Reform Bill, 1973 (Italy),
158, 162-3, 174, 177, 179
Hearing aids, Belg., 95; Italy, 178,
252; Lux., 152; W. Germ., 28
Home help, Ireland, 224-5; UK,
189; W. Germ., 13
Home treatment, Belg., 96; Neth.,
66; W. Germ., 28
Home visits, France, 119, 128, 130;

Ireland, 224; Neth., 49, 65;
UK, 202; W. Germ., 31
Hospital Act, 1969 (Denmark), 233
Hospital beds, 264-5; Belg., 101-3;
Denmark, 245-6; France, 138-43;
Ireland, 227-30; Italy, 181-2; Lux.
154-5; Neth., 70-2, 73-4, 102;
UK, 186, 198-9, 205-7;
W. Germ., 15, 20, 37-9
Hospital doctors, Denmark, 235,
242-4; France, 135; Italy, 176,
179, 200-1, 203-4; W. Germ.,
33-5, 36
Hospital fees, Belg., 87, 95;
Denmark, 238-40; France, 120,
130-1; Italy, 172-3, 176; Lux.,
149, 150; Neth., 66, 73;
W. Germ., 27
Hospital Law, 1968 (Italy), 160,
182, 183
Hospital Management Committees
(UK), 188
Hospital outpatient facilities,
Italy, 170, 172-3; UK, 198;
W. Germ., 33, 36, 41
Hospital Reform Law, 1970 (France),
140
Hospital Tariffs Act, 1964 (Neth.),
72
Hospital treatment, 260-1; Belg., 95,
97; Denmark, 234, 240; France,
119, 120, 127, 130-2, 133;
Ireland, 215, 218; Italy, 170,
172-3, 177, 252-3; Lux., 152,
153; Neth., 59-72, 89, 91; UK,
187, 197; W. Germ., 21-3, 26,
27-8, 249
Hospitals, 3, 264-5; Belg., 94,
101-3; Denmark, 234, 244-7;
France, 138-43; Ireland, 216-8,
222, 227-30; Italy, 158, 176,
181-3; Lux., 149, 154-5;
Neth., 70-4; UK, 187, 188, 198,
205-8; W. Germ., 6, 21-3, 25,
26, 27-8, 32, 33-5, 37-43, 44n
Hospitals, classes of treatment,
Belg., 93, 95-6; Italy, 183;
Neth., 66, 73; W. Germ., 15,
27, 34, 39
Hospitals, length of stay, 264-5;
Denmark, 247; France, 139;
Italy, 182, 185n; Lux., 152, 155;

Neth., 47, 48, 74; UK, 206,
207-8; W. Germ., 27, 37, 43
Hospitals, private, Belg., 102;
Denmark, 234; France, 139-40,
141; Ireland, 214, 221, 225, 227,
229, 253; Italy, 158, 161, 176,
181-3, 253; Lux., 154; Neth., 72,
249; UK, 186; W. Germ., 34, 38
Hospitals, public, Belg., 101, 102;
Denmark, 233, 234, 238-9;
France, 132, 139-43; Ireland,
225, 227, 229; Italy, 158, 161,
176, 181-2, 253; Lux., 150;
UK, 187, 188, 198, 205-8, 269;
W. Germ., 38, 72
Hospitals Trust Fund (Ireland), 223,
224

Incapacity Insurance Act, 1966
(Neth.), 46, 50, 53, 55, 62-3,
68, 74
Income maintenance benefits, see
Sickness benefits
Infant and child care, Ireland, 218,
223, 224; Neth., 67; UK, 189;
W. Germ., 13, 28
Infant mortality, 276
Innungskrankenkassen (IKK), 7-8,
11, 18, 31
*Institute Nazionale per l'Assicura-
xione contro le Malattie* (INAM),
157-8, 159-60, 161, 164-79,
183, 184n, 250
*Instituto Nazionale della Previdenza
Sociale* (INPS), 159, 167, 177-8,
184n
Insurance, health, see Health
insurance
Ireland, birth, death, infant
mortality rates, 276; GNP, 277;
pop., 275; medical care:
admin., 215, 250; benefits, 215,
218, 220, 223-5, 260-1;
coverage, 218-20, 253; expend.,
221-3, 257, 259; finance, 220-1,
227, 256; hist., 214-5;
hospitals, 227, 264-5;
personnel, 226, 262-3
Italy, birth, death, infant mortality
rates, 276; GNP, 277; pop., 275;
medical care: admin., 159-63,
250; benefits, 172, 174-9,
184-5n, 260-2; coverage, 163-7,
252-3; expend., 170-4, 257;

finance, 167-9, 256; hist., 157-9;
hospitals, 181-3, 264-5;
personnel, 179-81, 262-3

Joint Association of Sickness Find
Organisations (Neth.), 49, 64
Joint Consultative Committees (UK),
190, 199

Knappeschaft Uche Krankenkassen
(KNK), 7-8, 11, 12, 13, 18-9

Landeskrankenkassen (LKK), 7-8,
11, 31
Local Executive Councils (UK),
188-9, 190
Local Sickness Funds (W. Germ.),
7-8, 11, 18-9, 31
Luxembourg, birth, death, infant
mortality rates, 276; GNP, 277;
pop., 275; medical care:
admin., 146-7, 250; benefits, 148,
150-3, 260-1; coverage, 148, 252;
expend., 149-51; finance, 148,
254-6; hist., 146; hospitals, 154-5,
264-5; personnel, 153-4, 263

Manual workers, Belg., 84, 85, 98;
Ireland, 218; Italy, 157, 164,
168; Lux., 146, 148, 152, 156n;
W. Germ., 5, 7-8, 12, 13, 16, 18
Maternity benefits, France, 115,
117-8, 121, 124, 133-4; Ireland,
220; Italy, 164, 167-8, 169,
172, 178; Lux., 148, 153;
Neth., 48, 67-8; UK, 199;
W. Germ., 19, 20-1, 22, 29, 42
Maternity care, Belg., 87, 91, 96;
Denmark, 240-1; France, 107,
118, 121-3, 131-2, 138, 139;
Ireland, 218, 223, 224; Italy, 178;
Lux., 155; Neth., 48, 60, 66;
UK, 189, 197, 205; W. Germ., 25
Maternity hospitals, France, 138;
Ireland, 227, 228; Neth., 71
Medical care, see by country
Medical Practices Committee (UK),
196
Medical professions, 262-3, 270-2;
Belg., 94, 97-101, 104, 105n;
Denmark, 234-5, 241-4;
France, 132, 134-8; Ireland, 217,
226; Italy, 176-7, 179-81;
Lux., 153-4; Neth., 48, 69-70;

281

UK, 187, 200-5; W. Germ., 10, 14, 25, 29

Medical training, 271-2; Denmark, 242; France, 134-5, 136-8; Italy, 179-80; Neth., 69-70; UK, 200, 204-5; W. Germ., 25, 30

Medicines & appliances, 259, 260-1; Belg., 86, 91, 94, 95; Denmark, 238-9, 241, 244; France, 120-1, 127, 130, 143; Ireland, 219, 224; Italy, 170, 172, 175, 198; Lux., 150-1, 152; Neth., 59-62, 65; UK, 266n, 269-70; W. Germ., 21-3, 25, 27, 42, 266n

Midwives, Belg., 99; Denmark, 241, 247; France, 132, 136-7, 145n; Ireland, 226; Italy, 160, 174, 176, 178, 180-1; Lux., 153, 154; Neth., 66, 69, 70; UK., 196, 201, 204-5; W. Germ., 13, 37

Miners, Belg., 81, 85; France, 107, 109, 126, 250

Miners' Sickness Funds (W. Germ.), 7-8, 11, 12, 13, 18-9

Ministry of Health (Italy), 159, 160-3, 177, 182

Ministry of Labour and Social Affairs (Italy), 159, 161-2

Ministry of Labour and Social Security (Lux.), 146

Ministry of Local Affairs (Denmark), 235

Ministry of Public Health (Belg.), 94

Ministry of Public Health and Social Security (France), 108, 132, 144n

Ministry of Social Affairs (Belg.), 79-80, 249

Ministry of Social Affairs (Denmark), 235

Ministry of Social Affairs and Public Health (Neth.), 37, 48, 66, 76n

Ministry of Work and Social Welfare (W. Germ.), 6, 15, 20, 27, 35, 38, 41, 43n, 249

Monopsony, 3, 268-70; UK, 209

Mutual Societies, see Sickness Funds

National Health Service (Denmark), 235-6

National Health Service, see UK National Health Service, proposed,

(Italy), 158, 160, 162-3, 183-4, 250, 256, 266n

National Hospital Council (Neth.), 72

National Insurance Act (UK), 1911, 186, 187; 1946, 187

National Insurance Scheme (UK), 192, 195, 210n, 211n, 256

National Mutual Benefit Institution for Employees of Local Authorities (INADEL) (Italy), 159, 165-6, 171

National Provident and Mutual Benefit Institution for State Employees (Italy), 157-8, 159, 161, 164-6, 169, 171, 173, 174-5, 177, 178-9

National Provident Institution for Employees of Public Law Corporations (ENPDEDP) (Italy), 159, 165-6, 171

National Sickness Insurance Institution (Italy), 157-8, 159-60, 161, 164-79, 183, 184n, 250

National Sickness Insurance Scheme (France), 109, 110-2, 115-22, 126, 127-34, 144-5n, 250

National Sickness and Invalidity Insurance Institution (INAMI) (Belg.), 80, 84, 88, 93, 96

National Social Insurance Institute (Italy), 159, 167, 169, 177-8, 184n

National Social Security Organisation (ONSS) (Belg.), 80, 249

National Solidarity Fund (France), 116, 131

Netherlands, birth, death, infant mortality rates, 276; GNP, 277; pop., 275; medical care: admin., 47-50, 249; benefits, 50, 62-8; coverage, 50-3, 251, 252; expend., 55-63, 257-8; finance, 53-5, 253-4; hist., 46; hospitals, 70-4, 102, 254-5; personnel, 69-70, 262-4

Nurses, Belg., 86, 99; Denmark, 243-4; France, 137, 142-3; Ireland, 217; Italy, 180; Lux., 154; Neth., 66, 69. UK, 196, 201, 204-5, 269; W. Germ., 36-7

Opticians, Ireland, 226; UK, 188-9, 197-8, 205

283

CONTEMPORARY COMMUNITY HEALTH SERIES

Marriage and Mental Handicap: A Study of Subnormality in Marriage
Janet Mattinson

Methodology in Evaluating the Quality of Medical Care: An Annotated Selected Bibliography, 1955-1968
Isidore Altman, Alice J. Anderson, and Kathleen Barker

Migrants and Malaria in Africa
R. Mansell Prothero

A Psychiatric Record Manual for the Hospital
Dorothy Smith Keller

Racism and Mental Health
Charles V. Willie, Bernard M. Kramer, and Bertram S. Brown, Editors